Master Plan

For

Delhi
2021

(MPD - 2021)

**[As Notified on 7.2.2007 vide SO No. 141
Published in Gazette of India, Extraordinary,
Part II, Section-3, Sub-Section (ii)]**

Master Plan

For

Delhi

2021

(MPD - 2021)

[As Notified on 7.2.2007 vide SO No. 141
Published in Gazette of India, Extraordinary,
Part II, Section-3, Sub-Section (ii)]

Vivek Kr. Garg
Advocate

Manas Publications
New Delhi-110002 (INDIA)

Manas Publications
(Publishers, Distributors, Importers & Exporters)
4858, Prahlad Street,
24, Ansari Road, Darya Ganj,
New Delhi - 110 002 (INDIA)
Ph.: 23260783, 23265523; Fax: 011-23272766
E-mail: manaspublications@vsnl.com

2007

ISBN 81-7049-335-8

Rs. 250/-

Typeset at
Manas Publications

Printed in India at
Salasar Imaging System, Delhi
and Published by Mrs Suman Lata for
Manas Publications, 4858, Prahlad Street,
24, Ansari Road, Darya Ganj,
New Delhi - 110 002 (INDIA)

Preface

The Ministry of Urban Development, Government of India, *vide* their Notification No. S.O. 141, published in the Gazette of India, Extra Ordinary, Part II, Section-3, Sub-Section (ii) dated 7th February, 2007 has notified Master Plan for Delhi 2021 with the perspective for the year 2021. MPD 2021 is an extensive modification of the Master Plan with the perspective for the year 2001 alongwith all the amendments carried out till date. MPD 2021 has come into effect from 7.2.2007.

Highlights of MPD 2021 are given in the following pages. A few words about MPD 1962 & 2001 are given in subsequent pages.

Full text of the Master Plan of Delhi with the perspective for the year 2021 is given in this book. Contents have been especially prepared by us for facilitating easy location of the relevant matters.

PUBLISHER

MAJOR HIGHLIGHTS OF THE MASTER PLAN OF DELHI 2021

The Master Plan incorporates several innovations for the development of the National Capital. A critical reform has been envisaged in the prevailing land policy and facilitating public - private partnerships. Together with planned development of new areas, a major focus has been on incentivising the recycling of old, dilapidated areas for their rejuvenation. The Plan contemplates a mechanism for the restructuring of the city based on mass transport. The Perspective Plans of physical infrastructure prepared by the concerned service agencies should help in better coordination and augmentation of the services.

The Master Plan envisages vision and policy guidelines for the perspective period upto 2021. It is proposed that the Plan be reviewed at five yearly intervals to keep pace with the fast changing requirements of the society.

The following critical areas have been the focal points of the Plan:

(a) Land Policy:

The land policy would be based on the optimum utilisation of available resources, both, public and private in land assembly, development and housing.

(b) Public Participation and Plan Implementation:

- Decentralised local area planning by participatory approach;
- Performance oriented planning and development, with focus on implementation and monitoring.

(c) Redevelopment:

Incentivised redevelopment with additional FAR has been envisaged as a major element of city development covering all the areas;

(i) Planned Areas: Influence Zone along MRTS and Major Transport Corridor; underutilised / low-density areas; Special Area; shopping / commercial centres; Industrial areas / clusters and resettlement colonies.

(ii) Unplanned Areas: Villages; unauthorised colonies and JJ Clusters.

(d) Shelter:

- Shift from plotted housing to group housing for optimal utilization of land;
- Private sector participation for development / redevelopment of housing;
- Removing unnecessary controls (like height) for optimum utilization of land and to facilitate creation of 'signature projects.
- Enhancement of ground coverage, FAR and height for all categories of residential plots.

(e) Housing for poor:

- In-situ slum rehabilitation, including using land as a resource for private sector participation;
- In order to prevent growth of slums, mandatory provision of EWS housing / slum rehabilitation in all group housing to the extent of 15% of permissible FAR or 35 % of dwelling units on the plot, whichever is higher.
- Housing for urban poor to the extent of 50-55% of total;
- Recategorisation of housing types, development control norms and differential densities to make EWS /LIG housing viable and economical.

(f) Environment:

- Special emphasis on conservation of the Ridge.
- Rejuvenation of River Yamuna through a number of measures including ensuring adequate flow in river by release of water by riparian states, refurbishment of trunk sewers, treatment of drains, sewering of unsewered areas, treatment of industrial affluent, recycling of treated effluent and removal of coliforms at STPs .
- Provision of lung spaces / recreational areas and green belt to the extent of 15 to 20% of land use.
- Multipurpose grounds: A special category for marriages / public functions.

(g) Unauthorised Colonies:

Unauthorised colonies, which are to be regularised as per government policy, should be effectively incorporated in the mainstream of urban development. This requires provision of infrastructure development, services and facilities for which differential norms and procedures have been devised.

(h) Mixed Use:

- To meet the growing demand of commercial activities and overcome the shortfall of available commercial space, a liberalized provision of Mixed Use in residential areas has been adopted adhering to the requisites of the environment, while achieving better synergy between workplace, residence and transportation.
- 2183 streets have been notified by the GNCTD *vide* notification dated 15.09.06 for local commercial and mixed-use activities.
- Small shops of daily needs have been permitted on ground floor, in residential areas.

(i) Trade & Commerce:

- District & Community Centres are proposed to be developed as facility corridors along major transport networks to prevent unintended and unplanned ribbon development and for better synergy between public transport and work centres.

- Dovelopment of Integrated Freight Complexes / Wholesale Markets at the urban periphery.
- Mandatory provisions for service and repair activities.
- Informal shops, weekly markets, handicrafts bazaars, used books / furniture / building materials bazaars to be developed.
- Enhancement of FAR

(j) Informal Sector

- The informal and organised sector is a major source of employment in the economic fabric of the city for which the following approach is proposed:
- Earmarking of 'Hawking' and 'No Hawking' Zones at neighbourhood and cluster levels.
- The weekly markets to be identified and planned / developed.
- New areas for informal trade to be developed and integrated with housing, commercial, institutional and industrial areas.
- Provision of common basic services like toilets, water points, etc.
- Institutionalizing designs of stalls, push-carts and mobile vans.
- Involvement of NGOs envisaged.

(k) Industry:

- Environment as a major concern and listing of prohibited industries.
- Modernisation / up-gradation of existing industries including non-conforming industrial centres.
- Special provisions for service and repair centres.
- Inclusion of new activities like IT industry, etc.
- Enhancement of FAR.

(1) Conservation of Heritage:

- Identification of heritage zones and archaeological parks.
- Development of Special Conservation plans for listed buildings and precincts.

(m) Transportation:

- The proposals include the following:
- Unified Metro Transport Authority
- Synergy between landuse and transport
- A new parking policy including private sector development of parking facilities, increase in norms for parking space, multi level parking and underground parking.
- Integrated multimodal public transport system to reduce dependence on personalised vehicles.
- Road and rail based mass transport system to be a major mode of public transport, optimal use of existing road network and development of missing links.
- Restructuring of existing network through expressways, elevated roads, arterial roads, distributor roads and relief roads.
- Provision for introducing cycle tracks, pedestrian and disabled friendly features in arterial and sub-arterial roads.

(n) Health Infrastructure:

- Health facilities proposed to achieve norms of 5 beds / 1000 population
- Enhancement of FAR for hospitals and other health facilities.
- Nursing Homes, clinics etc. also allowed under relaxed Mixed Use norms.

(o) Educational Facilities:

- Rationalisation of planning norms with enhanced floor area.
- Locating new school sites adjacent to parks / playgrounds.
- Provision for vocational and other educational facilities.
- Schools and training centres for mentally /physically challenged with differential development norms.

(p) Disaster Management:

- Disaster Management centre provided in each administrative zone.
- Building regulations for safety of structures as per seismic zone.
- Land Use zoning as per microzonation.

(q) Provision of Sports Facilities:

- Provisions for sports infrastructure for local, national and international events.
- Incentives provided for sports facilities and swimming pools in schools, clubs and group housing.

(r) Focus on Infrastructure Development:

- Perspective Plans for Water, Power, Drainage & Solid Waste Management of Service Agencies part of MPD-2021. Alternative Sources of energy and new technology. The Plan gives emphasis on energy conservation, efficiency and exploring alternative sources of energy.
- Realistic standards of water supply for equitable distribution.

FEW WORDS ABOUT MASTER PLANS OF DELHI 1962 & 2001

The National Capital Territory of Delhi, admeasuring 1485 sq. kms, has established a continuous growth of population since independence, resulting sprawl of the city as well as densification in certain areas even beyond acceptable levels. As a result the infrastructural networks are getting excessively stressed and may soon be at thresholds if appropriate planned efforts are not done in recent future.

For the orderly development of National Capital, Delhi Development Provisional Authority (DDPA) was constituted in 1955. The enactment of Delhi Development Act 1957, gave a new impetus to it and Delhi Development Authority (DDA) came into existence in 1957 and was responsible for Planning and Development .

MASTER PLAN FOR DELHI 1962 (MPD 1962)

The first Comprehensive Plan, that is, Master Plan for Delhi was formulated by a team of Ford Foundation and TCPO, GOI in 1957-61, which was promulgated in September, 1962. The MPD-62, the first step towards modern planning in India, shall remain an exemplary document, being pioneer successful attempt of integrated Planning and Development of city of Delhi.

The MPD-62 recommended an area of about 45000 ha for Urbanization and projected the population of Delhi about 4.6 million by the year 1981. It envisaged urban and rural continuum and projected balanced growth of Region by shifting of identified activities in NCR from Delhi city. The main attributes of the MPD-62 are as under :

- Planning in regional context.
- Comprehensive planning for both urban & rural.
- Segregated land use for appropriate built environment.
- Perfect zoning and sub-division regulations.
- Multinodal hierarchical development.
- Harmonious neighbourhood planning.
- Performance based industrial development.
- Conservative surgery of outlived areas.
- Efficient traffic & transportation network.
- Extensive lung spaces/open spaces.

Experience of MPD-62

- The city, which was growing in a haphazard way, got planned direction for development.
- Several planned colonies could be developed with healthy & pleasant built environment benefiting a large number of families. A large number of EWS families as well as other families got option in terms of plots/flats depending upon their income structure, to house themselves.
- Three District Centres i.e., Nehru Place, Bhikaji Cama Place and Rajendra Place could be developed along with several Community Centres, Local Shopping Centres and Convenience Shopping centres.
- Almost all the Industrial areas as per plan were developed to house the industrial units based on their performance level. A large number of these units got shifted from their previous location, which was amidst residential areas resulting in decongestion and pollution free environment there.
- Social Infrastructure in form of large number of Schools, Hospitals and Cultural Centres could be provided in the city for better quality of life to the city population.
- A hierarchical network of roads could be developed to take care of city traffic facilitating ease in movement to the city population.
- The landuse intensity & permissibility helped in a balanced skyline and development of the city.
- A large number of Open Spaces could be created and a considerable proportion of developed land could be put to Regional Parks, Parks, etc. making healthy living environment.

Implementation Experience

- The population projection proved much less than the real growth of the city in the Plan Period.
- The envisaged dispersal of population and activity could not take place in the Region due to inadequate/non-development of Ring & Satellite Towns.
- The large scale Land Acquisition Policy did not prove very useful, as there was mismatch between the land acquisition and development, resulting into upcoming of Unauthorized Colonies, encroachments on Public land, violation of envisaged landuses, etc.
- The Segregated Landuse Concept did not work successfully everywhere and in many areas depending upon the economic profile / strategic location, misuse and mixed use appeared in alarming magnitude.

- Despite the identified planned Industrial Areas based on performance standards a large number of industries located themselves in other than planned area and mushroomed in residential areas & many of them became non-conforming even in planned areas due to change in their outputs/products.
- The Commercial Areas of higher order i.e., CBD's, District Centres, Community Centres, etc. could not be developed resulting in commercialization of major transport corridors and also in areas which suited the purpose due to their prestigious/strategic location. It further gave rise to informal sector and concentration of commercial activity in existing commercial areas especially in old built-up areas. The few centres, which could be developed, did not gain the desired status and became merely the Office Complexes.
- The densities recommended were low hence the city got horizontal sprawl. Housing provisions were favouring to economically capable class than to economically weaker section. The urban Villages were recommended to be conserved and retain their character but due to the changed economics most of them attracted non-compatible uses and acted as free market for land transactions leading to penetration of commercial and other uses in shape of multi-storeyed development disregarding the safety of human life.
- Balanced development in terms of Social Infrastructure could not be achieved as most of the facilities came up only in select part of the city and other remained neglected.
- The Physical Infrastructure could not be provided in the entire city and a large portion of the city remained un-served with regard to Water Supply, Sewerage and Drainage.
- The movement of the people could not be contained as envisaged due to non- development of higher order of Commercial Centres, dispersal of the activities within the city as well as in NCR, etc. The average speed of vehicle on roads reduced, trip length as well as travelling time increased resulting thereby congestion on roads and elongation of peak hours.
- Absence of monitoring framework and lack of coordination in various departments, several Plan Provisions could not be implemented resulting imbalances in use zones, activities and overall functioning of the city.

MASTER PLAN FOR DELHI 2001 (MPD 2001)

In order to cater to the increasing & changing requirements of the city and guide the development upto the year 2001, the MPD-62 was extensively modified by the DDA. The modified plan envisaged 24000 to 40000 ha. of additional urban area, projected a total population of 12.8 million in NCTD by the year 2001 & was promulgated on 1st August 1990.

The MPD-2001 envisaged the contiguous urban extensions to accommodate over spill of population with different activities, efficient circulation system, decongestion of core areas and densification of thinly built existing urban areas.

The main tenets of MPD-2001 are as under:

- Delhi to be an integral part of its region.
- Ecological balance to be maintained.
- The central city area to be the special area.
- Urban heritage of Delhi to be conserved.
- The city centre to be decentralised.
- Mass transport system to be multi-modal.
- Development to be low rise-high density.
- Development to be hierarchical.

The other contemporary issues/aspects which had emerged with time and gained increased eminence were also considered and incorporated in the Plan and are as under:

- Urban Design
- City Personality
- Policy on Tall Buildings & Hoarding
- Environment
- Heritage Conservation
- Mixed Use & Detailed Permissibility
- Pedestrianisation
- Plan Monitoring & Review

Experience of MPD-2001

- The population projection for the city proved almost realistic and the city population grew as envisaged in the Plan.
- The MPD 2001 could be incorporated more specifically in Sub-Regional & Regional Plans resulting thereby comparatively effective developments in terms of linkages, and use activities. Several activities on their own as well as multi-national companies located/considered for their location in NCR towns for economic reasons which otherwise could have come in NCTD.

- To house the increasing population two new Urban Extension Projects i.e., Dwarka & Narela could be taken up and further extension of Rohini has also been done for the purpose.
- A large quantum of land could be developed for residential activities giving option to the city population in form of Co-operative Housing Societies, Group Housing & Plotted Development as well as serviced plots for resettlement of EWS.
- Development with higher density and higher FAR could be achieved restricting the excessive horizontal sprawl of the city. Mixing of identified other uses in residential areas resulted convenience and economic upliftment of city population in different parts of the city.
- Several public & Semi-Public facilities came up in different parts of the city in form of Super-specialty Hospitals, Hospitals, University/Colleges, Schools, etc. Land could be given to DVB, MTNL, Fire Department, Police etc. which has improved the living environment as well as quality of life in the city.
- To facilitate ease in movement of the city population several roads could be improved in term of Right of Way, Flyovers/Grade Separators, etc. The MRTS could also be initiated for long term benefit for the commuters.
- Due importance could be given to the heritage of the city & such select monuments/area could be linked with open spaces for their conservation. Heritage award could be instituted for better awareness and judicious development in the city.
- A large number of organised play fields & other ecological wealth could be developed/saved for appropriate environment and for healthy living of the city population.

Implementation Experience

The NCR Towns grew at fast pace & some of them adjoining to the Delhi City did not remain a separate entity and became almost continuous Urban Agglomeration stressing the infrastructure of the Mother City.

Since the Plan did not have the spread of the city showing/accommodating population hence land acquisition became difficult and unintended growth started coming up in continuity to/fringes of existing urban areas for obvious reasons.

CONTENTS

DELHI MASTER PLAN 2021

- Introduction 1
- Vision 1
- Review of Past Experience 1
- Methodology Adopted for Plan Preparation 2
- Major Highlights of the Plan 3

1.0 Regional and Sub-Regional Frame 5
1.1 Balanced Regional Development 5
1.2 Policy Zones 6
  1.2.1 National Capital Territory of Delhi 6
  1.2.2 Central National Capital Region (Central NCR) 6
  1.2.3 Highway Corridor Zone 6
  1.2.4 Rest of NCR 6
1.3 Frame Work for Sub-Regional Development 6

2.0 Population and Employment 7
2.1 Population 7
2.2 Population Estimates at Five Year Intervals 7
2.3 Natural Growth and Immigration 8
2.4 Elderly and Children Population 8
2.5 Employment 8
2.6 Projected Work Force for NCTD-2021 9

3.0 Delhi Urban Area-2021 9
3.1 Population Holding Capacity of Delhi 9
3.2 Urban Extension 10
  3.2.1 Green Belt 10
  3.2.2 Hierarchy of Urban Development 10
3.3 Redevelopment of Existing Urban Area 14
  3.3.1 Redevelopment Strategy
    3.3.1.1 Planned Area 14
    3.3.1.2 Special Area 15
    3.3.1.3 Unplanned Areas 16
  3.3.2 Guidelines for Redevelopment Schemes 17

4. Shelter 18
4.1 Housing Need 18
4.2 Housing Strategy 19
  4.2.1 New Housing Area 19
  4.2.2 Restructuring and Up-gradation of the Existing Area 20
    4.2.2.1 Planned Area 20
    4.2.2.2 Traditional Inner City and Unplanned Areas 20
  4.2.3 Housing for Urban Poor 21
    4.2.3.1 Rehabilitation/Relocation of Slum & JJ Clusters 21
    4.2.3.2 Resettlement Colonies 22
    4.2.3.3 New Housing for Urban Poor 22
    4.2.3.4 Slum & JJ Redevelopment Regulations and Guidelines for Collective Community Rehabilitation/Relocation - *in-situ* Up-gradation/rehabilitation of Slum & JJ Clusters and Resettlement Colonies 22
4.3 Night Shelter 23
4.4 Development Controls for Residential use Zone 23
  4.4.1 Permission of Use Premises in the Sub Use Zone – Foreign Mission (RF) 23
  4.4.2 Sub-Division of Residential Zone (RD) into Use Premises 23
  4.4.3 Control for Building/Buildings within Residential Premises 25

5.0 Trade and Commerce 29
5.1 Pre 1962/MPD-1962 Commercial Areas 29
5.2 Hierarchy of Commercial Areas 29
5.3 Metropolitan City Centre 30
  5.3.1 Connaught Place & Extension 31
  5.3.2 Shahjahanabad (Walled City) and Extensions 31
  5.3.3 Karol Bagh 31

5.4 District Centre/Sub-Central Business District 31
5.5 Non-Hierarchical Commercial Centres 32
5.6 Community Centre (CC) Local Shopping Centre (LSC)/Convenience Shopping Centre (CSC) 32
5.7 Commercial Centres in Urban Extension
5.7.1 Sub-City Level Commercial Areas 32
5.7.2 Local Level Commercial Areas 32
5.8 Hotels 32
5.9 Service Markets 33
5.10 Informal Sector 33
5.10.1 Policy for Existing Areas 34
5.10.2 Organised Informal Sector Places (Haat) 34
5.10.3 Informal Bazaar 34
5.10.4 Weekly Markets 34
5.10.5 Planning Norms for Informal Trade 34
6.0 Wholesale Trade 38
6.1 City Level Wholesale Markets 38
6.1.1 Existing Markets in Special Area 38
6.1.2 Proposed Wholesale Markets within Integrated Freight Complexes 38
6.2 Sub-City Level Markets 39
6.3 Storage of Oil, CNG and LPG 39
7. Industry 40
7.1 Strategy 40
7.2 Classification of Industries 40
7.3 Permissibility of Industrial Units in Different Use Zones and Use Premises 40
7.4 Household/Service Industries 41
7.5 No Industrial Activity Zone 42
7.6 Industrial Area Redevelopment Schemes 42
7.6.1 Existing Planned Industrial Areas 42
7.6.2 Redevelopment of Unplanned Industrial Areas 42
7.6.2.1 Norms for Redevelopment of Clusters of Industrial Concentration in Non Conforming Areas 43
7.7 New Industrial Areas 44
7.8 Industry Use Zone – Guidelines 45
Annexure-I : Classification of Industries 46
Annexure-II : Industries Permissible in Commercial Centres 50
Annexure-III : Prohibited/Negative List of Industries 51
8.0 Government Offices 54
8.1 Decentralization of Offices 54
8.2 Optimium Utilization of Government Land 54
9.0 Environment 55
9.1 Natural Resources 56
9.1.1 Water (Surface and Ground) 56
9.1.2 Air 57
9.1.3 Noise 58
9.2 Natural Features 58
9.2.1 River Yamuna 58
9.2.2 Regional Park 59
9.3 Green/Recreational Areas 59
9.4 Multipurpose Grounds 60
9.5 Amusement Park 60
9.6 Green Belt 61
Annexure-I : List of Drains Out Falling into River Yamuna 62
Annexure-II : Recommendations of the Committee Under Secretary (UD) MOUD, Govt. of India, for Yamuna 62
10. Conservation of Built Heritage 63
10.1 Conservation of Built Heritage 63
10.2 Conservation Strategy 63
10.3 Heritage Zones 64
10.4 Archaeological Park 64
10.5 Special Conservation Plans 64
11. Urban Design 65
11.1 Significant Areas of Built Environment 65
11.1.1 Metropolitan City Centre 65
11.1.2 District Centres 66
11.1.3 Other Areas 66
11.2 Visual Integration 66
11.3 Tall Buildings 66

11.4 Urban Corridors ... 67
11.4.1 City Gateways ... 67
11.4.1 MRTS Corridors ... 67
11.5 Services ... 67
11.5.1 Public Amenities ... 67
11.5.2 Parking ... 67
11.6 Hoardings, Street Furniture & Signage ... 67
11.6.1 Street Furniture & Signage ... 67
11.6.2 Road Signage & Safety ... 68
11.7 Pedestrian Friendly City ... 68
11.8 Urban Design Scheme ... 68
12.0 Transportation ... 68
12.1 Integrated Multi-Modal Transport System ... 69
12.2 Metropolitan Transport Authority ... 69
12.3 Roads ... 70
12.3.1 Urban Relief Roads ... 70
12.3.2 Underground Roads ... 71
12.3.3 Grade Separators ... 71
12.3.4 Freeways ... 71
12.4 Mass Rapid Transit System (MRTS) ... 71
12.4.1 Synergy Between Transport and Land Use ... 72
12.5 Bus ... 72
12.6 Bicycle/Cycle-Rickshaw ... 73
12.7 Transportation for Special Areas ... 73
12.8 Rail ... 73
12.9 Modal Split ... 74
12.10 Intercity Passenger Movement ... 74
12.10.1 Rail ... 74
12.10.2 Bus ... 75
12.10.3 Air ... 75
12.10.4 Goods Movement ... 76
12.11 Integrated Freight Complexes ... 77
12.12 Fuel Stations ... 77
12.12.1 Fuel Stations in Urban Areas ... 77
12.12.2 Development Control Norms and Permissibility ... 78
12.12.3 CNG Service Stations ... 78
12.13 Parking ... 78
12.13.1 Park and Ride ... 79
12.13.2 Public Parking ... 79
12.13.3 Parking Facilities in DTC Depots ... 79
12.13.4 Underground Parking ... 79
12.13.5 Parking in Residential Areas ... 80
12.13.6 Parking Standards ... 80
12.13.7 Multi-Level Parking ... 80
12.14 Registration and Licensing ... 80
12.15 Barrier Free Environment ... 80
Annexure-I : Proposed Multi-Level Parking Sites ... 82
13. Social Infrastructure ... 83
13.1 Health ... 83
13.2 Education ... 85
13.3 Sports Facilities ... 88
13.3.1 Provision of Sports Facilities ... 88
13.3.2 International Sports Events ... 88
13.3.3 Development Controls ... 88
13.4 Communications - Post/Telegraph/Telephone Facility ... 89
13.4.1 Post and Telegraph ... 89
13.4.2 Telephone ... 89
13.5 Security - Police ... 90
13.6 Safety ... 91
13.6.1 Fire ... 91
13.6.2 Guidelines for Locating Fire Stations & Other Fire Fighting Facilities in Urban Extension ... 91
13.6.3 Disaster Management Centre ... 91
13.7 Distributive Facilities ... 92

13.8	Socio-Cultural Facilities	93
13.9	Other Community Facilities	94
13.10	Cremation Ground, Burial Ground & Cemetery	94
13.11	Public & Semi-Public Facilities/Premises	95
14.0	**Physical Infrastructure**	**104**
14.1	Projected Requirements for the Year 2021	104
14.2	Water	104
14.3	Sewerage	106
14.4	Drainage	107
14.5	Power	108
14.6	Solid Waste	110
15.0	**Mixed Use Regulations**	**111**
15.1	Governing Principles for Mixed Use	111
15.2	Mixed Use in Residential Areas	112
	15.2.1 Differentiated Approach	112
	15.2.2 Types of Mixed Use	112
15.3	Identification of Mixed Use Areas in Existing Urban Areas and Urbanizable Areas	112
	15.3.1 In already Urbanized/Urban Areas, mixed use shall be permissible	112
	15.3.2 The extent of Mixed use permissible in various categories of colonies	113
	15.3.3 Notification of Mixed use Streets in Urban Areas	114
	15.3.4 Notification of Mixed use Streets in Urbanisable Areas in Future	114
15.4	General Terms and Conditions Governing Mixed use	115
15.5	Permissible and Non-Permissible Uses	115
15.6	Retail Shops	115
15.7	Other Activity	116
15.8	Professional Activity	118
15.9	Registration of Mixed Use Premises and Payment of Charges	118
15.10	Consultation with RWAs	118
15.11	Conditions for Denial/Withdrawal/Restrictions of Mixed Use	119
15.12	Commercial Streets and Areas	119
	Annexure-I List of Pre-1962 Built up Residential and Rehabilitation Colonies	120
16.	**Land use Plan**	**121**
16.0	Land use Plan-2021	121
16.1	Zonal Development Plans	121
16.2	Special Area Regulations	122
17.	**Development Code**	**122**
	– Introduction	122
	– Enforcement of the Code	122
18.	**Plan Review and Monitoring**	**128**
18.2	Major Issues	131
18.3	Monitoring Unit	132
18.4	Management Action Groups	132
	18.4.1 Planning Indicators	132
	18.4.2 High Level Group for Sub-Regional Plan for Delhi	132
	18.4.3 Environment Planning and Coordination Group	132
	18.4.4 Delhi Unified Metropolitan Transport Group	132
	18.4.5 Infrastructure Development Group	133
	18.4.6 Enforcement and Plan Monitoring Group	133
	18.4.7 Spatial Data Infrastructure (SDI) Group	133
	18.4.8 Local Level Participatory Planning Group	133
	18.4.9 Common Platform for Building Approvals	133
	18.4.10 Slum Rehabilitation and Social Housing Group	133
	18.4.11 Legal Framework : Review Group	133
18.5	Review	133
18.6	Programme of Action	133
	Annexure-I : MPD-2021 - Perspective Plan for Infrastructural Services - Water Supply	140
	Annexure A : Proposed Draft Delhi Water Board (Amendment) Bill, 2006	146
	Annexure B : Water Management by Use of Recycled Waste Water	148
	Annexure-II : Perspective Plan for Infrastructure Services for Delhi-2021 - Sewerage	149
	Annexure- III : Draft MPD-2021	156
	Annexure-IV(i) : Strategies/Master Plan-2021 for Solid Waste for Delhi City	158
	Annexure-IV(ii) : Action Plan	161
	Annexure-V :	169

MINISTRY OF URBAN DEVELOPMENT

(Delhi Division)

NOTIFICATION

New Delhi, the 7th February, 2007

S.O. 141.—(E) Whereas extensive modifications which the Central Government proposed to make in the Master Plan for Delhi keeping in view the perspective for Delhi for the year 2021 and growing new dimensions in urban development, were published vide Public Notice in the Gazette of India Extraordinary S.O. No. 318(E) dated 16th March, 2005 by the Delhi Development Authority inviting objections/ suggestions as required by sub-section (3) of Section 11-A of the Delhi Development Act, 1957 (61 of 1957), within ninety days from the date of the said notice.

2. Whereas, the objections/suggestions received with regard to the said public notice have been considered by a Board of Enquiry set up by the Delhi Development Authority and also by the Delhi Development Authority, and the Central Government has, after carefully considering all aspects of the matter, decided to extensively modify the Master Plan for Delhi.

3. Now, therefore, in exercise of the powers conferred by sub-section (2) of Section 11-A of the said Act, the Central Government hereby approves the Master Plan for Delhi with the perspective for the year 2021, as an extensive modification to the Master Plan for Delhi with perspective for the year 2001, as notified vide Ministry of Urban Development Notification S.O. No. 606 (E) dated 1.8.1990 along with all the amendments carried out till date therein. The said Master Plan for Delhi with perspective for the 2021 as notified herein shall come into effect from the date of Publication of this Notification in the Gazette of India.

MASTER PLAN FOR DELHI—WITH THE PERSPECTIVE FOR THE YEAR 2021

INTRODUCTION

1. Delhi, the focus of the socio-economic and political life of India, a symbol of ancient values and aspirations and capital of the largest democracy, is assuming increasing eminence among the great cities of the world.

Growing at an unprecedented pace, the city needs to be able to integrate its elegant past as well as the modern developments into an organic whole, which demands a purposeful transformation of the socio-economic, natural and built environment. The city will be a prime mover and nerve centre of ideas and actions, the seat of national governance and a centre of business, culture, education and sports.

2. Apart from critical issues such as land, physical infrastructure, transport, ecology and environment, housing, socio-cultural and other institutional facilities, the cornerstone for making Delhi a world-class city is the planning process itself and related aspects of governance and management. This needs a co-ordinated and integrated approach amongst several agencies involved with urban services and development along with a participatory planning process at local levels.

VISION

3. Vision-2021 is to make Delhi a global metropolis and a world-class city, where all the people would be engaged in productive work with a better quality of life, living in a sustainable environment. This will, amongst other things, necessitate planning and action to meet the challenge of population growth and in- migration into Delhi; provision of adequate housing, particularly for the weaker sections of the society; addressing the problems of small enterprises, particularly in the unorganized informal sector; dealing with the issue of slums, up-gradation of old and dilapidated areas of the city; provision of adequate infrastructure services; conservation of the environment; preservation of Delhi's heritage and blending it with the new and complex modern patterns of development; and doing all this within a framework of sustainable development, public-private and community participation and a spirit of ownership and a sense of belonging among its citizens.

REVIEW OF PAST EXPERIENCE

4. The process of planned development of the National Capital began with enactment of the Delhi Development Act 1957, followed by the promulgation of the Master Plan of Delhi in 1962 (MPD-62).

5. The MPD-62 set out the broad vision for the development of Delhi and, with a view to realizing the development plan underlying this vision, a scheme of Large Scale Acquisition and Development of Land was also formulated. The aim of the latter was to ensure that the spatial pattern of development and use of land could conform to the development plan and infrastructure and services could be laid out to match the same. At that early stage, the process of planned development was envisaged as a public sector led process with very little private participation in terms of development of both, shelter and infrastructure services. The philosophy of public sector led growth and development process continued in general till the process of economic reforms was initiated in the early nineties. Therefore, the Master Plan for Delhi 2001 (MPD-2001) also substantially reiterated the planning process, which had been outlined in MPD-62. These plans could be seen mainly as land use plans with a three level hierarchy i.e. Master Plan, Zonal Plans and Layout Plans for specific development schemes within each zone.

6. The population of Delhi in 2001 was 138 lakh as against the MPD-2001 projection of 128 lakh. This has had its inevitable implications and impact in terms of shelter, including squatter settlements, and other infrastructure facilities.

Some issues that arise for consideration and are also directions for policy include:

(i) Review of the scheme of large scale development and acquisition and its relevance in the present context;

(ii) Alternative options for development of areas identified for urbanization in MPD-2021;

(iii) Evolving a system under which planning for, and provision of basic infrastructure could take place simultaneously with reference to (i) and (ii) above; and

(iv) Involving the private sector in the assembly and development of land and provision of infrastructure services.

7. One of the most important aspects of planned development pertains to the provision of adequate well-planned shelter and housing for the different categories of inhabitants of the city. The quantitative and qualitative shortages and deficiencies in this regard have been observed while formulating the MPD-2021. In turn, this should also be seen in concert with the involvement of the private sector in land assembly and development.

8. Two major challenges which have emerged in the wake of the developments outlined above relate to the phenomenon of unauthorized colonies and squatter / jhuggi jhompri settlements. This reality will have to be dealt with not only in its present manifestation, but also in terms of future growth and proliferation.

9. The exercises done for the MPD-2021 show that there is a need for redevelopment and densification of the existing urban areas and city improvement. This aspect is a major component of the new Master Plan. It calls for a comprehensive redevelopment strategy for accommodating a larger population, strengthening of infrastructure facilities accompanied by creation of more open spaces at the local level by undertaking measures for redevelopment of congested areas.

10. Another important development observed during the period of the last Master Plan is the phenomenal growth of automobiles in Delhi. This has resulted in a variety of problems pertaining to congestion, pollution, safety of travel and parking etc., which need to be addressed.

11. The NCT of Delhi has been divided into 15 Zones from A to H and J to P, of which 8 Zones are in the urban area, one in Riverbed and remaining 6 in the rural area. So far, Zonal Plans in respect of 11 zones (including sub cities of Dwaraka, Rohini and Narela) have been notified with the approval of the Government of India. It is pertinent to finalise the Zonal Plans for all the planning zones within a year from the date of notification of the MPD-2021.

12. The experience of the past two Master Plans shows that projections regarding various basic infrastructure services have been made with reference to the population growth projections and the increased urbanization requirements. However, the infrastructure provisions especially those related to water and power have not matched the pace of development.

METHODOLOGY ADOPTED FOR PLAN PREPARATION

13. Keeping in view the democratic procedure and statutory obligations, the Draft Plan was prepared after obtaining the views of the public. It also included extensive consultations at the pre-planning stage by involving local bodies, Government of NCT of Delhi, public sector agencies, professional groups, resident welfare associations, elected representatives, etc.

14. The Ministry of Urban development issued guidelines in 2003 for the preparation of the MPD 2021 which inter alia emphasised the need to explore alternate methods of land assembly, private sector participation, and flexible land use and development norms. The Authority also had the benefit of the reports of 12 study groups set up with experts and stakeholders on various aspects such as shelter, demography, conservation, transportation, industry, environment, mixed use, infrastructure, trade and commerce etc. Details of the study groups are given in Annexure–V. Five seminars were organised on various aspects involving experts in the field, representatives of GNCTD and local bodies and NGOs.

15. The DDA has also made presentations on the draft MPD 2021 before various forums including the Consultative Committee of Parliament, Lt Governor, Delhi, Chief Minister Delhi and the Cabinet of GNCTD and the Group of Ministers set up by the central Government. The Draft MPD 2021 was also discussed at length in the Legislative Assembly of NCT of Delhi and the suggestions made by the members were considered and forwarded by the Delhi cabinet to the Authority and the Ministry of Urban Development for its consideration. A large number of representations received in the Ministry of Urban development from various interest groups such as lawyer, doctors, Chartered Accountants, traders, residents, etc were also considered. Personal interaction with various interest groups as well as elected representatives including Members of Parliament, Members of Legislative assembly, Municipal Councillors were held by the Minister and Minister of state for Urban development at various points in time.

16. The Draft Master Plan was notified for inviting public objections / suggestions through Gazette Notification dated 16.03.2005 and public notice in newspapers on 08.04.2005. In response, about 7000 objections / suggestions were received, which were considered by the Board of Enquiry which met on 17 occasions and also afforded personal hearing to about 611 persons/ organizations. The Authority considered the revised draft MPD 2021 along with the report of the Board of Enquiry in three sittings held on 29.12.2006, 4.1.2007 and 19.1.2007 before it was sent to the Ministry of Urban Development for approval. The Ministry of Urban development considered the proposal in the light of the inputs received from DDA and from various quarters and finally approved the Master Plan for Delhi 2021 in the present form.

17. The success of Master Plan depends on conversion of the policies and strategies outlined in it into time bound development and action plans, periodic reviews and close monitoring, besides the people's will and willingness to adhere to discipline in the use of land, roads, public space and infrastructure. Any issue arising from interpretation of the provisions of this Master Plan will be settled by DDA in consultation if required with central Government.

MAJOR HIGHLIGHTS OF THE PLAN

18. The Master Plan incorporates several innovations for the development of the National Capital. A critical reform has been envisaged in the prevailing land policy and facilitating public - private partnerships. Together with planned development of new areas, a major focus has been on incentivising the recycling of old, dilapidated areas for their rejuvenation. The Plan contemplates a mechanism for the restructuring of the city based on mass transport. The Perspective Plans of physical infrastructure prepared by the concerned service agencies should help in better coordination and augmentation of the services.

19. The Master Plan envisages vision and policy guidelines for the perspective period upto 2021. It is proposed that the Plan be reviewed at five yearly intervals to keep pace with the fast changing requirements of the society.

20. The following critical areas have been the focal points of the Plan:

(a) Land Policy:

The land policy would be based on the optimum utilisation of available resources, both, public and private in land assembly, development and housing.

(b) Public Participation and Plan Implementation:

•Decentralised local area planning by participatory approach;

•Performance oriented planning and development, with focus on implementation and monitoring.

(c) Redevelopment:

Incentivised redevelopment with additional FAR has been envisaged as a major element of city development covering all the areas;

(i) Planned Areas: Influence Zone along MRTS and Major Transport Corridor; underutilised / low-density areas; Special Area; shopping / commercial centres; Industrial areas / clusters and resettlement colonies.

(ii) Unplanned Areas: Villages; unauthorised colonies and JJ Clusters.

(d) Shelter:

•Shift from plotted housing to group housing for optimal utilization of land;

•Private sector participation for development / redevelopment of housing;

•Removing unnecessary controls (like height) for optimum utilization of land and to facilitate creation of 'signature' projects.

•Enhancement of ground coverage, FAR and height for all categories of residential plots.

(e) Housing for poor:

•In-situ slum rehabilitation, including using land as a resource for private sector participation;

•In order to prevent growth of slums, mandatory provision of EWS housing / slum rehabilitation in all group housing to the extent of 15% of permissible FAR or 35 % of dwelling units on the plot, whichever is higher.

•Housing for urban poor to the extent of 50-55% of total;

•Recategorisation of housing types, development control norms and differential densities to make EWS /LIG housing viable and economical.

(f) Environment:

•Special emphasis on conservation of the Ridge.

•Rejuvenation of River Yamuna through a number of measures including ensuring adequate flow in river by release of water by riparian states, refurbishment of trunk sewers, treatment of drains, sewering of unsewered areas, treatment of industrial affluent, recycling of treated effluent and removal of coliforms at STPs .

•Provision of lung spaces / recreational areas and green belt to the extent of 15 to 20% of land use.

•Multipurpose grounds: A special category for marriages / public functions.

(g) Unauthorised Colonies:

Unauthorised colonies, which are to be regularised as per government policy, should be effectively incorporated in the mainstream of urban development. This requires provision of infrastructure development, services and facilities for which differential norms and procedures have been devised.

(h) Mixed Use:

•To meet the growing demand of commercial activities and overcome the shortfall of available commercial space, a liberalized provision of Mixed Use in residential areas has been adopted adhering to the requisites of the environment, while achieving better synergy between workplace, residence and transportation.

•2183 streets have been notified by the GNCTD vide notification dated 15.09.06 for local commercial and mixed-use activities.

•Small shops of daily needs have been permitted on ground floor, in residential areas.

(i) Trade & Commerce:

•District & Community Centres are proposed to be developed as facility corridors along major transport networks to prevent unintended and unplanned ribbon development and for better synergy between public transport and work centres.

•Development of Integrated Freight Complexes / Wholesale Markets at the urban periphery.

•Mandatory provisions for service and repair activities.

•Informal shops, weekly markets, handicrafts bazaars, used books / furniture / building materials bazaars to be developed.

•Enhancement of FAR.

(j) Informal Sector:

•The informal and organised sector is a major source of employment in the economic fabric of the city for which the following approach is proposed:

•Earmarking of 'Hawking' and 'No Hawking' Zones at neighbourhood and cluster levels.

•The weekly markets to be identified and planned / developed.

•New areas for informal trade to be developed and integrated with housing, commercial, institutional and industrial areas.

•Provision of common basic services like toilets, water points, etc.

•Institutionalizing designs of stalls, push-carts and mobile vans.

•Involvement of NGOs envisaged.

(k) Industry:

•Environment as a major concern and listing of prohibited industries.

•Modernisation / up-gradation of existing industries including non-conforming industrial centres.

•Special provisions for service and repair centres.

•Inclusion of new activities like IT industry, etc.

•Enhancement of FAR.

(l) Conservation of Heritage:

●Identification of heritage zones and archaeological parks.

●Development of Special Conservation plans for listed buildings and precincts.

(m) Transportation:

●The proposals include the following:

●Unified Metro Transport Authority

●Synergy between landuse and transport

●A new parking policy including private sector development of parking facilities, increase in norms for parking space, multi level parking and under ground parking.

●Integrated multimodal public transport system to reduce dependence on personalised vehicles.

●Road and rail based mass transport system to be a major mode of public transport, optimal use of existing road network and development of missing links.

●Restructuring of existing network through expressways, elevated roads, arterial roads, distributor roads and relief roads.

●Provision for introducing cycle tracks, pedestrian and disabled friendly features in arterial and sub-arterial roads.

(n) Health Infrastructure:

●Health facilities proposed to achieve norms of 5 beds / 1000 population

●Enhancement of FAR for hospitals and other health facilities.

●Nursing Homes, clinics etc. also allowed under relaxed Mixed Use norms.

(o) Educational Facilities:

●Rationalisation of planning norms with enhanced floor area.

●Locating new school sites adjacent to parks / playgrounds.

●Provision for vocational and other educational facilities.

●Schools and training centres for mentally / physically challenged with differential development norms.

(p) Disaster Management:

●Disaster Management centre provided in each administrative zone.

●Building regulations for safety of structures as per seismic zone.

●Land Use zoning as per microzonation.

(q) Provision of Sports Facilities:

●Provisions for sports infrastructure for local, national and international events.

●Incentives provided for sports facilities and swimming pools in schools, clubs and group housing.

(r) Focus on Infrastructure Development:

●Perspective Plans for Water, Power, Drainage & Solid Waste Management of Service Agencies part of MPD-2021. Alternative Sources of energy and new technology. The Plan gives emphasis on energy conservation, efficiency and exploring alternative sources of energy.

●Realistic standards of water supply for equitable distribution.

1.0 REGIONAL AND SUB-REGIONAL FRAME

Delhi as the National Capital has a distinct and unique character. It is a growing and expanding magnet of attraction for people from all across the country and also a hub for the region surrounding it. Planning for a metropolis like Delhi, therefore, cannot be limited within its boundaries.

The physical potential for further urbanization within the NCT is reducing although there is a virtual urban continuum between Delhi and the surrounding areas, which lie in the States of Uttar Pradesh and Haryana. With the imperatives of growth and development, the problems of Delhi have become complex, which have to be viewed both as a challenge in terms of the pressures of regular and floating in-migration, as well as an opportunity in terms of planning and development in a regional context.

1.1 BALANCED REGIONAL DEVELOPMENT

In recognition of the above factors, the Central Government enacted the National Capital Region Planning Board Act, 1985. The National Capital Region (NCR) Planning Board, constituted under the Act, is charged with the responsibility of coordinating the efforts of the adjoining States through the instrumentality of Regional and Sub-Regional Plans.

The present National Capital Region (NCR) comprises of a total area of 33,578 sq. km. including areas of Delhi (1483 sq. kms), Haryana (13413 sq. kms.), Uttar Pradesh (10853 sq. kms.) and Rajasthan (7829 sq. kms).

1.2 POLICY ZONES

The Regional Plan 2021 has been drawn up with reference to the following four Policy Zones: -

i. NCT of Delhi.

ii. Central National Capital Region - Central NCR

iii. Highway Corridor Zone

iv. Rest of NCR.

1.2.1 NATIONAL CAPITAL TERRITORY OF DELHI

In the National Capital Territory of Delhi, the basic policy is to achieve environmentally sustainable development/re-development considering the limitations of land and water with significantly improved quality of infrastructure.

1.2.2 CENTRAL NATIONAL CAPITAL REGION (CENTRAL NCR)

The Central NCR (earlier the Delhi Metropolitan Area) as defined in the Regional Plan - 2021, comprises of the notified / controlled development areas of the neighboring towns of Ghaziabad - Loni, NOIDA, Gurgaon-Manesar, Faridabad-Ballabhgarh, Bahadurgarh and Sonepat-Kundli, and the extension of the ridge in Haryana, having an area of about 2000 sq. kms.

It has been suggested that the opportunities presented by the Central NCR should be maximized to enable it to compete effectively with the NCT of Delhi, offering comparable employment, economic activities, comprehensive transport system, housing, social infrastructure and quality of life and environment. Together with this larger industries should be located in the urbanisable areas in this zone.

1.2.3 HIGHWAY CORRIDOR ZONE

The NCR Plan has proposed promotion of planned and regulated development along the National Highways. However, while planning for these Zones, due care has to be taken to ensure that the activities being permitted are segregated from highway traffic through proper green belts, and regulated and controlled access to the Highways. The identified Highway Corridor Zones will also have to be notified by the respective State Governments with appropriate regulations for their development.

1.2.4 REST OF NCR

In the Rest of the NCR (approximately 29,795 sq. kms.), the basic policy of the Regional Plan - 2021 is aimed at accelerated development of the urban and rural areas. For this, infrastructure has to be substantially upgraded at local and regional level (both by the State and Central Government) in order to induce growth in these areas, specifically in identified settlements / Metro Centres. It is felt that this will make them more attractive for locating economic and allied activities and for attracting private sector investment.

1.3. FRAME WORK FOR SUB-REGIONAL DEVELOPMENT

As a follow up of the Regional Plan-2021 and in consonance with, under Section 17 of the NCRPB Act, 1985, a Sub-Regional Plan for Delhi is to be prepared by GNCT-Delhi. It is suggested that a High Level Group may be constituted by GNCT-Delhi to implement the policies of the Regional Plan and ensure timely preparation of the Sub-Regional Plan.

As already mentioned Delhi has a limited area of 1483 sq. kms., out of which about half of the area is already urbanized. For the remaining area, optimum utilization of land is required so that while providing for the urbanization requirements, the natural features like the ridge and other major green areas, defined water bodies and areas of ecological importance could be conserved.

In this background, it has been suggested that:

i) As per NCR Plan, no new Central Government and Public Sector Undertaking offices should be located in NCTD. However, this would be possible only after a time bound action plan is prepared together with suitable incentives and disincentives.

ii) Industrial growth in Delhi should be restricted to high-tech with emphasis on units, which require skill, less manpower and energy and do not create pollution / nuisance.

iii) Legal and fiscal measures should be adopted to restrict employment in industries and distributive trade.

iv) Major regional transport corridor and communication network needs to be strengthened to enhance economic development within the region and decentralization of the distributive trade.

v) The natural features such as Forest, Wild life Sanctuary, Ridge, River Yamuna and other water bodies should be conserved and kept free from unrestricted and unplanned urban development.

NCR Plan-2021 has proposed the availability of urbanisable land in NCT-Delhi for 2021, which is given in Table 1.0.

Table 1.0: Availability of Urbanisable Land in NCT-Delhi for 2021

S.No.	Land Use	Area (Ha.)	Percentage to Total Area (Ha.)
1	Total Geographical Area - NCT Delhi	148300	100
2	Built -up Area (As per IRS IC LISS III Satellite data 1999)	70162	47.31
3	Natural Features (Forest, Wild Life Sanctuary, Ridge, River Yamuna and Other Water Bodies / Drains)	19509.10	13.16
4	Sub- Total (Built-Up + Natural Features)	89671.10	60.47
5	Balanced land available in NCT - Delhi (1-4)	58628.90	39.53
6	Land to be kept reserved for:		
	(i) Disposal of Solid Waste generated up to 2051 (sanitary landfill & statutory green belts)	10000	6.74
	(ii) Metro Services / Utilities e.g. power plant, grid station water and sewerage treatment plant, etc.	10000	6.74
	(iii) Agriculture zone in NCT Delhi including dairy farming, horticulture, greenbelts etc.	11000	7.42
7	Sub Total - 6	31000	20.90
8	Proposed/Actual Land available for urbanization (5-7)	27628.90*	18.63
9	Total Urbanisable area 2021 (including built up area 1999) (2+8)	97790.90	65.94
10	Population, which can be accommodated in 97790.90 ha. @ 225 PPH = 220 lakh		

*This included unplanned and built up area

Source : NCR Plan 2021

2.0 POPULATION AND EMPLOYMENT

As per 2001 Census, NCT of Delhi had a total population of 138 lakh. NCT Delhi is highly urbanized with 93.18% of its population living in urban areas as against the national average of 27.81%. During 1991-2001, the urban population of Delhi increased at 3.87 % annual growth rate. With the continuation of the present population trend, the total population of NCTD by the year 2011 and 2021 would be 182 lakh and 225 lakh respectively. Envisaging a balanced regional development, the population for the NCTD has been projected as under:

2.1 POPULATION

The population assignment stipulated in the Regional Plan-2021 for the National Capital Region (NCR) and National Capital Territory of Delhi (NCTD) are as given below:

Table 2.1. Population Assignment - 2021

Area	Population (In lakh)
NCR	641.38
NCTD	220-230

Source: NCR Plan - 2021.

While it may not be possible to make an accurate forecast, the expectation is that the population of Delhi may range between 220 to 230 lakh in the year 2021. However, requirement of land, provision of infrastructure and transportation, etc. should be planned for the projected population of 230 lakh.

2.2 POPULATION ESTIMATES AT FIVE YEAR INTERVALS

The population estimates for NCTD at five year intervals are given in the following table:

Table 2.2. Five Yearly estimates of Projected Population

Year	Population (In lakh)
2001	138.0
2006	162.0
2011	182.0
2016	199.0
2021	230.0

Source: Census of India and projections by DDA Sub-Group (MPD- 2021)

During the course of implementation of the plan, attempts should be made to restrict the population of Delhi lower than 220 lakh by 2021. To a substantial extent, this depends on the effective implementation of the policies and proposals of the Regional Plan -2021 NCR by the Government of NCT Delhi/Agencies, DDA, concerned Central Govt. Department. and other NCR participating States.

2.3. NATURAL GROWTH AND INMIGRATION

There has been increase in natural growth from 55.80% in 1981 to 59.21% in 1991 and 60.18% in 2001 and decrease in the net migrants from 44.20% in 1981 to 40.78% in 1991 and 39.82% in 2001. However, a reduction in the rate of natural growth and increase in migration between 2001and 2021 is envisaged in the MPD 2021. The net increase of population in NCT-Delhi is given below:

Table 2.3. Population in NCT-Delhi

Year	Addition by Natural Growth	Increase by Migration	Net Increase (in lakh)
1981	12.0 (55.8%)	9.52 (44.2%)	21.54 (100%)
1991	18.9 (59.2%)	13.05 (40.8%)	32.0 (100%)
2001	26.66 (60.18%)	17.64 (39.82%)	44.30 (100%)
2011	24.2 (54.8%)	20.0 (45.2%)	44.2 (100%)
2021	24.0 (50%)	24.0 (50%)	48.0 (100%)

Note: Figures (in bracket) indicate percentage to total net increase.

Source: Census of India and projections by DDA Sub-Group (MPD- 2021)

2.4 ELDERLY AND CHILDREN POPULATION

The DDA Sub-group (MPD-2021) projected that the Rate of elderly population (persons aged +60) is expected to increase from 5.9% in 2001 to 10.7% in 2021. At the same time population of children (aged 0-14 years) would decrease from 29.5% in 2001 to 21.75 % in 2021. The details break-up of elderly people and children are given below.

Table 2.4. Elderly and Children population

Year		Population in lakh	
		Elderly (+60year)	Children (0-14year)
1991		4.5 (4.8%)	32.8 (34.8%)
2001		8.1 (5.9%)	40.6 (29.5%)
2011		14.2 (7.8%)	45.0 (24.7%)
2021		24.6 (10.7%)	49.9 (21.7%)

Figures (in bracket) indicate percentages to the total population.

Source: Census of India and projections by DDA Sub-Group (MPD- 2021)

The above age-group wise distribution of population should form the basis for providing special facilities to the elderly such as old age homes, low floor buses, special seats in buses, special seats in public toilets and ramps in public buildings.

2.5 EMPLOYMENT

The participation rate (Working Population / Total Population × 100) for the last two decades for Delhi is as given below :

Table 2.5. Participation rate of population

Year	Male	Female	Total
1991	28.8	3.7	32.5
2001	28.3	4.4	32.72

Source: Census of India and projections by DDA Sub-Group (MPD- 2021)

With the generation of employment in different sectors, the participation rate for 2021 would be 38.1 percent in NCTD. Based on the assigned population of 220 lakh, this would generate a total work force of 83.82 lakh by 2021.

2.6 PROJECTED WORK FORCE FOR NCTD-2021.

The work force in different economic sectors has been assigned as follows:

Sectors	Work Force (in lakh)	%
1) Agricultural etc.	0.67	0.8
2) Manufacturing, Processing, Servicing, Repairs Household Industry	0.34	0.4
3) Other than Household Industry	17.52	20.9
4) Construction	5.95	7.1
5) Trade and Commerce	25.31	30.2
6) Transport, Storage & Communications	6.20	7.4
7) Other Services *	27.83	33.2
Total	83.82	100

Source: Census of India and projections by DDA Sub-Group (MPD- 2021).

*Includes Central Govt., Quasi Govt., Delhi Admin., Local Bodies and Private Sector etc.

The demographic trends indicate the following:

(i) The rate of growth of the elderly population is expected to show an increasing trend from 5.9% in 2001 to 10.7% in 2021.

(ii) It is projected that the gender composition will shift significantly to a greater parity between numbers of males and females with 102 lakh females and 106 lakh males in 2021.

The trend discerned from a comparison of the 1991 Census and 2001 Census shows that the percentage of combined workforce in 'Primary activities, Industry & Construction' is declining and that in 'Services' is increasing. In keeping with this decline, emphasis should be laid on tertiary sector activities such as commerce, sports, IT applications, cultural activities and tourism.

3.0 DELHI URBAN AREA -2021

In 2001, about 702 sq km of area was estimated to have been built up, accommodating about 138 lakh population. To accommodate the projected population of 230 lakh by the year 2021, a three-pronged strategy is recommended:

(i) To encourage the population to deflect in the NCR towns.

(ii) To increase the population holding capacity of the area within existing urban limits through redevelopment; and

(iii) Extension of the present urban limits to the extent necessary.

3.1 POPULATION HOLDING CAPACITY OF DELHI

The area within the existing urbanisable limits of Delhi Urban Area-2001 consists of the planning zones A to H and the Dwarka, Rohini, Narela Sub-city projects. Population holding capacity of A to H zones is to be enhanced through a redevelopment strategy and modified development norms. This will be related with:

(i) Residential development types and their potential for higher absorption.

(ii) Redensification of housing areas developed at lower densities and along selected sections of the Metro corridor.

(iii) Redevelopment areas should be identified by the concerned agencies and Special Redevelopment Schemes should be prepared with regard thereto for implementation within a stipulated time framework.

(iv) Employment areas / centres

(v) Augmentation and rationalisation of infrastructure physical and social.

(vi) Increase in transportation network capacity.

The holding capacity of Dwarka, Rohini Phase III, IV & V and Narela is proposed to be enhanced through:

(i) Early and full utilisation of the planned areas and,

(ii) Implementation of the schemes under planning stages.

Existing residential areas may provide a potential to accommodate about 153 lakh population ultimately i.e. 114 lakh in Zones A to H and 39 lakh in Dwarka, Rohini Phase III, IV & V and Narela.

Table 3.1: Zonewise Estimated Holding Capacity of Existing Urban Area

(Population in '000)

Zone	Holding capacity MPD 2001	Existing population 2001	Holding capacity 2021
A	420	570	570
B	630	624	630
C	751	679	788
D	755	587	813
E	1789	2798	2800
F	1278	1717	1975
G	1490	1629	1955
H	1865	1226	1865
Sub total	8978	9830	11400
Dwarka		597	1300
Rohini III		96	160
Rohini IV& V		198	820
Narela		179	1620
Sub total	3222	1070	3900
GRAND TOTAL	122 Lakh	109 lakh	153 Lakh

Note: Population figures are only broad planning guidelines.

The remaining population for the year 2021 will have to be accommodated in the planned new urban extensions.

3.2 URBAN EXTENSION

Out of the remaining 77 lakh (230-153 lakh) population, 29 lakh already exists in villages, census towns, unauthorised colonies and JJ clusters in the present rural areas. Therefore about 48 lakh additional population is to be accommodated in the future urban extensions.

Due to land constraint in the NCTD, the areas earmarked as rural / agricultural in the previous Master Plans have always been under pressure for utilisation for various urban activities and have virtually lost their original character. In future, urbanisation has to be in the areas that have development pressure/potential like the areas along the major transport corridors and fringes of already urbanised areas. It is envisaged that major rural areas would be absorbed as urban extension from time to time with due regard to balanced city development.

At the first instance, to accommodate the projected additional population @ 250-300 pph average city level density, the requirement for urban extension would be 20,000-22,000 ha. of land within development time frame of 15-16 years. The immediate urban extension could be in the zones of J to L, N & P (I & II). The land required for urban extension, will have to be assembled for planned development. Considering the constant pressure on the rural land, new farmhouses and motels shall not be permitted in the proposed Urban Extension as per MPD-2021.

3.2.1 GREEN BELT

The previous Master Plan proposals for retention of Green Belt have not been maintained and a considerable part has already been utilised for both, planned and unplanned developments.

The Plan stipulates that the land upto the depth of one peripheral village revenue boundary along the border of NCTD, wherever available, would be maintained as Green Belt. Considering the constant pressure on the rural land, new motels shall not be permitted in the green belt. However, existing village abadis, regularized unauthorized colonies and approved motels may continue in the green belt. (Refer Table 9.4, Chapter 9.0 Environment, for permissibility). GNCTD shall be responsible for ensuring utilization of land in Green belt in accordance with permissible uses.

Land in the Urban Extension is proposed to be broadly distributed in different land uses in the following manner as shown in Table 3.2.

Table 3.2: Land use Distribution

Land use	% of Land
Residential	45-55
Commercial	4-5
Industrial	4-5
Green/ Recreational*	15-20
Public & Semi-Public Facilities	8-10
Circulation	10-12

* This does not include green areas within the various gross land use categories.

On an average the space required per person would be 40 sqm, covering about 920 sqkm of urban area for the projected population of 230 lakh in year 2021.

3.2.2 HIERARCHY OF URBAN DEVELOPMENT

A planned city for an environment of convenience should have a hierarchical cellular structure; with nuclei to contain essential facilities and services at different levels. The pattern of a community module is conceived as residential area containing a 'neighbourhood' with senior secondary school and shopping facilities for day-to-day needs. The higher level of additional facilities is to be provided at Community, District and Zonal/sub-city levels. Such a structure could be maintained in the process of the preparation of plans on the basis of the standards set in the Table 3.3:

Table 3.3 Hierarchy of Urban Development

Level	Facilities	Area in sq.m.			To be provided/ indicated	
		No.	Per Unit	Total	LOP	ZP*
1. Housing Area Population –5,000	1. Convenience shopping	1	1000	1000	●	
	2. Totlot	20	125	2500	●	
	3. Housing area Park	1	5000	5000	●	
	4. Housing area Play ground	1	5000	5000		
	5. Anganwari	1	200-300	400-600	●	
	6. Milk Booth	1	As per standard design of the concerned Department		●	
2. Neighborhood Population -10,000	1. Primary School	1	2000-4000	2000-4000	●	
	2. Sr. Secondary School	1	6000-8000	6000-8000	●	
	3. Religious building	2	400	800	●	
	4. Electric Sub Station 11 KV	1	80	80	●	
	5. Banquet Halls	1	800-2000	800-2000	●	
	6. Local shopping	1	3000	3000	●	
	7. Service Market	1	2000	2000	●	
	8. Informal Bazaar/ Rehri Bazar	1	1000	1000		
	9. Three wheeler & Taxi Stand	1	400	400	●	
	10. Neighborhood Park	1	10000	10000	●	
	11. Neighborhood Play Area	1	5000-10000	5000-10000	●	
	12. Underground water tank with booster station and OHT	1	2000	2000	●	
	13. Sewage Pumping Station	1	500	500	●	
	14. Coaching centres, IT & language training centres	1	500	500	●	
	15. Dhalao including segregation	1	200	200	●	
	16. Dispensary	1	800-1200	800-1200	●	
	17. Local level waste water treatment facility		As per requirement		●	
3. Community Population-1,00,000	1. Hospital 'C' (101 beds & 200 beds)	1	5000-10000	5,000-10,000	●	●
	2. Hospital 'D' (upto 100 beds)	1	2,500-5,000	2,500-5,000	●	●
	3. a) Family Welfare Centre b) Pediatric Centre c) Geriatric centre d) Diagnostic center	1 1 1 1	500-800 each	500-800 each	●	
	4. Maternity Home	2	1,000-2,000	2,000-4,000	●	●
	5. Nursing Home/ Polyclinic	2	1,000-2,000	2,000-4,000	●	●
	6. Dispensary for pet animals & birds	1	300	300	●	
	7. Police Post	1	1,000	1,000	●	
	8. Community Recreational club	1	2,000	2,000	●	
	9. Socio-Cultural activities (auditorium, music, dance & drama centre/ meditation & spiritual centre)	1	1,000	1,000	●	
	10. Night Shelter	1	1,000	1,000	●	

	11. Multipurpose Community hall (provision for marriages, small public gathering, function, eating joint and library, gym etc.)	1	2000	2000	•	•
	12. LPG Godowns	3 LPG Godowns per 1 lakh population			•	
	13. SKO/ LDO outlet	As per standard design of the concerned department			•	
	14. Electric sub station 66 KV	2	8,550	17,000		•
	15. Community Centre	As per norms / requirement			•	•
	16. Informal Bazaar	1	1,000	1,000	•	•
	17. Community Park	1				
	a) Park	1	50,000			•
	b) Multipurpose Park/ground	1	20,000			•
	18. Community Sports Centre	1	10,000-30,000	10,000-30,000	•	
	19. Bus Terminal	1	1,000	1,000		•
	20. Waste water treatment facility	As per requirement				•
	21. Sewage Pumping Station	1	2000	2000		•
	22. Parking space for parking of buses, LMVs, IPTs, etc.	2	3000	6000		•
4. District Population-5,00,000	1. Hospital 'A' (501 beds & above)	1	25,000 -45000	25,000-45,000	•	•
	2. Hospital 'B' (201 beds to 500 beds)	2	15,000-25000	30,000-50000	•	•
	3. Veterinary Hospital for pet animals & birds	1	2,000	2,000	•	•
	4. Vocational Training Centre: (ITI/ Polytechnic/ Vocational Training Institute/ Management Institute/ Teacher Training Institute etc.) Research and Development Centre	1	4,000	4,000	•	•
	5. School for Mentally Challenged	2	2,000	4,000	•	
	6. School for Physically Challenged	2	2,000	4,000	•	
	7. General College	1	As per the UGC norms			
	8. Professional College (Engineering)	1	As per the AICTE norms			•
	9. Police Station	2	10,000	20,000		•
	10. Fire Station (5 to 7 km radius)	3	10,000	30,000	•	•
	11. Old Age Home	1	1,000	1,000	•	
	12. Care Centre for Physically/ Mentally challenged	1	1,000	1,000		•
	13. Working women-men hostel	1	1,000	1,000		•
	14. Adult Education Centre	1	1,000	1,000		•
	15. Orphanage/ Children's Centre (one each)	1	1,000	1,000		•
	16. Electric sub station 220 KV	1	29,600	29,600	•	•
	17. District Centre	1	4,00,000	4,00,000	•	•
	18. Service Market	1	60,000	60,000	•	•
	19. Bus Terminal	1	2,000	2,000		•

	20. Bus Depot	1	4,000	4,000		●
	21. District park			2,90,000		●
	a. Park	1	2,50,000			
	b. Multipurpose ground/ Park	1	40,000			
	22. District Sports Centre	1	30,000-1,00,000	30,000-1,00,000		●
	23. Recreational club	1	5,000	5,000		●
	24. Cremation ground	1	4,000	4,000		●
5. Zonal/ Sub City Population 10,00,000	1. Medical College	1	As per Medical Council of India / Regulatory Body			●
	2. Nursing and Paramedic Institute	1	2,000	2,000	●	
	3. Telephone Exchange	1	2,500	2,500		●
	4. RSU (Remote Subscribe Unit)	1 for 3 km radius	300	300	●	
	5. Sub City Wholesale Market	1	1,50,000	1,50,000		●
	6. Bus Depot		As per requirement			●
	7. Head Post Office & Administration Office	1	2,500	2,500		●
	8. Sewage Pumping Station	1	2,500	2,500		●
	9. Municipal Office for water & sewerage	1	1,000	1,000		●
	10. Sewerage Treatment Plant (180 mld)	1	2,34,000	2,34,000		●
	11. City Park			10,80,000		●
	a. Park	1	10,00,000			
	b. Multipurpose ground	1	80,000			
	12. Old Age Home	2	1,000	2,000		●
	13. Divisional Sports Centre	1	3,00,000	3,00,000		●
	14. Burial ground/ Cemetery	1	10000	10000		●
	15. Religious Centre	1	40,000	40,000		●
	16. Science Centre		As per requirement			●

LOP – Layout Plan ZP – Zonal Plan

In addition, the following facilities shall also be provided at city level:

Table 3.4 City Level Facilities

Facilities	No.	Area (in ha.)
1. University Campus a) Academic incl. Administration b) Residential c) Sports & Cultural Activities d) Parks & Landscape	4 sites in Urban Extension	Up to 20.0
2. District office and battalion	1 for each administrative zone	1.0
3. Police Lines		2.0
4. District Jail	1 / 25 lakh population	5.0
5. Police Training Institute/ College	City level (To be located in fringe area)	5.0
6. Police Firing Range		Up to 10.0
7. Police Camp		Up to 10.0
8. Interstate Bus Terminus (ISBT)	As per requirement	10.0

9. International Conventional Centre	At city level		As per requirement
10. Fire Training Institute/ College	City level (One site in Urban Extension)		3.0
11. Disaster Management Centre	1 for each administrative zone.		1.0 Ha along with suitable open area (2Ha) for soft parking, temporary shelter, parade ground etc.
12. Exhibition-cum-Fair Ground	2 sites in Urban Extension.		Up to 40.0 each
13. Religious Centre	1	25 lakh population	4.0
14. Integrated Office Complex	1 for each administrative zone.		1.5
15. Amusement Park	Up to 10 ha., in District Park.		
16. International Sports Complex	About 200 Ha to be reserved wherever possible in Urban Extension.		
17. Veterinary Institute	As per Veterinary Council of India / Ministry norms (subject to availability of land.		

Note:

i. Post office counter, telegraph office, courier service counter, Internet counter, bank counter/ATM permitted in all use zones / under mixed use as per requirement.

ii. These are suggestive norms and lower norms could be adopted in built up areas / special areas, etc.

iii. For the Zonal Development Plans in Urban Extension, the facility belts/corridors shall be detailed out in the layout plans.

3.3. REDEVELOPMENT OF EXISTING URBAN AREA

The scope for development of urban extensions on a large scale is restricted due to limitations of buildable / urbanizable land in Delhi. Therefore, the option of redevelopment through a process of reorganisation and utilisation of the land already developed will be a major element of the overall city development plan.

A redevelopment strategy for accommodating more population in a planned manner is to be taken up on priority in all use zones for efficient and optimum utilization of the existing urban land, both in planned and unplanned areas. This would have to be based on provision of infrastructure viz. water supply, sewerage, road network, open spaces and the essential social infrastructure.

To encourage the growth impulse for regeneration in the target redevelopment areas, the possible incentives and modalities recommended include grant of planning permission at the scheme level with permission to reorganize/pool properties for planning purposes, provision of social infrastructure through Transferable Development Rights or Accommodation Reservation and reduced space standards for unplanned areas, enhanced FAR for specified redevelopment areas and application of flexible concept of mix-use zones in Special Area & Villages on scheme basis.

3.3.1. REDEVELOPMENT STRATEGY

The target areas for redevelopment will have to be identified on the basis of their need for up-gradation and potential for development. Redevelopment Schemes will be prepared by the respective local body / land owners / residents. The concerned local body should promote private land owners to take up assembly and redevelopment of a minimum area of 4 hectares. Some of the areas identified are:

3.3.1.1. Planned Areas

A. Influence Zone along MRTS and major Transport Corridor

Growth of Delhi over the years has been on the ring and radial pattern with reliance on road based public transport. The development envisaged by the previous Plans was poly nodal with hierarchy of Commercial Centres located either on ring or radial roads. The proposed MRTS network will bring sizable urban area within walking distance from the proposed stations. This will have an impact on the existing structure of the city and consequently its development. This changed scenario provides opportunities for city restructuring and optimum utilization of the land along the MRTS corridors. In this process, a sizable proportion of the additional population with requisite facilities and employment can be absorbed along these corridors.

Influence Zone along MRTS corridor is envisaged as intensive development zone. The scheme for Redevelopment of Influence Zone shall be prepared on the basis of the following:

i. Maximum upto 500 m. wide belt on both sides of centre line of the MRTS / Major Transport Corridor (to be identified in consultation with GNCTD) will be designated as Influence Zone which will be identified in the respective Zonal Development Plans.

ii. Entire approved layout plan of a scheme will be included in the zone if more than 70% of the plan area falls inside the influence zone. In case of large schemes, block / pocket boundary should be considered as one scheme for this purpose.

iii. The approval of schemes will be granted only after commencement of execution of the respective phase of MRTS.

iv. Development Controls applicable will be as permissible for the respective use zones / use premises.

v. Higher FAR and height can be availed of through the preparation and approval of comprehensive integrated scheme.

vi. In the proposed Urban Extension areas the land uses will be integrated with the proposed movement corridors at planning stages only.

vii. The following areas shall be excluded from the enhancement of FAR: -

- Lutyens' Bungalow Zone, Chanakya Puri., DIZ Area and Matasundari Area.
- Civil Lines Bungalow Area.
- Monument Regulated Zone (As per ASI guidelines).
- Property development of DMRC.
- Comprehensive commercial schemes.

B. Re-densification of low-density areas.

There is a large proportion of underused land with a number of vacant sites as well as dilapidated built-up areas lying vacant in the city. Many of such areas are owned by Government of India. Such areas are recommended to be planned for redevelopment with higher density in order to make optimum use of land resource as per the prescribed norms.

C. Redevelopment of Other Developed areas

In Delhi, including New Delhi (NDMC area), a large number of housing, commercial and industrial areas are old and characterized by poor structural condition, sub-optimal utilisation of land, congestion, poor urban form, inadequate infrastructure services, lack of community facilities, etc. These are to be redeveloped as per the prescribed norms and development controls and with the initiative / consultation with the Residents' society / RWA / Traders' Associations.

3.3.1.2. Special Area

The Special Area as defined in the Plan has been divided into three separate parts, namely (i) Walled City (ii) Walled City and Extension and (iii) Karol Bagh. These are characterized by a mix of different land uses and have similarities in compact built form, narrow circulation space and low-rise high-density developments, mainly accommodating residential, commercial - both retail or wholesale and industrial uses. Therefore, it is important that the areas, which are already established with identified uses, continue to play an active economic role. The Authority may further designate certain other areas as 'Special Area'.

The strategy is to provide suitable framework for allowing mix-use activities appropriate to the character of the areas as per the individual schemes having greater flexibility in terms of permitting variety of uses namely, commercial use (shops, offices, banks etc.), household industries or outlets for specialized services etc. However, the criterion of selection of the mix-use activities shall be as per Mixed Use Regulations.

Required parking and open spaces will have to be provided as per the norms, while reduced space norms for other facilities may be accepted. The redevelopment areas should ensure modern services and amenities, thereby eliminating risk generating structures and activities.

The regulations for Special Area shall be different from other areas. All these areas are to be brought within the planning purview. For this, the owners can jointly redevelop on the basis of the norms and regulations to be prescribed.

A. Shahjahanabad (Walled City)

The most important part of the Special Area is the traditional City of Shahjahanabad, part of which is a core of the business district. The area is prone to commercialisation, particularly with improved accessibility due to the MRTS. The Plan proposes to regulate and shift noxious and hazardous wholesale trades and industrial activity from this area.

Traditional areas in Walled City need special treatment to conserve its heritage value while retaining the residential character. Redevelopment of government owned katras is to be taken on priority. However, redevelopment would also be promoted in privately owned katras simultaneously. Permission of activities in use premises and building control regulations shall be as follows:

(i) The area surrendered for public facilities or for heritage value to be used as tradable FAR.

(ii) Street pattern:

The street pattern in residential area is proposed to be restructured with linkages from the metro stations. The minimum road width and prioritizing of road widening are dictated by fire and other disaster management criteria. The streets, having 30m to 50m lengths, shall have a minimum of 3m width and streets having more than 50m length shall have a minimum of 4.5m width. Common facilities shall be located with linkages to pedestrian roads and metro stations.

(iii) Subject to preparation and approval of an Integrated Redevelopment Scheme, higher FAR and other development controls can be considered. This provision is also subject to requirement of heritage controls, parking, accessibility of emergency vehicles and basic services.

B. Walled City Extension

Pahar Ganj, Sadar Bazar, Roshanara Road and their adjoining areas comprise the Walled City and Extension. These are old congested built-up areas and for up-gradation of the environment in these areas, minimum level of infrastructure and parking facilities should be provided.

The redevelopment in these areas shall be in accordance with the respective comprehensive redevelopment schemes with conservative surgery as a planning tool, as far as possible.

In the Special Area Plan, use zones have been marked in different pockets of the `Other Urban Renewal Areas'. These pockets shall be planned for the respective use zones assigned. The redevelopment schemes for different use zones shall generally adopt regulations prescribed in the Development Code except in cases where special provisions have been made / proposed in this Plan.

C. Karol Bagh

Karol Bagh has become one of the important commercial centre outside the Walled City. The invasion of commercial activity has pushed out the residential use substantially. Karol Bagh area is due for comprehensive redevelopment on the basis of mixed-use concept with provisions of parking and up-gradation of facilities and utilities. The gridiron pattern should be treated as an asset to regulate and pedestrianize the traffic movement.

3.3.1.3. Unplanned Areas

A. Slum and JJ Clusters, Resettlement Colonies and Unauthorised Colonies

In-situ up-gradation of the land pockets of slum and JJ Clusters, which are not required for public / priority use is the first option for provision of affordable housing for rehabilitation of squatters. Resettlement colonies though planned, are also to be upgraded in a similar way for infrastructure provision. Similarly, unauthorized colonies slated for regularization are also proposed to be improved through redevelopment by ensuring participation of the inhabitants.

B. Villages

The villages in Delhi have undergone significant physical and functional transformation related with their specific location. Villages are characterized by a mix of different land uses and have similarities in compact built form, narrow circulation space and low-rise high-density developments. These mainly accommodate residential, commercial and industrial uses and function as a mix. It is important that these areas, which are already established with identified uses, continue to play an active economic role.

Comprehensive schemes for the development of villages should be prepared by the concerned local bodies with the aim of provision of optimal facilities and services within the abadis and integration with the surrounding areas. Towards the latter objective, development along the peripheries of the villages should be carefully planned, wherever necessary for the provision of services and green / open areas, circulation, etc. This aspect should also be kept in view while preparing layout plans for urban extension areas.

For provision of social and educational facilities, reduced space standards shall be adopted. The facilities like community hall, dispensary etc. may be grouped together depending on the availability land. Small shops shall be permissible in residential plots on ground floor as per provisions of Mixed Use Regulations in village abadi including rural (para 15.6.3).

3.3.2 GUIDELINES FOR REDEVELOPMENT SCHEMES

The basic objective of redevelopment is to upgrade the area by implementing specific schemes on the basis of existing physical and socio-economic conditions in the following way:

(i) Influence Zone along MRTS Corridor and the Sub-Zones for redevelopment and renewal should be identified on the basis of physical features such as metro, roads, drains, high tension lines and control zones of Monuments / Heritage areas, etc.

(ii) The residents / cooperative societies/ private developers should get the layout and services plan prepared in consultation with the concerned authority for approval.

(iii) Within the overall Redevelopment / Regularisation plans, building plan approval shall be at following two stages:

(a) Planning Permission for an area of around 4 Ha. This permission may not be required in case an approved layout / Redevelopment / Regularisation plan exists.

(b) 1. Cluster Block for a minimum area of 3000 sq.m. The owners should pool together and reorganise their individual properties so as to provide minimum 30% of area as common green / soft parking besides circulation areas and common facilities.

2. Individual buildings shall be given sanction by the concerned authority within the framework of cluster block approval.

(c) The norms of Group Housing with respect to ground coverage, basement, parking, set backs etc. (except FAR) shall be applicable.

(iv) Amalgamation and reconstitution of the plots for planning purpose will be permitted.

(v) To incentivise the redevelopment a maximum overall FAR of 50% over and above the existing permissible FAR on individual plots subject to a maximum of 400 shall be permissible. Higher FAR shall however not be permissible in redevelopment of Lutyens Bungalow Zone, Civil Lines Bungalows Area and Monument regulated Zone.

(vi) In case of plots with service lanes, the lane area may be included in the scheme. However, no FAR / coverage will be granted and the area shall be used as public area.

(vii) The standards of housing density, minimum width of roads and community facilities can be relaxed, wherever justified, by planning considerations (e.g., pedestrianization of the area).

(viii) The Public and Semi-public uses and services like hospitals, dispensaries, colleges, schools, police stations, fire stations, post offices, local government offices, parking etc. shall be retained in their present locations as far as possible and if not, relocated as part of the redevelopment scheme. Alternative sites shall be indicated in the Redevelopment Schemes / Zonal Development Plans. Any change or addition thereof shall be in accordance with the overall policy frame prescribed in the plan.

(ix) Reduced space standards may be adopted for community facilities / social infrastructure for the areas mentioned in 4.2.2.2 B sub para (ii) 'social'. The land required for any public purpose may be acquired with the consent of the owner through issue of Development Rights Certificate in lieu of payment towards cost of land as per the prescribed regulations. The concept of Accommodation Reservation i.e. allowing construction of community facilities without counting in FAR may also be utilized.

(x) Subject to preparation and approval of integrated / comprehensive Redevelopment schemes and provision of parking and services, up to 10% of the FAR may be allowed for commercial use and 10% of the FAR for community facilities with a view to trigger a process of self-generating redevelopment.

(xi) The circulation pattern should include segregation of pedestrian and vehicular traffic, entry control, access of emergency vehicles to every block, provision of adequate parking etc.

(xii) Appropriate levies for increased FAR, and landuse conversion shall be charged from the beneficiaries by the competent authority as per prevailing rules / orders.

(xiii) Urban Design and Heritage to be ensured as per the guidelines.

(xiv) The land use shall be governed as per the Master Plan / Zonal Development Plan. The non-residential use will be permitted as per the provisions of the Mixed Use Regulations and Special Area Regulations.

4. SHELTER

The policy regarding "Shelter" is based on the goal of ensuring 'Shelter for All' by harnessing the potential of the public, private / corporate and household sectors. It aims to ensure effective housing and shelter options for all citizens, especially for the vulnerable groups and the poor, by creation of adequate housing stock on either rental or ownership basis. It envisages the role of the public agencies as facilitator through policy and strategic interventions.

Housing has a strong spatial relationship with employment, social services and other urban activities. The policy for development of housing could act as major tool for influencing the efficiency and equity of urban areas, besides its direct role in the provision of shelter.

4.1 HOUSING NEED

As per the Census 2001, Delhi has 24.5 lakh Census houses under the category of residence and residence-cum-other uses, in which 25.5 lakh households are residing. This reflects a net housing shortage of about 1.0 lakh houses / dwelling units. The households are accommodated in a variety of housing types including different categories of planned built housing, squatter settlements, unauthorized colonies, traditional areas and villages. The Sub-group on Shelter noted that up to the year 1991, the contribution to housing stock through institutional agencies was only 53% (excluding squatter housing). Therefore, the component of housing through non-institutional sources, viz., unauthorized colonies, squatter / JJ clusters, etc., is quite significant. This trend has continued in the current decade as well and has to be kept in view while determining the plan and strategy for housing.

Based on the projected population of 230 lakh by 2021, the estimated additional housing stock required will be around 24 lakh dwelling units. This includes an estimated housing requirement of 20 lakh dwelling units for additional population and backlog of about 4 lakh units comprising of 1 lakh net shortage and the rest by dilapidated and Kutcha structures requiring replacement.

It has also been assessed that around 40% of housing need can potentially be satisfied through redevelopment / up-gradation of existing areas of Delhi. This may be met in the present urban limits of A to H zones and in the sub cities of Dwarka, Rohini and Narela. This implies that the remaining 60% of the requirement would have to be met through 14.4 lakh new housing units to be provided in new areas. In order to ensure that housing need is accommodated in the urban extension, the Zonal Plans for 2021 should be prepared within 12 months.

Keeping in view the socio-economic composition of the population, it is estimated that around 50-55% of the housing requirement would be for the urban poor and the economically weaker sections in the form of houses of two rooms or less. Based on past experience it is necessary to distinguish between the urban poor comprising the inhabitants of squatter settlements / pavement dwellers, etc. and other economically weaker sections of the society, conventionally classified in the form of EWS, LIG, etc. The role of the government would have to be both as a provider and facilitator. The category of the urban poor is to be broadly catered in old and new urban areas through up-gradation of old / traditional areas, employers and industrial housing, group housing and also in unauthorised regularised colony infills.

A possible indicative scenario in terms of mode of housing supply in different types of development for the next two decades emerges as under:

Table 4.1 Indicative Distribution of Housing Types

Housing Type	Developm Agencies	Housing Component %		
		EWS/ LIG	Others	Total
Slum & JJ - In-situ Rehabilitation; Relocation / Reconstruction & Up-gradation.	Public Private, Co-op Society	25	-	25
Houses on Independent Plots & Redevelopment	Public, Private	4	4	8
Group Housing (Min. 35% of total DUs mandatory 2 room or less)	Public, Private Co-op Society	14	28	42
Employer Housing	Central / State Govt.	2	2	4
Unauthorised Regularised colonies infill	Co-op Society/ / Residents'/Association /Private	6	9	15
Other Housing areas/ Up-gradation of Old areas Traditional areas/ Villages	Public, Private Co-op Society	3	3	6
TOTAL		54	46	100

4.2 HOUSING STRATEGY

The proposed housing strategy incorporates specific approaches for development of new housing areas, upgradation and re-densification through redevelopment of existing housing areas including unauthorized colonies, housing in villages and Special Area. Looking at the possible distribution of housing types, the future requirement of shelter provision will be dominated by small dwelling units. In view of the limited availability of land and increased requirement of housing, plotted residential development shall be discouraged.

It is proposed to adopt a multi-pronged housing strategy for provision of housing stock and for delivery of serviced land, involving the private sector to a significant extent, public agencies and co-operative societies etc. The overall responsibility for provision of land and facilitation of adequate housing to meet the projected demand lies with the DDA in collaboration with GNCTD and other agencies.

Planning norms, land use zoning, density, FAR, and building controls have been reviewed for housing, both in new areas to be opened up and for redevelopment of existing areas. In the context of housing strategy, it is essential to optimise utilization of land and space with a view to increasing net residential density. These norms and controls should also be reviewed periodically (preferably every five years) by DDA and suitably modified / updated to meet the requirements of the citizens. It has been observed that the practice of prescribing FAR / density norms without distinguishing between housing categories in terms of plinth area, can result in over population or under population on the one hand, and non-optimal design and under-utilisation of the utility network, on the other. The norms should provide options to achieve the density and FAR both in Ground + 3 or 4 storeyed walk-up structures, without lift or in high-rise construction. A fixed density could lead to under utilisation of FAR or imposition of artificial limits to optimal use of land, which is a scarce commodity. Therefore, the following density norms, with corresponding category of dwelling unit (DU) sizes are proposed:

Slum/EWS housing (upto 30 sq.m)-600 DUs/Ha

Category I (above30-upto40sq.m.)-500 DUs/ Ha

Category II (above40-upto80sq.m.)-250 DUs/ Ha

Category III (above80sqm) - 175 DUs/Ha

The Central Government may relax density and other norms in consultation with DDA for public housing and projects of national importance.

In case of plotted development, the permissible number of dwelling units will be as prescribed for different plot sizes given in the development controls.

In case of Bungalow area (Part zone D) any residential density in group housing pockets shall be prescribed on the basis of detailed scheme.

In case of Civil Lines Bungalow Area, the development controls for group housing shall be as prescribed in the Zonal Development Plan of zone 'C'.

To make the construction activity more environment friendly, the choice of alternative building materials and techniques have to be reoriented and promoted for construction activity. Building technology parks and mobile expositions for cost effective materials and techniques are to be explored for new housing areas and redevelopment schemes. Standard specifications may also be incorporated in the Government Schedule and may be adopted for public buildings and housing schemes.

4.2.1 NEW HOUSING AREAS

Even if the assumptions regarding the extent of housing that could be met by redevelopment of the existing areas actually materialize, there would still be a need for the development of housing to the extent of at least 75,000 DUs per annum in different categories. This implies that specific plans would have to be evolved by DDA with the approval of the Competent Authority and action be taken with reference to the following:

(i) Determination of area requirement;

(ii) Identification of the areas for urbanization / housing development;

(iii) Evolving the pattern and norms for new housing development;

(iv) The mode and manner of development, and the roles of the private and public sectors in this process.

As already indicated, more than 50% of the new housing would be in the form of one and two room units with average plinth area of about 25 sq.m. to 40 sq.m. The average plinth area per house to be achieved in various neighbourhoods will also depend on composition of various income groups to be accommodated in the composite housing schemes.

The policy should indicate that EWS & LIG houses after construction by a private group shall be handed over to the nodal agency/ agencies and these should be allotted to eligible beneficiaries.

The new housing developed through the aforementioned methods should be based on a composite area basis and should cater to the special needs of elderly, handicapped and single occupants. With these aspects and planning norms, the land required to be developed in new housing will be to the tune of around 450-500 ha. per annum.

4.2.2 RESTRUCTURING AND UP-GRADATION OF THE EXISTING AREAS

In Delhi, a large number of areas are old and are characterized by poor structural condition of buildings, sub-optimal utilisation of land, congestion, poor urban form, inadequate infrastructure services, lack of community facilities, etc. The housing stock in both planned and unplanned areas can be enhanced through various approaches as given below.

4.2.2.1. Planned Areas

A. Plotted / Group Housing

The flats built by DDA, particularly those, which have become aged, may be redeveloped with permission and subject to the condition that the structural safety of other flats is not impinged. Already developed group housing inclusive of public (DDA and others), co-operative housing may be redeveloped on the basis of prescribed norms and regulations by formulating co-operative societies or self-managing communities. The funds for redevelopment should be contributed by the residents.

B. Employer Housing

In Delhi after Independence, substantial areas were developed at low density and have potential for densification. These are mainly government and cantonment areas. In order to optimally utilise these prime lands there is need of intensive development. On a conservative estimate the present housing stock can be increased to more than double. Infrastructure enhancement and provision for additional housing can be financed from the funds generated through cross-subsidisation between commercial and residential use for EWS and LIG categories.

C. Bungalow Area

Lutyens' Bungalow Zone comprises of large size plots and has a very pleasant green environment. The essential character of wide avenues, large plots, extensive landscape and low rise development, has a heritage value which has to be conserved. Mixed use, high intensity development along MRTS corridor and de-densification of trees / reduction of green cover is not permitted at all. The strategy for development in this zone will be as per the approved plans and the LBZ guidelines, as may be issued by the Government of India from time to time.

Civil Lines also has Bungalow Area of which the basic character has to be maintained.

4.2.2.2. Traditional Inner City and Unplanned Areas

The congested areas of the city have a predominant residential component like Shahjehanabad (Walled City), and its Extensions, Karol Bagh (Special Area) and villages. The unauthorised / regularised colonies, which are unplanned areas, have a role to play as a housing stock provider. All these areas should be redeveloped ensuring modern services and amenities for a safe residential environment and in the process, eliminating risk prone structures and activities. The owners can jointly redevelop the areas based on the prescribed guidelines.

A. Special Area and Villages

The Old City areas, Shahjehanabad (Walled City), and its Extensions, Karol Bagh (designated as Special Area) are fast changing their residential character to non-residential use, but still have a residential component. The non-residential uses of varying degrees have developed with time depending on their location, related with accessibility and the established trade.

In the case of traditional inner city areas, it is essential first to distinguish between the heritage segment of the area and the non-heritage segment of the area. Well-designed Special Area Redevelopment Schemes must be prepared for traditional areas giving the development control parameters for the heritage areas keeping in view archaeological norms / architectural character and general parameters for the non-heritage segment of the traditional area. Each Special Area Redevelopment Scheme should entail an enumeration of the monuments and old buildings within the heritage areas, which must be conserved. The MCD is the nodal agency who should prepare Special Area Redevelopment Schemes for all traditional areas within a time frame.

The basic objective of Special Area Redevelopment Scheme in traditional areas is to bring about in situ improvements which help in improving architectural character of the area, i.e., design and layout, as well as revitalising trade and commerce in the area.

The villages are also considered at par with these as they also have the same traits. The socio-economic changes in these old unplanned areas, especially in villages, have been substantial. The redevelopment plans should ensure that the permissibility of mixed use zoning at property or within the premise level is compatible to the predominant residential areas.

B. Unauthorised / Regularised Unauthorised Colonies

Unauthorised colonies in Delhi pose a serious human problem as a huge population is living in these colonies. The issue of existing unauthorized colonies has engaged attention since the mid-seventies when a policy for regularization was formulated. 567 out of 607 listed unauthorized colonies were regularised till October 1993, but many more unauthorized colonies have come up since then. Such colonies are to be identified by the Govt. of NCTD.

The present method of regularization of unauthorized colonies is by the provision of basic infrastructure to improve the environment. However, regularization has not really brought in any tangible improvement. Effectively, the process has only led to de-facto tenure rights on the land and access to services.

In all unauthorised colonies whether on private or public land, regularization should be done as per the government orders issued from time to time. It must be ensured that for improvement of physical and social infrastructure, the minimum necessary / feasible level of services and community facilities are provided.

(i) Physical: Plans for provision of services shall be prepared by the concerned local bodies.

(ii) Social: For provision of social facilities, reduced space standards shall be adopted. Depending on the availability of land, facilities like community hall, dispensary etc. can be grouped together.

(a)	Primary school	800 sq.m. per 5000 population
(b)	Sr. Secondary School	2000 sq.m per 10000 population

The above norms can be further relaxed for existing recognised schools on the basis of minimum norms prescribed by the Education Department, GNCTD / Central Board of Secondary Education.

(c) The following facilities can be clubbed in a composite facility centre (500-1000 sqm.)

(i) Multi-purpose community hall - 100 sqm.

(ii) BastiVikas Kendra - 100 sqm.

(iii) Religious site - 100 sqm.

(iv) Police Post - 100 sqm.

(v) Health Centre - 100 sqm.

(vi) Park/Shishu Vatika- 200 sqm.

(vii) Area for essential retail outlets e.g., Milk Booth, Fair Price Shop, Kerosene shop, etc. may be provided.

(viii) Provisions for informal trade units and weekly market to be made, wherever necessary.

4.2.3. HOUSING FOR URBAN POOR

The category of urban poor for purpose of the Plan would mainly comprise the inhabitants of squatter settlements and informal service providers. Such services could include domestic help, hawkers and vendors, low paid workers in the industrial, commercial and trade / business sectors, etc. These include both existing population and future migrants. In terms of housing requirements of the city, this continues to be the single biggest challenge and would require a mix of approaches and innovative solutions.

4.2.3.1. Rehabilitation/Relocation of Slum & JJ Clusters

In so far as the existing squatter settlements are concerned, the present three-fold strategy of relocation from areas required for public purpose, in-situ up-gradation at other sites to be selected on the basis of specific parameters and environmental up-gradation to basic minimum standards shall be allowed as an interim measure. Rest of the clusters, till they are covered by either of the first two components of the strategy, should be continued.

During the Plan period 1981-2001, sites and services approach based relocation was employed in which resettlement of squatter slums was done on 18 sqm and 12.5sqm. plots (transit accommodation) allotted to eligible persons on licence basis. This has led to a number of aberrations and there are several aspects, due to which this approach needs to be progressively abandoned and substituted by an alternate approach. Broadly speaking this alternate approach should have the following components:

(i) Resettlement, whether in the form of in-situ up-gradation or relocation, should be based mainly on built up accommodation of around 25 sq. m with common areas and facilities, rather than on the model of horizontal plotted development.

(ii) The concept of land as a resource should be adopted to develop such accommodation with private sector participation and investment, to the extent possible.

(iii) Incentives by way of higher FAR, part commercial use of the land and, if necessary and feasible, Transfer of Development Rights should be provided.

(iv) A cooperative resettlement model with adequate safeguards may be adopted with tenure rights being provided through the institution of Co-operative Societies.

(v) The provision of accommodation should be based on cost with suitable arrangements for funding / financing, keeping in view the aspect of affordability and capacity to pay.

(vi) In cases of relocation, the sites should be identified with a view to develop relatively small clusters in a manner that they can be integrated with the overall planned development of the area, particularly keeping in view the availability of employment avenues in the vicinity. Very large resettlement sites could lead to a phenomenon of planned slums.

(vii) Suitable arrangement for temporary transit accommodation for families to be rehabilitated should be made. This may preferably be near or at the same site and the utilization of these may be synchronised with the phases of implementation of the scheme of in-situ up-gradation.

(viii) Community Based Organisations (CBOs) and Non-Governmental Organisations (NGOs) should be closely involved in the resettlement process.

4.2.3.2. Resettlement Colonies

Most of the resettlement colonies have been provided with essential services, but the immediate need is of individual services i.e. water, sewerage and electricity. To ensure healthy and better environment, the construction of houses needs to be based on approved / standard building plans.

Co-operative societies / private developers / govt. agencies may come forward for redevelopment based on the incentives as applicable for the Squatter Rehabilitation Scheme. Reconstruction of existing plotted development, group housing should be encouraged as per the Redevelopment Guidelines given in para 4.2.3.4.

4.2.3.3. New Housing for Urban Poor

New housing should be in the form of one or two room units, which would be developed through public and private agencies and through Cooperative societies. As this category constitutes bulk of the housing stock that has to be catered at an affordable price to the lowest income bracket as housing for Economically Weaker Sections (EWS), this is often done by cross-subsidization.

For this purpose, adequate land would be earmarked for EWS housing. The developers of group housing shall ensure that minimum 15% of FAR or 35% of the dwelling units, whichever is more, are constructed for Community-Service Personnel / EWS and lower income category. In old built up areas, this may be as redevelopment schemes or industrial housing, etc., whereas, in urban extensions, the acquisition and development cost of this land should be borne by rest of the project. Such reserved lands should be handed over to a designated agency for promoting housing for low income and weaker sections.

The pattern of EWS housing shall be such as to ensure optimal utilization of land in a sustainable manner. For that purpose, multi- storied housing will be the preferred option. Apart from mandatory provision for EWS housing in all group housing projects/ schemes, the primary responsibility for creating adequate stock of housing for urban poor shall be borne by public agencies.

4.2.3.4. Slum & JJ Redevelopment Regulations and Guidelines for Collective Community Rehabilitation / Relocation - In-situ Up-gradation / Rehabilitation of Slum & JJ Clusters and Resettlement Colonies

The concerned implementing agency / corporate body should work out schemes for collective community rehabilitation/ relocation and explore the possibility of involving private sector/slum cooperatives. In existing resettlement colonies, redevelopment, regular servicing and maintenance, which are overdue, are to be based on the guidelines and incentives as applicable for the Slum& JJ Rehabilitation Scheme.

The following guidelines with site-specific relaxations may be adopted as required. Regular monitoring of executed schemes and revision of these guidelines at the time of preparation of new schemes is essential. Group housing norms shall be applicable with the following conditions:

(i) Minimum plot size 2000 sqm (facing a min. road of 9m).

(ii) Maximum density - 600 units per ha. + 10% variation, on residential component of the land.

(iii) The scheme should be designed in a composite manner with an overall maximum FAR of 400 on the residential component of the land and FAR on the remunerative component of the land shall be as applicable for the relevant land use.

(iv) Mixed land use / commercial component up to 10% of permissible FAR in the residential component of the land.

(v) Specific situations may require clubbing of scattered squatters with JJ sites in the neighbourhood to work out an overall comprehensive scheme.

(vi) The minimum residential component of the land area for rehabilitation of squatters has to be 60% and maximum area for remunerative use has to be 40%.

(vii) Area of dwelling unit for rehabilitation shall be around 25 to 30 sqm..

(viii) Common parking is to be provided which can be relaxed wherever required, except for the parking for remunerative purposes.

(ix) No restriction on ground coverage (except set backs)

(x) Schemes shall be approved by concerned local body.

(xi) Schemes / designs should be compatible for disabled.

(xii) Norms for Social Infrastructure shall be as per 4.2.2.2 B sub para (ii) 'Social'.

(xiii) Norms for Physical Infrastructure shall be as per note (iv) of Table 4.2.

4.3. NIGHT SHELTER

The provision of night shelters is envisaged to cater to the shelter less, which are proposed to be provided near the Railway Terminals, Bus Terminals, Wholesale / Retail markets, Freight Complexes etc. as per requirements, and should be identified keeping in view major work centres. Special provisions should be made for the homeless, women and children including the disabled, orphans and old. In addition, multi-purpose use of the existing facility buildings may be allowed for night shelter purpose. Provision should also be made for converting existing buildings, wherever available, with suitable modifications into night shelters.

On the basis of the 2001 Census of houseless population, at least 25 sites should be earmarked in Delhi for night shelters. In order to make the provision of this facility financially sustainable for the local body, innovative concepts such as integrated complex with commercial space on the ground floor and night shelter on the first floor should be explored. The guidelines and incentive package should be designed by the concerned local agency in collaboration with the Govt of NCT-Delhi with a view to develop self-sustaining night shelters. One night shelter shall be provided for 1 lakh population.

4.4. DEVELOPMENT CONTROLS FOR RESIDENTIAL USE ZONE

In the residential use zone there are two sub-zones, RD - Residential Area (including villages within Laldora located in any use zone) and RF - Foreign Mission. Permission of use premises in sub-use zone RD shall be as per permissibility given in the respective chapters.

4.4.1 PERMISSION OF USE PREMISES IN THE SUB USE ZONE - FOREIGN MISSION (RF)

Use premises in the Foreign Mission sub use zone as part of the approved layout plan.

(i) Foreign Mission

(ii) Housing (for the Mission Employees)

(iii) Guest House

(iv) Local Shopping

(v) Bank

(vi) Recreational Club

(vii) Health Centre- Hospital, Dispensary

(viii) Integrated Residential School

(ix) Cultural and Information Centre

(x) Police Post and Fire Station

(xi) Post and Telegraph office

4.4.2 SUB-DIVISION OF RESIDENTIAL ZONE (RD) INTO USE PREMISES

The sub-division of residential use zone into use premises and subsequent approval of the layout plans shall be governed by the following norms:

The residential area can have both the plotted and group housing. In case of group and cluster court housing the minimum plot size shall be 3000 sqm. (2000 sqm for slum re-housing plot with differential infrastructure norms).

The provision of requisite social infrastructure shall be governed by the norms for residential neighbourhood of 10,000 population. In any residential sub division plan the minimum area reserved for social infrastructure shall be about 7 sqm per person.

Table 4.2 Infrastructure Requirement for layout at Residential Neighbourhood level

S.No	Use Premises	No. of units	Unit Area (ha.)	Total land (ha.)
(a)	**Education**			
	1. Primary School	1	0.20-0.40	0.20-0.40
	2. Senior Secondary School	1	0.60-0.80	0.60-0.80
(b)	**Shopping**			
	3. Local Convenience shopping	1	0.40	0.40
	4. Service Market	1	0.20	0.20
	5. Informal Bazaar	1	0.10	0.10

(c)	**Other Community Facilities**			
	6. Milk Booth	–	As per standard norms (in LSC)	
	7. Banquet Hall	1	0.08-0.20	0.08-0.20
	8. Religious Building	2	0.04	0.08
	9. Housing Area Play ground	2	0.5	1.0
	10. Neighbourhood Play area	1	1.0	1.0
	11. Anganwari	2	0.02-0.03	0.04-0.06
(d)	**Recreational**			
	12. Tot lot @ 0.50sq.m./person		0.0125	0.5
	13. Housing Area Park	2	0.5	1.0
	14. Neighbourhood Park	1	1.0	1.0
(c)	**Utilities**			
	15. Dhalao including segregation facility	1	0.02	0 2
	16. Underground water tank	1	0.20	0.20
	17. Local level waste water treatment facility		Wherever	feasible
(f)	**Transportation**			
	18. Three wheeler and Taxi Stand	1	0.04	0.04

Notes:

(i) These facilities should preferably be located along internal roads with minimum 12 m ROW, unless specified. The development of the infrastructure should be monitored to assess the achievement in the relevant sectors.

(ii) The open space at the neighbourhood level shall be provided @ 4.5 sq.m. per person Minimum size of tot lot at cluster level shall be 125 sq.m.

(iii) The location of schools and Anganwaris should be made in the layout plan in cluster form to facilitate sharing of common parking space and playground.

(iv) The planning of physical infrastructure shall be governed by the following norms:

(a) Under ground tank, sewerage-pumping system shall be provided as per requirement.

(b) Rainwater harvesting shall be an integral part of the storm water drainage plan at the time of sanction of layout plan for all the plots.

(c) The natural drainage pattern is not to be disturbed.

(d) Dual pipe system of recycled water is recommended in new areas and redevelopment schemes.

(e) Dhalaos including facility of segregation of biodegradable and recyclable solid waste should be provided.

(f) Electric sub station shall be provided as per requirement.

(g) Pole mounted electric transformers for augmenting electric supply in already developed areas are recommended.

(h) Non-conventional sources i.e. solar energy etc. is recommended for public areas in all the establishments.

(i) Provisions for decentralised sewerage treatment plant and segregated waste disposal shall be made where centralised system is not available. It shall be ensured that no untreated effluent is allowed to exit / spill out of the scheme area.

(v) Planning of the residential neighbourhood regarding circulation system, including safety requirements shall be governed by the BIS standards or as per the norms of the concerned agencies.

(vi) Suitable landscape plans for the neighbourhood shall be prepared, indicating in reasonable detail, the landscape development of the parks and roadside plantation etc.

(vii) These are suggestive norms and lower norms could be adopted in built up areas / Special Areas, etc.

Table 4.3: Uses / Use Activities Permitted in Use Premises

Use Premises	Definition	Use/ Use Activities Permitted
* Residential Plot - Plotted Housing	A Premise for one or more than one dwelling unit and may have on it one main building block and one accessory block for garages and service personnel.	Residence, mixed use activity as per the Master Plan provisions/ Registered RWA/Society Office (50 sq.m.)
Residential Plot - Group Housing	A premise of size not less than 3000 sqm (2000 sqm. for Slum/ JJ rehabilitation) comprising of residential flats with basic amenities like parking, park, convenience shops, public utility etc.	Residential flat, mixed use activity as per the Master Plan provisions, retail shops of confectionery, grocery & general merchandise, books and stationery, Chemist, Barber, Laundry, Tailor, Vegetable Shop (On ground floor with an area up to 20 sqm. each). Community Room, Society office, Crèche / Day Care Centre, religious, Senior citizen recreation room, swimming pool.
Residential Flat	Residential accommodation for one family / household as part of group housing.	Residence, mixed use activity as per the Master Plan provisions.
Residential Premises Special Area	A residential premise in Special Area.	As per Special Area Regulations
Slum/ rehabilitation	Residential accommodation provided JJ as part of slum area resettlement/ rehabilitation	As per Slum Area Redevelopment Regulations
Foreign Mission	A Premise for the foreign mission.	Foreign Mission and related facilities / offices (with max. 25% of FAR for residential component)
Hostel	A premise in which residential accommodation in the form of rooms is provided, usually attached to an institution, with or without dining facility.	Hostel, Old Age Home, Watch and Ward Residence (20 sqm), Service Shops of Barber, Laundry, Soft Drink and Snack Stall (max. 20 sq.m. each)
Guest House Lodging & Boarding House	A premise providing temporary accommodation for short durations.	Guest Rooms, Watch and Ward Residence (20 sqm), Service Shops of Barber, Laundry, Soft Drink and Snack Stall (upto 20 sqm each)
Dharamshala its equivalent	A premise providing temporary accommodation or for short durations.on no-profit basis.	Dharamshala, Service Personnel Shops of Barber & Laundry, Soft Drink & Snack Stall (upto 20 sqm each)
Rain Basera (Night Shelter)	A premise having the facility for providing the night accommodation to individuals without any charges or with token charges. It may run by local government or voluntary agencies.	Night Shelter and related facilities.
Farm House	A dwelling house on a farm.	Farm House, Watch and Ward Residence (up to 20 sqm)

* Pre 1962 plotted double storied flats shall be treated as Residential Plots.

* Bed and Breakfast accommodation may be a permissible activity in residential plot/ flat, if registered under the Scheme notified by Ministry of Tourism, GoI/ GNCTD from time to time.

4.4.3 CONTROL FOR BUILDING/BUILDINGS WITHIN RESIDENTIAL PREMISES

A. Residential Plot-Plotted Housing

Maximum ground coverage, FAR, number of dwelling units for different size of residential plots shall be as per the following table:

	Area of Plot (sq. m)	Max. Ground Coverage %	FAR	No. of DUs
1	Below 32	90*	350	3
2	Above 32 to 50	90*	350	3
3	Above 50 to 100	90*	350	4

4	Above 100 to 250	75**	300**	4
5	Above 250 to 750	75	225	6
6	Above 750 to 1000	50	150	9
7	Above 1000 to 1500	40	120	9
8	Above 1500 to 2250	40	120	12
9	Above 2250 to 3000	40	120	15
10	Above 3000 to3750	40	120	18
11	Above 3750	40	120	21

Notes:

1. The local body concerned shall be competent to disregard variation of upto 2% in plot size, arising from conversion of area from sq. yard to sq.m. and to grant the norms applicable to the lower category of plot size in accordance to para (ii) below.

2. *100% ground coverage shall be eligible for regularization of construction, already existing as on 22.09.06 on payment of charges as notified.

3. Minimum size of the residential plot shall be 32 sqm. However, in case of Government sponsored economically weaker section schemes, size could be reduced further.

4. **100% ground coverage and 350 FAR shall be eligible for regularization of construction already existing as on 22.09.06 on payment of charges as per the notification, in respect plot size between 100 to 175 sqm.

5. Permissible FAR and Dwelling Units shall not be less than MPD-2001 norms.

Terms and Conditions:

(i) The additional number of dwelling units would be subject to payment of levy for the augmentation of civic infrastructure.

(ii) The total coverage and FAR permissible in any plot in a category, shall not be less than that permissible and available to the largest plot in the next lower category.

(iii) Height:

The maximum height of the building in all plots shall be 15 metres.

(iv) Subdivision of plots is not permitted. However, if there are more than one buildings in one residential plot, the sum of the built up area and ground coverage of all such buildings, shall not exceed the built up area and ground coverage permissible in that plot.

(v) The mezzanine floor, and service floor, if constructed, shall be counted in the FAR.

(vi) Basement:

Basement shall not be counted towards FAR if used for purposes permissible under Building byelaws namely household storage and parking. Basement area shall not extend beyond the coverage on the ground floor as per permissible and sanctioned built up area, but may extend to the area below the internal courtyard and shaft. Basement if used in terms of Chapter 15.0. Mixed Use regulations shall count towards FAR and shall be liable to payment of appropriate charges, if it exceeds the permissible FAR.

(vii) Stilts:

If the building is constructed with stilt area of non-habitable height (less than 2.4m), used for parking, such stilt area shall not be included in FAR but would be counted towards the height of the building.

(viii) Parking:

Parking space shall be provided for within the residential plot as follows:

(a) 2 Equivalent Car Space (ECS) in plots of size 250-300 sq.m.

(b) 1 ECS for every 100 sq.m. built up area, in plots exceeding 300 sq.m., provided that, if the permissible coverage and FAR is not achieved with the above-mentioned parking norms in a plot, the parking norms of the preceding category shall be allowed.

(ix) Density:

For the purpose of density calculations, the dwelling unit shall be considered to accommodate 4.5 persons and the servant quarter to accommodate 2.25 persons.

(x) The minimum setbacks shall be as given in the following table :

S. No.	Plot size (in sq.m.)	Minimum Setbacks (in metre)			
		Front	Rear	Side(1)	Side(2)
1	Below 100	0	0	0	0
2	Above 100 and upto 250	3	0	0	0
3	Above 250 and upto 500	3	3	3	0
4	Above 500 and upto 2000	6	3	3	3
5	Above 2000 and upto 10000	9	6	6	6
6	Above 10000	15	9	9	9

(a) In case the permissible coverage is not achieved with the above-mentioned setbacks in a plot, the setbacks of the preceding category may be allowed.

(b) In the case of construction in the future, a minimum 2m x 2m open courtyard shall be provided for in residential plots of area of 50 sqm. to 100 sqm.

(xi) Number of servant quarters shall be provided as per approved layout plan and shall be constructed within the stipulated height. However, if the garage block space is merged with the main building, no separate servant quarter block or servant quarter, as part of main building shall be allowed. However, provision for a servant's room as part of the dwelling unit within the permissible coverage FAR shall be allowed.

(xii) Each servant quarter shall comprise of one habitable room of area not less than 11 sqm. floor area, exclusive of cooking verandah, bathroom and lavatory. The maximum size of servant quarter shall be 25 sqm. If larger in size, the servant's quarter shall be counted in density as a full dwelling unit.

(xiii) Plot owners / allottees seeking extra coverage, additional floor or part thereof, over and above Gazette Notification dated 23.07.98, as per above mentioned norms shall be charged betterment levy (or additional FAR charges) at the rates notified with the approval the Government from time to time. This is in addition to the levy payable on the additional FAR allowed vide notification dated 23.07.98 and over the FAR allowed vide notification dated 15.05.95.

(xiv) Plot owners / allottees seeking regularization of construction in terms of the additional coverage allowed under this notification, shall have to pay a penalty and compounding charges notified with the approval of the Government, over and above the betterment levy referred to in para (xiii) above.

(xv) Plot owners / allottees seeking regularization of additional height in terms of this notification, will have to pay penalty and special compounding charges notified with the approval of the Government, in addition to betterment levy referred to in para (xiv).

(xvi) The amount so collected be deposited in an escrow account by the local body concerned for incurring expenditure for developing parking sites, augmentation of amenities / infrastructure and environmental improvement programmes and a quarterly statement of the income and expenditure of the account shall be rendered by the local bodies to the Government.

(xvii) Encroachment on public land shall not be regularized and shall be removed before the local body grants sanction for regularization of additional construction or height.

(xviii) Every applicant seeking sanction or regularization of additional FAR and/ or height shall submit a certificate of structural safety obtained from a structural engineer. Where such certificate is not submitted or the Building is otherwise found to be structurally unsafe, formal notice shall be given to the owner by the local body concerned, to rectify the structural weakness within a reasonable stipulated period, falling which the building shall be declared unsafe by the local body concerned and shall be demolished by owner or the local body.

(xix) Standard Plans:

There are a number of standard building plans designed and approved by the Authority. Such plans shall continue to operate whenever applicable. Such plans shall be modified as per the applicable development controls.

B. Residential Plot -Group Housing

Minimum size of plot	3000 sq.m.
Maximum Ground Coverage	33.3%
Maximum FAR	200

Height NR (Subject to clearance from AAI/Fire Department and other statutory bodies.

Parking 2.0 ECS/100 sqm built up area

(i) The density may vary (10% variation permissible in all categories) for specific categories as given below:

(a) Category I (upto 40 sq.m) - 500 DUs/Ha.

(b) Category II (above 40-upto 80 sqm) 250 DUs/Ha.

(c) Category III - 175 Dus/Ha. (above 80sqm)

(ii) Plots for group housing should be located on roads facing a minimum width of 18 m ROW (13.5 m ROW for redevelopment areas and 9m ROW for Slum Rehabilitation / Special Area and Villages).

(iii) Additional floor area up to a maximum of 400 sq.m shall be allowed to cater to community needs such as community / recreational hall, crèche, library, reading room and society office. In addition to above, 100 sq.m. area shall be permissible for Senior Citizen Recreation Room.

(iv) The Central Government in consultation with the DDA may relax density and other norms for public housing and projects of national importance.

(v) The developer shall ensure that minimum 15% of FAR or 35% of the dwelling units, whichever is more, are constructed for Community-Service Personnel / EWS and lower category. Such flats should have a carpet area between 25 - 40 sqm.

(vi) Ground coverage up to 40% may be allowed to achieve low-rise high-density housing without lifts.

(vii) Levy on additional FAR shall be at rates notified with the approval of Government from time to time.

(viii) Stilts: If the building is constructed with stilt area of non- habitable height and is proposed to be used for parking, landscaping etc. the stilt floor need not be included in FAR and shall be counted towards height.

(ix) Basement, if constructed, and used only for parking, utilities and services shall not be counted towards FAR.

C. Cluster Court Housing

Minimum size of plot	3000 sqm.
Maximum FAR	175
Maximum height	15.0m with maximum coverage 100% subject to light and ventilation condition

(i) The net housing density permissible shall be 225 DUs per Ha. with 15% variation on either side and could be averaged for more than one pocket.

(ii) Minimum street in front of pocket to be 12 m.

(iii) No projection outside the building envelope allowed.

(iv) Each cluster court house is for one dwelling for a single family.

(v) Basement:

(a) Basement if constructed shall not be included in FAR calculations.

(b) Basement shall be below the ground floor. Basement area may, however, be extended below the internal courtyard and shaft.

(vi) Stilts:

If the building is constructed with the stilt area of non-habitable height and is proposed to be used for parking, landscaping etc., the stilt floor need not be included in the FAR but would be counted towards height (within stipulated height).

(vii) Parking:

Parking shall be provided as per group housing norms.

(viii) Density:

For the purpose of density calculations, the dwelling unit shall be considered to accommodate 4.5 persons and the servant quarter to accommodate 2.25 persons.

(ix) Servant quarter:

No separate servant quarter block or servant quarter as part of main building shall be allowed if the garage block space is merged with the main building. Provision for a servant's room as part of the dwelling unit within the permissible coverage and FAR shall be allowed with maximum size of servant quarter as 25 sqm and if larger in size would be counted as a full dwelling unit.

D. Foreign Mission

Maximum Ground Coverage	25%
Maximum FAR	75
Maximum height	15m.

Basement upto the building envelope line to the maximum extent of 50% of plot area shall be allowed and if used for parking and services should not be counted in FAR.

E. Hostel/Guest House/Lodging & Boarding House/Dharamshala

Min. Plot size	500 sqm.
Maximum ground coverage	30%
Maximum floor area ratio	120
Maximum height	15m

(i) Parking to be provided @ 2 ECS per 100 sq.m. of built up area.

(ii) These norms shall not be applicable for Guest House under Mixed Use Regulations.

F. Night Shelter

Min. Plot Size	1000 sqm.
Max. Ground Coverage	30%
Max. FAR	120
Max. Height	26m

G. Farm House

	Plot Area	
	1.0 ha. and above but less than 2.0 ha.	2.0 ha. and above
Maximum Floor Area	100 sq.m.	150 sq.m.
Maximum Height	6 m.(Single storey)	6 m. (Single storey)

Other Controls for farmhouses:

(i) Setback in dwelling house should be 15 m away from any boundary line of the property.

(ii) Where the property abuts to urban road, the dwelling house building should be setback from the centre line of that road by 60m. Where the property abuts to village road, the building setback from the centre line of that road should be by 30m.

(iii) No dwelling units should be built within 400m of the right of way of any National Highway.

5.0 TRADE AND COMMERCE

Shopping and commercial areas reflect the economy and the image of the city. As per the Economic Survey of Delhi 2001-2002, there were about 2.3 lakhs retail enterprises in Delhi with an employment of 5.4 lakhs engaged in trade, commerce and allied services. It is expected that the number of enterprises in retail trade are likely to increase to about 4.15 lakhs by 2021 and the corresponding employment is likely to increase to about 9.63 lakhs. In addition to these, large number of enterprises in sectors such as restaurants and hotels, finance & insurance, real estate & business operate from commercial centres. This indicates the predominance of retail and allied service activities in the economic structure of the city.

The major changes in the economic structure are due to liberalization of the economy, entry of multinational companies in the consumer sector, improved telecommunication system, increased per capita income and the purchasing power of the people.

5.1. PRE 1962/MPD-1962 COMMERCIAL AREAS

Residential areas and streets/ stretches earlier declared as commercial areas/ streets or where commercial use was allowed in MPD-1962 shall continue such use at least to the extent as permissible in MPD-1962. Commercial activity existing from prior to 1962 in residential areas are also permitted subject to documentary proof thereof.

5.2. HIERARCHY OF COMMERCIAL AREAS

The following five-tier system of Commercial Areas is envisaged to accommodate required shopping, commercial office and other service activities like cinema, hotel and restaurant and various community services and facilities in an integrated manner.

In addition, some components of commercial use are also provided under mixed use, non-hierarchical commercial centres, and informal sector in the selected areas along the MRTS corridor.

Table 5.1: Five-Tier System of Commercial Areas

Tier	I	II	III	IV	V
Population		About 5 lakhs	About 1lakh	About 10,000	About 5,000
	Metropolitan City Centre (Pertains to already developed Central Business District)	District Centre	Community Centre	Local Shopping Cetre	Convenience Shopping Centre
Arca (Ha.)	-	40	4.0	0.3	0.1
Activities Permitted	Retail Shopping, Stockists and dealers of medicines and drugs, Commercial and Offices of local bodies, PSUs, Cinema, Cineplex, Hotels, Restaurants, Banquet Halls, Socio-Cultural activities / Recreational Club, Service Apptts, Coaching Centres/ Training Institutes, Police Post, Fire Post. Tel. Exchange, Post & Telegraph Office, Petrol Pump/ CNG Station, Bus Terminal, Informal Trade.	Retail Shopping, Stockists and dealers of medicines and drugs, Commercial and Offices of local bodies, PSUs, Cinema,Cineplex, Hotels, Restaurants, Banquet Halls, Socio-Cultural activities/Recreational Club, Service Apptts, Coaching Centres/ Training Institutes, Police Post, Fire Post. Tel. Exchange,Post & Telegraph Office, Petrol Pump / CNG Stn. Bus Terminal, , Repair /Services, Bank, ATM, Guest House, Nursing Home, Informal Trade.	Retail Shopping, Stockists and dealers of medicines and drugs, Commercial and Offices of local bodies, PSUs, Cinema, Cineplex, Hotels, Service Apptts. Restaurants, halls, Guest House, Nursing Home, Dispensary, Clinical Lab. Clinic & Poly Clinic, Coaching Centres/ Training Institutes, Police Post, Post Office, Petrol Pump/ CNG Station, Repair /Services, Bank, ATM, Informal Trade, Multi level parking.	Retail Shopping, Stockists and dealers of medicines and drugs, Commercial Offices, Clinical Laboratory, Clinic & Poly Clinic, Repair / Services, Bank, ATM, Guest Home, Informal Trade. Coaching Centres/Training Institutes, Restaurant.	Retail Shopping, Local level service activities. Repair, Office, Bank. ATM, Informal Trade, Restaurant.

Notes:

(i) Besides the above, retail shopping of desired level shall also be provided in all work centres and transportation nodes.

(ii) Utilities, Public Conveniences shall be provided as per requirement.

(iii) Service & Repair and Informal activities should be provided as Service markets and Informal bazaar.

(iv) The mandatory requirement of parking as per prescribed standards would be met through multi level parking as far as possible in Metropolitan City Centre, District Centre and Community Centre.

5.3 METROPOLITAN CITY CENTRE

The existing CBDs are Connaught Place and its Extension, commercial areas in Walled City and its Extension and Karol Bagh. These have all the necessary ingredients to emerge as Metropolitan City Centres.

These Metropolitan City Centres, need to be seen in the light of the historical legacy of the pre-colonial and post-colonial capital cities of the so called old and new Delhi, are envisaged as a city level centre for shopping, entertainment, socio-cultural and all other activities indicated in respect of District Centres. A comprehensively planned and attractive built environment will therefore need to be conceptualized and implemented to develop these as unique centres and major attraction of the city, apart from their commercial and social value for the citizens.

The Urban Design guidelines for Metropolitan City Centre are given in Chapter 11.0 Urban Design.

5.3.1 CONNAUGHT PLACE & EXTENSION

The development of the Metropolitan City Centre in harmony with the existing urban form of the classical Connaught Circus and multi-storeyed buildings in its extension is envisaged to bring in visual integration in the overall urban form.

The areas included in the Metropolitan City Centre would be Connaught Place & Extension (Janpath, Sansad Marg, Baba Kharag Singh Marg, Panchkuian Road, Barakhamba Road, Kasturba Gandhi Marg), Gole Market, Mandi House, Pragati Maidan, Indraprastha Estate.

An integrated plan incorporating urban design, landscape, traffic and transportation schemes, safe pedestrian walkways, parking areas, recreational and cultural areas etc. is to be prepared for its development.

5.3.2 SHAHJAHANABAD (WALLED CITY) AND EXTENSIONS

The commercial areas in Shahjahanabad (Walled City) and Extensions would be delineated in Special Area / Zonal Plan (as provided for in para 16.3 (5)). These traditional areas need to be treated carefully and sensitively in view of their high density and multiple uses. The aim is to revitalize the glory of Walled city and its economic & tourism potential.

5.3.3. KAROL BAGH

Commercial area of Karol Bagh has become one of the important centre in the Special Area, for which development norms/regulations have been given in Chapter 17.0 Development Code.

5.4. DISTRICT CENTRE /SUB-CENTRAL BUSINESS DISTRICT

The District Centres are meant to serve as the apex of the multi-nodal activities of the community, whieh should be conceived as major shopping centers, while serving the community with a reasonable variety of other services and facilities and also centres of socio-cultural activity where the community can get together. MPD-2001 proposed two sub CBDs with norms of District Centres (namely Shahadara and in Urban Extension). These are now proposed to be dealt as District Centres. The emphasis in these centers should be on commerce and their related activities.

The District Centres already developed or in advanced stages of development are:

(i) Nehru Place
(ii) Rajendra Place
(iii) Bhikaji Cama Place
(iv) Janakpuri
(v) Laxmi Nagar
(vi) Shivaji Place (Raja Garden)
(vii) Jhandewalan
(viii) Netaji Subhash Place (Wazirpur)
(ix) Saket
(x) Manglam Place (Rohini)

These centres were developed on the basis of integrated schemes and some of these need upgradation in terms of infrastructure, parking spaces, hawking plazas, physical infrastructure and built environment. The implementing agency / land owning agency can undertake review of the schemes for their upgradation and optimum utilisation of land. The implementing agency should formulate action plans by involving developers and owners associations to improve the environment through self-sustaining schemes, which should include provisions for their subsequent maintenance and upkeep.

Other District Centres in Delhi Urban Area (DUA)-2001, in the process of development yet to be developed are as indicated below:

(i) Trans Yamuna Area- Shahdra
(ii) Rohini - Twin District Centre
(iii) Peeragarhi (Rohtak Road)

(iv) Paschim Vihar

(v) Shalimar Bagh

(vi) Dheerpur Extension (Jahangirpuri)

(vii) Majnu ka Tila (Khyber Pass)

(viii) Dilshad Garden

(ix) Shastri Park (Shahdara)

(x) Mayur V ihar

(xi) Rohini Ph-III /IV /V

(xii) Dwarka

(xiii) Narela

5.5 NON-HIERARCHICAL COMMERCIAL CENTRES

Besides the above District Centres, the following Non Hierarchical Commercial Centres shall be developed with specific schemes for each centre:

(i) Commercial Centre at Asaf Ali Road

(ii) Commercial Centre adjoining Metropolitan Passenger Terminal, Okhla (Jasola)

(iii) Commercial Centre Laxmi Bai Nagar

(iv) Commercial Centre, Nehru Nagar (Near Ring Rail)

The following other existing non-hierarchical commercial centres, which are also providing services at city level, would also need to be redeveloped:

(i) Central market - Lajpat Nagar

(ii) INA market

(iii) Sarojini Nagar market

(iv) Any other area as may be identified.

The development control norms for the above areas shall be as per approved schemes and any enhancement in FAR wherever approved shall be subject to charging appropriate levies from the beneficiaries.

5.6 COMMUNITY CENTRE (CC) LOCAL SHOPPING CENTRE (LSC) / CONVENIENCE SHOPPING CENTRE (CSC)

5.6.1 The Community Centres should be conceived as shopping and business centres catering to the needs of the population at community level. These centres may have Retail Shopping, Commercial and Government Offices, Local Body/Public Sector Undertaking offices, Cinema / Cineplexes, Hotels, Restaurants, Banquet halls and Guest House, Nursing Home, Dispensary, Clinical Laboratory, Clinic & Poly Clinic facilities together with other community facilities as indicated in table 5.1.

5.6.2 The LSC / CSC will cater to the day-to-day needs of the local population. Some areas developed prior to 1962 like Lajpat Nagar, Rajouri Garden, Tilak Nagar, Kamla Nagar etc. having concentration of commercial activities, may continue subject to conditions prescribed under the Mixed Use Regulations. The existing built-up commercial centres may be redeveloped if need be with enhanced FAR subject to payment of appropriate levies.

5.7. COMMERCIAL CENTRES IN URBAN EXTENSION

5.7.1 SUB CITY LEVEL COMMERCIAL AREAS

In Urban Extension, District Centres and Community Centres could be developed wherever possible, in a linear form as commercial cum facility corridors along major transport networks. Such corridors will have non-residential uses like Commercial, Recreational, Public and Semi public, Utilities, Service and Repair, etc. with detailed Urban Design and landscape schemes. The aim is to prevent unintended and unplanned ribbon development. The proposed MRTS stations and bus terminals, as the case may be, shall be integrated within these facility corridors.

5.7.2. LOCAL LEVEL COMMERCIAL AREAS

In case of Urban Extensions it is proposed to combine and integrate LSC and CSC at neighborhood level to ensure their location within walkable distance.

5.8 HOTELS

Delhi is emerging as an international centre of education, health care, tourism, sports and business, which require complimentary facilities such as hotels catering to various economic groups. Such uses are proposed as part of commercial use (Community Centres and above), Public Semi-Public facilities, wholesale markets, transport nodes, etc.

To cater to low tariff accommodation, a hierarchy of Guest House, Lodging and Boarding House / Dharamshala / Hostel have been proposed under respective land uses.

Hotel is permitted in Commercial Use Zone, Commercial Centres in Industrial Use Zone, and Transport Nodes (ISBT, Bus Depot/ Terminal, Railway Station, Airport, Integrated Freight Complex, Metropolitan Passenger Terminal) and other use zones - where already existing and where building plans are approved by the Competent Authority. The maximum ground coverage and FAR in such cases shall be as per the sanctioned building plans but in no case exceeding the permissible ground coverage and FAR of that use zone. This is subject to the provision of parking as per norms.

5.9. SERVICE MARKETS

Special attention is required for the low turnover and space extensive shops for fruits and vegetables, service and repair, junk and scrap materials (kabari), building materials, automobile workshops etc. The grouping of such activities with planned retail markets leads to conversion of shops into high profit commercial activity. To avoid continuance of this situation, about 10% of the unutilized sites of LSC / CSC are proposed to be converted into Service Markets.

In Urban Extensions, sites for such service markets at two levels should be established in the initial stages of development to avoid unauthorized ribbon development and misuse of residential premises.

Table 5.2 : Norms for Service Markets & Organised Informal Bazaars

	Sub City level (DC/CC)	Community Level (LSC/CC)
Population	Abolut 5 lakhs	About 100,000
Service Market		
Area (ha.)	6.0	0.2
Activities Permitted	Service and repair activities as specified as specified in industries chaper. Retail and Limited Wholesale for low turnover activities, like . Auto workshops, Fruit & vegetable, General Merchandise, Hardware and Building materials, Gas Godowns.	Service and repair activities as specified in the Industries chapter. Low turnover activities, like Auto workshops, Fruit & vegetable, General Marchandise, Hardware and Building materials, Kabari.
Informal Bazaar		
Area (ha.)	5.0	0.1
Activities Permitted	Informal Shops, Weekly markets, Organised easting places, Handicraft bazaar, used Book/ Furniture/Building materials bazaar, Cycle & Rickshaw repair, Kabari, etc.	Informal shops, Weekly markets, Handicraft bazaar, Cycle & Rickshaw repair, Kabari, etc.

Note ; Utilities, Public Conveniences shall be provided as per requirement.

5.10. INFORMAL SECTOR

Large sections of unemployed and under employed population in rural areas and small towns look forward to the metropolitan cities like Delhi for employment and enter the city to move up the economy ladder. This brings forth a multitude of small enterprises and petty trading activities in the informal sector. Thus, a metropolis like Delhi has organized sector and an equally large informal sector. This sector with highly reduced needs of floor space and investment is important as a source of employment and services in the economic fabric of the city.

A survey conducted by the Directorate of Economics and Statistics on unorganized trading activity in Delhi estimated the total number of unorganized trading enterprises as 2 lakh and the number of persons employed about as 3.18 lakh. The contribution of this sector, which is measured in terms of Gross Value added to the economy of Delhi, was estimated at Rs. 1.01 lakh per enterprise per annum.

The informal sector units locate themselves strategically near work centres, commercial areas, outside the boundaries of schools colleges, hospitals and transport nodes and near large housing clusters. A very high percentage of this activity has been observed in the Walled city, Trans Yamuna area and old commercial areas. A large number of units are mobile in nature.

5.10.1. POLICY FOR EXISTING AREAS

Keeping in view the National Policy on Urban Street vendors the following provisions are made:

(i) The location / concentration of present stationary informal units shall be considered on case to case basis and steps for relocation / improvement shall be taken. It should be ensured that such activities do not spill over on the right of way. The Government / concerned local agency should coordinate the policy.

(ii) The areas of informal sector shall have suitable public conveniences and solid waste disposal arrangements.

(iii) Formulation of guidelines for schemes would include 'Hawking' and 'No Hawking' Zones. Specific areas should be earmarked for stationary and mobile street vendors by the concerned local authority in consultation with RWAs.

(iv) The local authorities should take up new designs of stalls, push-carts and mobile vans of various sizes and with cleaning facilities, giving due consideration to urban design requirement of specific area, where informal shopping is being permitted.

(v) Defining the role and responsibility of NGOs along with specific obligations on part of hawkers towards the society for maintenance of law and order within the hawking zones and weekly markets.

(vi) An informal unit shall not be permitted within a distance equivalent to half the width of the road, from an intersection.

5.10.2. ORGANISED INFORMAL SECTOR PLACES (Haat)

There are large numbers of informal sector units in the city but no organized clusters. There is a need to provide for organised informal eating-places along with casual shopping, etc. to be located strategically in the city and at the following locations:

(i) Near TV Tower Pitampura.

(ii) Near sub C.B.D. Trans Yamuna Area.

(iii) Rohini.

(iv) Geeta colony

(v) Adjacent to transport nodes including ISBT.

Implementing agency may identify locations as per requirement for such activities.

5.10.3 INFORMAL BAZAAR

In new urban areas, informal bazaars could form part of the planned commercial areas at two levels. These could be implemented in the initial planning stages along with development of residential areas. The planning norms are given in the Table 5.3.

5.10.4 WEEKLY MARKETS

Weekly market, which is the traditional style of retail shopping, is quite popular in Delhi especially among the lower and middle-income groups. These markets are held in various areas. Further, parking and other open spaces within the service markets and commercial centres should be so planned that weekly markets can operate in these areas. The specific locations and timings of operation of such markets should be specified and regulated by the concerned local body.

5.10.5. PLANNING NORMS FOR INFORMAL TRADE

The informal sector trade should be incorporated in the planned development in various use zones. The provision of informal sector trade units should be ensured at the time of sanction of building plans / layout plans as per the norms given in the Table5.3.

Table 5.3 : Planning Norms

S. No.	Use Zones/Use premises	No. of Informal shops/Units
(i)	Retail trade : Metropolitan City Centre, District Centre, Community Centre, Convenience Shopping Centre,	3 to 4 units per 10 formal shops (to be provided in informal bazaar/service market components
(ii)	Government and Commercial Offices	5 to 6 units per 1000 employees
(iii)	Wholesale trade and Freight Complexes.	3 to 4 units per 10 formal shops

(iv)	Hospital	3 to 4 units per 100 beds
(v)	Bus Terminal	1 unit for two bus bay
(vi)	Schools Primary Secondary/ Senor Secondary/Integrated	 3 to 4 units 5 to 6 units
(vii)	Parks District Parks Neighbourhood parks	 8 to 10 units at each major entry 2 to 3 units
(viii)	Residential	1 unit/1000 population
(ix)	Industrial	5 to 6 units per 1000 employees
(x)	Railways Terminus/MRTS Stations	To be based on surveys at the time of preparation of the project.

Table 5.4 : Development Controls - Commercial Centres

Use/use premises	Maximum Coverage (%)	FAR	Height (mts)	Parking Standard ECS/100 sqm. Of floor area	Other controls
(a) Commercial Centres					
i. Convenience Shopping Centre / Local Shopping Centre / Local Level Commercial areas	40	100	15	2	Max. 10% additional Ground Coverage shall be allowed for providing atrium only in LSC.
ii. Service Market	40	100	15	2	
iii. Organised Informal Bazaar.	40	40	8		
iv. Community Centre / Non-hierarchical Commercial Centre	25	125	NR*	3	Maximum 10% additional ground coverage shall be allowed for providing atrium
v. District Centre/ Sub-Central Business District / Sub-City Level Commercial areas	25	150	NR*	3	Maximum 10% additional ground coverage shall be allowed for providing atrium
(b) Metropolitan City Centre/ Central Business District					
i. Commercial Plot: Retail & Commerce Metropolitan City Centre i.e. Connaught Place & its Extension	25	150	NR*	3	i. The size of the plot shall be as in the layout of commercial area and any subdivisional of the plot in Connaught Place and its extension should not be permitted ii. The development controls shall be in accordance with the comprehensive plan of the area to be reframed by the local body. iii. (a) In case of Connaught Place, the existing height shall be maintained and FAR could be achieved by increasing proportionate ground coverage. (b) No basement shall be permitted in middle circle of Connaught Place. (c) Mandatory Architectural Controls shall be applicable.

ii. Commercial Complex at Fire Brigade Lane and Janpath Lane	25	150	NR*	3		i. Ground coverage and FAR shall be calculated on the area of presently available plots. ii. The area shall be developed on the basis of compre hensive scheme.
(c) Hotel	30	150	NR*	3		i. Maximum 5 10% additional ground coverage shall be allowed for providing atrium. In case, the permissible additional ground coverage for atrium is utilised, 25% of the utilised ground coverage shall be counted towards FAR. ii. Maximum 20 % of the FAR can be used for the Commercial offices, Retail & Service shops. iii. These norms shall apply for new hotel sites disposed off after the date of notification i.e. 21-01-06.
(d) Service Apartments	30	150	NR*	3		
(e) Any other Commercial Centre	25	100	NR*	3		Subject to ststutory clearances. The development controls can vary subject to approved scheme.
i (Including Commercial component along with Railway / MRTS Stations / ISBT)						
ii. Asaf Ali Road (the area shown as commercial strip in Delhi Gate - Ajmeri Gate scheme)	80	200	20	3		Setbacks are not mandatory In case of rebuilding stilts shall be provided for parking.

* NR - No Restriction, subject to clearance from AAI, Delhi Fire Service and other statutory bodies.

Notes:

(i) The utilities such as, underground water storage tank, roof top water harvesting system, separate dry and wet dustbins, post delivery counter etc. are to be provided within the plot. All hotels, restaurants, auto workshops, hospitals etc. will have to make arrangements for solid waste disposal and primary effluent treatment.

(ii) Individual plot with floor area of 5000 sq.m. or above will provide ESS and generator within the plot. They have to submit energy consumption/ audit at the time of sanction of building plans.

(iii) Height subject to clearance from ASI, Airport Authority of India, Delhi Fire Service and concerned authority.

(iv) Wherever parking is provided within the plot / basement and is misused, the same is liable to muncipalisation / taken over by the authority.

(v) Wherever redevelopment of existing commercial areas stipulate preparation of a comprehensive scheme, the same can be initiated jointly by the lessees / owners themselves and submitted to land owning agency / planning authority for approval. Wherever any enhancement in FAR is approved, the same will be subject to charging appropriate levies from the beneficiaries. For Metropolitan City Centre, in Special Area, development controls shall be as per approved scheme.

Table 5.5: Definitions and Activities Permitted in Use Premises

Use premise	Definition	Activities permitted
Retail Shop	A premise for sale of commodities directly to consumer with necessary storage.	Retail Shop, Repair Shop, Personnel Service Shop.
Repair Shop	A premise equivalent of a of a retail shop for carrying out repair of household goods, electronic gadgets, automobiles, cycles etc.	Retail Shop, Repair Shop, Personnel Service Shop.
Personnel Service Shop	A premise equivalent of retail shop providing personnel services like tailor barber etc.	Retail Shop, Repair Shop, Personnel Service Shop.
Vending Booth	A premise in the form of booth for sale of commodities of daily needs either through a mechanical installation or otherwise.	Vending Booth
Convenience Shopping Centre	A group of shops in residential area serving a population of about 5,000 persons.	As given in table 5.1.
Local Shopping Centre	A group of shops in residential area serving a population of 10,000 persons	As given in table 5.1
Commercial Office	A premise used for offices of profit making organizations.	Commercial Office, retail & personal Service Shop, Restaurant, Bank, Post & Telegraph Office.
Bank	A premise for offices to perform banking function and operation.	Bank, Watch & Ward Residence (upto 20 sqm.) commercial office, Canteen
Motor Garage and workshop	A premise for servicing and repair of automobiles.	Motor garage and Work Shop, retail shop (spare parts), Soft drinks and Snacks stall)
Cinema / Cineplex	A premise with facilities for projection of movies and stills with a covered space to seat audience.	Cinema, Watch & Ward Residence (upto 20 sqm.) Administrative Office, Soft Drink & Snack Stall, Retail Shop & Commercial office.
Restaurant	A premise used for serving food items on commercial basis including cooking facilities. It may have covered or open space or both for sitting arrangement.	Restaurant
Hotel	A premise used for lodging of 15 persons or more.	Hotel, Banquet / Conferencing facilities, Restaurant, Swimming pool, Health Club, Food court, Discotheque. Commercial offices, retail & service shops to be restricted to 20% of floor area.
Service Apartment	A premise fully furnished, serviced and self contained with meal preparation and used for short-term corporate accommodation.	Guest suite, Conference facilities, Office, Retail and Service shops to be restricted up to 20% of floor area.

Informal Sector		
Weekly Market/	An area used once in a week by a group of informal shop establishments in the form of a market. These markets shift from one area to another on different days of the week.	Weekly market, informal Retail trade, Soft Drink and Snack Stall (All structures will be either temporary or mobile, only for one day in a week.
Informal Sector Unit	Retail/ service unit, stationary or mobile, working without roof including small khokhas on roadside. Street vendor- A person who offers goods or services for sale to the public without having a permanent built up structure but with a temporary static structure or mobile stall (or head load).	Informal Sector Unit

6.0 WHOLESALE TRADE

Delhi is the biggest consumption centre in North India. It has attained the status of a major distribution centre by virtue of its geographical location and other historical factors.

As per Economic Survey of Delhi 2001-2002, there are about 37,000 wholesale enterprises in Delhi with an employment of about 1.6 lakh. In addition there are about 6,500 enterprises of storage and warehousing providing employment to 27,000 persons. It is expected that the number of enterprises in wholesale trade may increase to about 66,000 by 2021 leading to increase in employment to about 2.85 lakh persons. Some of the major commodities involved in the wholesale trade are textile and related products, food items, auto-parts and machinery, hardware and building materials, paper and stationery, fruits and vegetables and Iron and Steel.

Around 20% of the total wholesale trade enterprises of urban Delhi are located in the walled city, accounting for around 12% of the employment. The average enterprise in the Walled City has less employment but high turnover in comparison to units in other areas. In order to decentralise wholesale trade, the planned markets were developed at Azadpur, Naraina, Okhla, Narela, Keshopur, etc.

6.1 CITY LEVEL WHOLESALE MARKETS

6.1.1 EXISTING MARKETS IN SPECIAL AREA

In case of existing developed areas, all wholesale markets generated with hazardous materials should be developed in decentralized manner and shifted to the areas assigned for these. All unauthorized encroachments / projections on roads/ government land should be removed to facilitate easy movement of traffic. Further extension of the wholesale activity in the Walled City and its Extension shall be totally stopped by giving incentives and disincentives as under:

(i) Incentives:

(a) The liasioning offices of the traders/ agents to continue in the present location;

(b) Development of New counter markets for wholesale trade and warehousing;

(c) The new counter markets should have access from National Highway, arterial networks and connectivity with MRTS; and

(d) Incentives such as Transferable Development Rights (TDR) and reduced taxes to enable start up / expanding of activity in the new markets.

(ii) Disincentives:

(a) Restriction on the entry of heavy goods vehicles in the Special area;

(b) Storage of hazardous / inflammable commodities like paper, plastic / PVC, chemicals, petroleum and its products; should be discouraged.

(c) Restriction on storage / warehousing of bulky commodities like food grains, fruits and vegetables, dairy, poultry / fish products, iron and steel, and building materials; and

(d) Non-renewal of trade licenses for Wholesale Trade in non-conforming areas.

Sadar Bazar

The old congested built up areas like Sadar bazaar have serious problems of traffic congestion, inadequate physical and social infrastructure, lack of open spaces etc. The wholesale market of Sadar bazaar needs to be redeveloped at the same location with necessary infrastructure and parking required for wholesale trade.

6.1.2 PROPOSED WHOLESALE MARKETS WITHIN INTEGRATED FREIGHT COMPLEXES

It is proposed to develop new wholesale markets as counter markets to cater to the demands of the growing population of Delhi only, near the rail and road entry points of NCTD. These should be linked with the proposed Wholesale Markets within Integrated Freight Complexes where the wholesale business could be operated more efficiently in a better environment. The break up of land requirement for different commodities at various locations should be decided at the time of preparation of schemes for the complex by the implementing agency.

Wholesale markets within Integrated Freight Complexes are to be developed as per requirement.

The new wholesale markets shall provide facilities for:

(i) Intra-urban freight movement and interchange of mode.

(ii) Warehousing and storage facilities.

(iii) Servicing, lodging and boarding, idle parking and other required facilities.

6.2. SUB-CITY LEVEL MARKETS

Delhi has become an agglomeration of cities over a period of time. Sub-City level wholesale markets shall cater to the needs of population at local level. These markets of medium size need to be dispersed throughout the city to enable even distribution of commodities from these complexes to the retail outlets.

Most of the existing planned markets and warehousing were developed in early seventies for specific commodities. Due to their proximity to residential area, these markets need to be redeveloped to overcome the environmental and traffic problems. The traders associations shall share the responsibility of redevelopment to modern wholesale markets. The beneficiaries will have to pay the betterment charges to the implementing agency. Space for commodities that are not permissible in mixed-use streets under para 15.6. shall be made available in wholesale city level market and sub-city level market to enable their relocation.

Some of the existing planned Wholesale Markets, Warehousing and Transport Centres are as given in Table 6.1.

Table 6.1: Sub-City Level Markets

Sl. No.	Location	Commodity / Activities
(i)	Azadpur	Fruit and vegetable
(ii)	Okhla	Fruit and vegetable
(iii)	Keshopur	Fruit and vegetable
(iv)	Naraina	Iron and Steel
(v)	Sanjay Gandhi Transport Centre	Transport / Warehousing
(vi)	Rohtak Road Transport Centre	Transport / Warehousing
(vii)	Narela	Food grains
(viii)	Najafgarh	Food grains

In addition to above, the following wholesale markets are to be developed:

(i) Loni Road
(ii) Rohini Ph-IV/V
(iii) Dwarka Sub-City
(iv) Narela Sub-City

In Urban Extension, about 8-10 ha. of land for about one million population should be provided for such Sub-City level markets. The different commodities to be provided at various locations should be decided at the time of preparation of schemes by the implementing agency. These markets shall have adequate parking, repair and servicing facilities. Land should be identified in each zone accordingly.

6.3. STORAGE OF OIL, CNG AND LPG

Shakurbasti Oil Depot has been shifted to a site between Ghevra and Tikri Kalan, which will be a major storage site for oil. The land thus vacated should be partly utilized for Disaster Management Centre and rest for recreational activities.

No new Depots for oil and LPG shall be developed in NCT of Delhi. The new depots required for the increased energy requirement shall be developed in the National Capital Region and the supply of Oil / LPG/ CNG etc. to Delhi should be through pipelines.

Table 6.2: Development Controls - Wholesale Trade

Use/Use Premises	Maximum			Parking Standard ECS/100 sq.m. of floor area	Definition	Activities Permitted
	Ground Coverage %	FAR	Height (m)			
Integrated Freight Complex/ Wholesale Market	30	80	No Restriction subject to (i)	3	Wholesale Market. A premise from where goods and commodities are sold and delivered to retailers. The premises include storage and godown, loading and unloading faculties.	Wholesale shop, Godown and storage, Commercial office (restricted to 25% of the total floor area)

Notes :

(i) Height subject to clearance from Airport Authority of India, Fire Department and other statutory bodies.

(ii) In case of plots upto 300 sqm. common parking is to be provided.

(iii) In case of plots of size 300 sqm and above, the utilities such as E.S.S., underground water storage tank, roof top water harvesting system, separate dry and wet dustbins, solar heating/lighting system etc. are to be provided within the plot.

(iv) In case of individual plots not forming part of any comprehensive / integrated development scheme, the development controls shall be as per already approved scheme / layout plan.

7. INDUSTRY

As per Economic Survey of Delhi 2001-02, there were about 1,29,000 industrial units in Delhi in 1998 against 85,050 units in 1991. A door-to-door industrial survey revealed that an average unit employed 9 workers while 30% of the units employed 4 workers or less. The survey also revealed that textiles products (garments) units constitute the largest number, followed by repair services and electrical machinery. The table below shows the growth of industrial units and employment.

Year	No. Of Industries	No. of Employees
1981	42,000	5,68,910
1991	85,050	7,30,951
1998	1,29,000	14,40,000

Source : Economic Survey of Delhi 2001-02

The issue of industries in Delhi has been a subject of extensive debate, controversy and concern over the past decade. This has centred mainly on the aspects of pollution and negative environmental impact of industries, the existence and continued growth of industries in non-conforming areas and the issue of classification and permissibility with reference to household industries. Serious concern has been expressed regarding the continued existence and further proliferation of industries in contravention of Master Plan provisions.

7.1 STRATEGY

Keeping in view the position brought out above as also in the context of the continuing pressure of population growth in Delhi, the following broad policy would be required for the industrial sector:

(i) Promote hi-tech and low volume -high value added industries, which are not labor intensive.

(ii) Encourage modernization and technological up-gradation of existing industries required for day-to-day needs of the people of the city.

(ii) Take corrective measures with regard to industries in non-conforming industrial areas in terms of environmental and other norms as may be prescribed.

(iii) Provide suitable incentives and disincentives, and other measures, for shifting and relocation of industrial units not conforming to the land use norms.

(iv) Review, and possibly widen, the scope of permissibility of household industrial units subject to adherence to pollution control norms and environmental considerations, fire safety regulations and other relevant factors, particularly the aspect of infrastructure services.

7.2 CLASSIFICATION OF INDUSTRIES

The classification of Industries is proposed to be simplified with prohibited category and non-prohibited category subject to proposals regarding specific category of industries permitted in different use zones. Further, all planned industrial areas are designated under a single landuse category namely Industry. The standards prescribed by the pollution control authorities would have to be met by all industrial units, in addition to specific conditions in terms of number of workers and power load in specified categories.

Industries listed under prohibited category shall not be permitted to be set up in Delhi (Annexure - III). The existing industrial units under prohibited category need to relocate themselves outside Delhi, within a period of three years.

7.3 PERMISSIBILITY OF INDUSTRIAL UNITS IN DIFFERENT USE ZONES AND USE PREMISES

For the industrial classification, the limits of aforesaid parameters shall be fixed according to the nature of industries, area and the nature of industrial development. The threshold parameters for industrial units are given in Table 7.1.

Table 7.1 : Parameters for Industrial Units in Different Use Zones and Use Premises

Use Zone / Use Premises	Groups Permitted (Refer Annexure)	Conditions: Max. no. of workers	Conditions: Max. Industrial Power Load (KW)
Residential Use			
(a) Residential	A	5	5
(b) Villages (Abadi)	A+A1	5	5
Commercial Use			
(a) Convenience Shopping Centre, Local Shopping Centre.	A+ A1+B Service / repair / packaging/assembly (without manufacturing) of permissible industries.	5	11
(b) Community Centre.		9	11
(c) District Centre,		19	11
(d) Service Market, Service Centre.			
Industrial Use			
(a) Plotted development	All industries except those prohibited and of Non-polluting and non-hazardous nature.	As per need	As per need
(b) Flatted Industries	All industries except those prohibited, and of Non-polluting and non-hazardous nature, excluding industries producing noise/water/ vibrations/odour pollution	20	As per need

Notes:

(i) Maximum no. of workers shall be as per notification issued by the competent authority from time to time.

(ii) The power requirement for operating pollution control devices and non-manufacturing use shall be over and above the aforesaid permissible load.

(iii) Existing Industrial Estates in the Growth Centres shall be considered as industrial use.

7.4 HOUSEHOLD/SERVICE INDUSTRIES

(i) Household industrial units with maximum 5 workers and 5 kilowatt power may be allowed to continue in residential areas and new industrial units of this type could be permitted in residential areas subject to the condition that no polluting industrial unit shall be permitted as household industry.

(ii) The industrial units could be permitted only after provisional registration by the Govt. of NCTD.

(iii) Household industrial units shall be allowed on any floor to the extent of 50% of permissible floor area of the dwelling unit.

(iv) Further additions / alterations to the list of Household Industries could be made, if considered appropriate and in public interest by the Central Government to do so.

(v) No inflammable or hazardous substance is permitted to be stored.

(vi) Separate industrial electric connection (single phase) and Municipal License, would be necessary to set up a household industry.

7.5 NO INDUSTRIAL ACTIVITY ZONE

In order to maintain the city's ambience and pollution free environment in important and historic areas of Delhi, following locations are categorized as 'No Industrial Activity Zone' where no industrial activity including household industry, shall be permitted.

(a) Lutyens' Bungalow Zone

(b) Civil Lines Bungalow Area

(c) Employer Housing

(d) Group Housing (excluding Janata Flats)

7.6 INDUSTRIAL AREA REDEVELOPMENT SCHEMES

The redevelopment schemes cover the following aspects :

(i) Modernization and upgradation of existing planned industrial areas; and,

(ii) Redevelopment of areas, which have become industrialized over the period of the two Master Plans even though not designated as such.

7.6.1 EXISTING PLANNED INDUSTRIAL AREAS

These industrialized areas were developed in the 70's and over the years, have deteriorated considerably in terms of physical infrastructure and, in some cases deficiencies on this score have persisted in an overall sense. Besides, there have been changes in the nature of activities in some of the areas and there have also been demands for using part of the plots for activities, which could be classified as commercial. There may also be a need to see whether further densification is possible in terms of creating smaller plots by sub-divisions to accommodate a larger number of industries / units. Guidelines for redevelopment of existing industrial areas shall be framed within 2 years by DDA in consultation with GNCTD and the local body. Till such time, the existing sub divisions may continue.

There is, therefore, a need for modernization and up-gradation of the existing industrial areas with due regard to environmental considerations. Since most of the Industrial areas are located along the Mass Public Transport Corridors, there is also a need for optimizing the use around these areas through the process of redevelopment.

This process of upgradation and redevelopment will need to be carried out in a planned manner, and in a public-private partnership framework, in which the entrepreneurs contribute to the betterment and subsequent maintenance through suitable Operation and Maintenance arrangements.

7.6.1.1 Industrial activity shall be conducted at the following locations in the Industrial Use Zone, as indicated in the Land Use Plan :

ZONES A to H :

Naraina Indl. Area, Jhandewallan Flatted Factory, Motia Khan Scheme, DCM Flatted Factory Complex, Shahzada Bagh Indl. Area, Gulabi Bagh Indl. Area, Rajasthan Udyog Nagar G.T. Road near Jahangirpuri, SMA Co-op. Indl. Estate G.T. Road near Jahangirpuri, SISI Indl. Area G.T. road near Jahangirpuri, G.T. Karnal Road Indl. Area near Rana Pratap Bagh, Hindustan Prefab Ltd., Indl. Area near Shivaji Rly Stn. (Minto Road), Okhla Indl. Area Ph.I, II & III, Mohan Co-op Indl. Area, SISI Complex Okhla near Modi Flour Mills, Najafgarh Road Indl. Area near Zakhira, Kirti Nagar Indl. Area, Mayapuri Ph. I & II, Udyog Nagar Rohtak Road, Keshav Pur Leather Tannery Scheme (part of Service Centre) near Vikaspuri, Wazirpur Industrial Area, Lawrence Road Indl. Area, Mangolpuri Indl. Area Ph.I & II, Jhilmil Indl. Area, Patparganj Indl. Area, Friends Colony Indl. Area, Narela Indl. Estate, Bawana Indl. Estate, Khanjhawala Indl. Estate, PVC Bazar Tikri Kalan.

(a) Additional Industrial Areas will be indicated while preparing plans for Urban Extension Areas.

(b) The approved Work-cum-Industries Centres, Service Centres etc., where development has been undertaken in accordance with the land use/earlier Master Plans, shall continue to be industrial subject to conformity with provisions stipulated.

7.6.2 REDEVELOPMENT OF UNPLANNED INDUSTRIAL AREAS

Besides the planned Industrial Areas, the Govt. of Delhi has notified following non-conforming clusters of industrial concentration having more than 70% plots in the cluster with industrial activities for redevelopment.

1. Anand Parbat
2. Shahdara
3. Samai Pur Badli

4. Jawahar Nagar
5. Sultanpur Mazra
6. Hastsal Pocket - A
7. Naresh Park Extension.
8. Libaspur
9. Peeragarhi Village
10. Khyala
11. Hastsal Pocket - D
12. Shalamar Village
13. New Mandoli
14. Nawada
15. Rithala
16. Swarn Park Mundka
17. Haiderpur
18. Karawal Nagar
19. Dabri
20. Basai Darapur

The redevelopment process involves preparation of redevelopment plans for widening of roads; laying of services, development of open space and parking etc.

In practical terms, these areas are deficient in terms of services and endanger the environment. The redevelopment of such areas needs to be based on clearly defined parameters in terms of the types of industries which may be permitted, spatial planning norms and environment related conditionalities regarding the provision of essential infrastructure with the participation of the owners / entrepreneur in a systematic manner.

7.6.2.1 Norms for Redevelopment of clusters of Industrial Concentration in Non Conforming Areas

Keeping in view the existing realities, as well as the imperatives of planned development, the following norms will have to be followed in the redevelopment process.

Non-conforming clusters of industrial concentration of minimum 4 hectare contiguous area, having more than 70% plots within the cluster under industrial activity / use may be considered for redevelopment of area identified on the basis of actual surveys. After notification of such clusters by GNCTD, the redevelopment scheme will have to be prepared by the concerned local body / land owning agency in consultation with the Society (to be formed by the land owners) based on the following norms / conditions:

(i) The cluster should have direct approach from a road of at least 18 m R/W.

(ii) Formation of Society shall be mandatory to facilitate preparation of redevelopment plan, pollution control and environmental management, development of services and parking and maintenance.

(iii) Only permissible industries having clearance from DPCC shall be permitted.

(iv) Amalgamation and reconstitution of plots shall be permissible for redevelopment.

(v) All the units shall have to obtain the statutory clearances. The industrial units shall have separate electric connections.

(vi) Other stipulations shall include—

(a) Minimum 10% area is to be reserved for circulation / roads / service lanes.

(b) Minimum 10% of semi-permeable surface for parking and loading / unloading areas.

(c) Minimum 10% of total area to be reserved for infrastructure requirements like CETP, Sub-Stations. Pump House, Fire Station, Police post, etc. as per the norms.

(d) Preparation of:

—Plan for water supply from DJB / Central Ground Water Authority (wherever required) along with requirement for pumping stations, storage tanks, ground water recharging / rainwater harvesting.

—Drainage plan as per norms.

(e) 8% of the cluster area shall be reserved for parks / green buffer.

(f) Plots measuring more than 100 sqm to have minimum 9.0 m. ROW.

(g) Plots measuring less than 100 sqm to have minimum 7.5 m. ROW.

(h) Common parking to be provided for plots below 60 sqm, whereas for plots above 60 sqm front set back (min. 3 m) shall be provided without boundary wall for parking and loading and unloading.

(vii) Other provisions / development control norms shall be applicable as prescribed. Depending upon ground conditions, the Technical Committee of DDA may relax the norms up to 10%.

The redevelopment work may be undertaken by the societies voluntarily or by the concerned local body / agencies. In case the agencies take up the redevelopment work for execution, they shall collect the charges from the individual industries themselves directly. Requisite charges for change in land use, enhanced FAR and land (wherever applicable) would be required to be paid to the concerned Authority.

The redevelopment shall be completed within the period specified by the Delhi Development Authority, Local Bodies in this regard. Clusters, which fail to complete the redevelopment proposals within the period specified as above, shall have to shift to other conforming industrial areas and the units functioning in non-conforming clusters shall have to close down. In such cases, the licensing authority will not renew / issue the licenses to industrial units without obtaining land use clearance from the competent authority. Further, no new licenses will be issued in non-conforming areas, without obtaining land use clearance.

The following areas shall not be eligible for industrial clusters redevelopment scheme :

Bungalow Zones (New Delhi & Civil Lines), the Ridge, River Bed (Zone-O), areas along water bodies, canals, sensitive areas from security point of view, conservation & heritage areas, reserved/protected forests, DDA flats, Cooperative Group Housing Societies, Government flats/bungalows/employer housing etc. and their immediate proximity.

7.7 NEW INDUSTRIAL AREAS

Development of new industrial areas in Greenfield areas of NCT of Delhi should be largely planned for the purpose of relocation of existing industries and for the development of a limited type of new industries for the following purposes:

(a) Relocation of permissible industries from the non-conforming clusters that are not eligible for regularization development; and

(b) Green field sites for Hi-tech industries.

New industrial activity in the NCT of Delhi should be restricted to hi-tech areas as given below :

i. Computer hardware and software industry and industries doing system integration using computer hardware and software.

ii. Packaging

iii. Industries integrating and manipulating the interfaces of the computers and telecom facilities.

iv. Industries catering to the information needs of uses by providing databases or access to databases spread throughout the globe.

v. Industries providing the facilities for sophisticated testing of different or all components of the information technology.

vi. Electronic goods.

vii. Service and repair of TV and other electronic items.

viii. Photo composing and desktop publication.

ix. TV and video programme production.

x. Textile designing and fabric testing, etc.

xi. Biotechnology.

xii. Telecommunications and enabling services.

xiii. Gems and jewellery.

7.8 INDUSTRY USE ZONE - GUIDELINES

The subdivision of industrial use zone into use premises and subsequent approval of layout plans for industrial estates shall be governed by the following norms :

(i) The new industrial areas to be developed may have plotted development for individual industrial units. The maximum size of industrial plots in new industrial areas shall be 400 sqm. except in already approved schemes.

(ii) The provision of land for the required facilities in industrial areas shall conform to norms given in the Table 7.2.

(iii) All new Industrial Estates shall have approach from a road of at least 30 m ROW.

(iv) Plots measuring less than 100 sqm. and will face 9 m ROW roads whereas plots measuring more than 100 sqm. will face 12 m ROW roads.

(v) Individual industrial plots facing main peripheral roads shall have access from dedicated service road after leaving green buffer.

(vi) The listed water bodies and / or any water body above 1 Ha. size are mandatory to be systematically included in the landscape plan.

(vii) Minimum 10m wide green buffer shall be provided along peripheral / access roads in the industrial areas.

(viii) The provision of Rainwater harvesting as an integral part of the landscape and storm water drainage plan at the time of sanction of layout plan shall be prepared.

(ix) The provision of minimum 30% of semi-permeable surface in all parking and loading / unloading areas.

(x) Grease traps should be provided near automobile washing area.

(xi) New Industrial areas should be located along major arterial roads. Major infrastructure network like CNG, LPG, oil, optical fibre, electricity, etc. to be made available along this corridor through underground pipelines.

(xii) Optimum utilisation of industrial areas should be made by way of development of flatted factories complexes.

(xiii) All industries should have provision for separating the solid waste before disposal. No untreated effluent shall be allowed to be discharged in the water bodies, open areas etc., outside the Industrial area. Primary treatment of the effluent shall be done at the plot level as per requirement.

(xiv) The provision of CETPs, solid waste separation / treatment plants shall be made at the industrial cluster level.

(xv) Proper disaster arrangements shall be made by the concerned agency for meeting any emergency situation arising due to fire, explosion, sudden leakage of gas or other natural calamities like earthquake, flood, etc.

(xvi) Industries in future may be grouped on the basis of common requirements such as effluent treatment, interdependence and nuisance value (fire hazard, noise, etc.).

(xvii) Selection of trees and plants shall be made keeping in view aspects such as distinctive avenue development, round the year flowering in park areas (either mixed or in cluster form) and shade requirements in specific areas.

Table 7.2: Norms for Land Distribution in Industrial Areas

S. No.	Use Premises	Percentage
1.	Industrial Plots (Net Area)	55-60
2.	Recreational: Buffer Zone, Parks, Water Bodies, Green under HT lines, etc.	10-12
3.	Commercial: Shopping Centre, Petrol Pumps, Guest House/ Budget hotels, Lodging and Boarding, Service and Repair shops, Communication/ Telephone Exchange, etc.	2-3
4.	Facilities •Public and Semi-Public: Fire Station/Fire Post, Police Station / Police Post, Hospital/ Dispensary, ITI / Polytechnic, Dharamshala, Night Shelter, Day Care Centre, etc. •Utilities: Electric Sub-Station, CETPs, Pumping Stations, Underground Reservoirs/ Fire Fighting Tanks and other utilities, etc.	8-10
5.	Transportation: Circulation, Loading/Unloading Area, Parking, ideal truck Parking, Goods Vehicle Parking etc.	18-20
	Total	100

Table7.3 : Development Control Norms

<table>
<tr><th rowspan="2">Use Premises</th><th colspan="3">Maximum</th><th>Parking standard</th><th rowspan="2">Activities Permitted</th><th rowspan="2">Definition</th></tr>
<tr><th>Gr. Cov. (%)</th><th>FAR</th><th>Ht (m)</th><th>BCS/ 100 sqm of floor area</th></tr>
<tr><td>Industrial Plot
(i) 50 sqm. and below
(ii) 51 sqm to 400 sqm.
(iii) 401 sqm and above</td><td>
100

60

50</td><td>
200

180

150</td><td>
8

15

15</td><td>
2

2

2</td><td>Industrial units: unit retail sales outlet and administrative office upto maximum 10% of floor area on ground floor only; residential flat upto the maximum extent of 5% of the floor space or 50 sqm. whichever is less for watch & ward and supervision, incidental storage [--]related to the industrial activity, commercial activity as per footnote (vi).</td><td>A premise for industrial activity having upto 50 workers with non-hazardous, non-poluting performance.</td></tr>
<tr><td>Flatted group Industry (Minimum plot size - 400 sqm.)</td><td>30</td><td>150</td><td>26</td><td>2</td><td>Industrial units; administrative office, watch and ward, maximum upto 5% of floor area or 20 sqm. whichever is less, storage related to the manufacturing activity, commercial activity as per footnote (vi).</td><td>A premise having a group of small industrial units having upto 20 workers with common services and facilities of non-hazardous, non-polluting nature.</td></tr>
</table>

Notes :

(i) In case of plots upto 60 sqm. common parking shall be provided.

(ii) In case of plots of size 500 sqm and above, the utilities such as E.S.S., underground water storage tank, roof top water harvesting system, separate dry and wet dustbins, solar heating/lighting system etc. shall be provided within the plot.

(iii) Identified Service Centres shall be planned as per plotted industrial area norms.

(iv) Development of IT hardware and software permissible under industrial use.

(v) Banquet hall shall be permissible in Industrial premise subject to specifications / regulations as may be prescribed, along with conversion charges.

(vi) Industrial units / plots abutting roads of 24m ROW and above shall be eligible for conversion to commercial use within the existing development control norms, subject to payment of conversion charges computed on current market value of commercial area and cost of parking as decided by Government from the time to time. The activities permissible in local shopping centres will be permitted in such plots. In addition, multilevel parking shall be permissible activity. However, this shall not be permitted on non-conforming/regularized industrial cluster. The above provision shall not affect the Supreme Court orders in any way.

ANNEXURE I

CLASSIFICATION OF INDUSTRIES

GROUP - A

HOUSEHOLD INDUSTRIES

1. Agarbatti and similar products
2. Aluminium hanger (excluding wire drawing and anodizing).
3. Ayurvedic / Homoeopathic/Unani medicines.
4. Assembly and repair of electronic goods.
5. Assembly and repair of sewing machines.
6. Assembly of hand tools.

7. Assembly of Badminton shuttlecocks.
8. Assembly and repair of electrical gadgets, cooler/heater etc.
9. Assembly and repair of typewriter (excluding Font Casting).
10. Assembly of Bakelite Switches.
11. Assembly and repair of measuring instruments (excluding handling of Mercury and hazardous materials).
12. Atta Chakkies.
13. Batik works.
14. Block making and photo enlarging.
15. Biscuit, pappey, cakes and cookies making.
16. Button making, fixing of button and hooks.
17. Bookbinding.
18. Brushes and brooms (by hand).
19. Calico and Textile products.
20. Cane and bamboo products.
21. Cassettes recording.
22. Clay and modeling with/without Plaster of Paris.
23. Coir and jute products.
24. Cardboard boxes.
25. Candles.
26. Copper and brass art wares.
27. Cordage, rope and twine making.
28. Carpentary.
29. Contact Lens.
30. Canvas bags and hold-alls making.
31. Candies, sweets, rasmalai etc. (when not canned).
32. Cotton/silk printing (by hand).
33. Computer repairing and cyber information Centre.
34. Computer Software.
35. Dari and carpet weaving.
36. Detergent (without bhatti).
37. Data processing.
38. Dairy products e.g. Cream, ghee, paneer, etc.
39. Dry Cleaning (excluding big workshops).
40. Desk Top Publishing.
41. Embroidery.
42. Enameling Vitreous (without use of coal).
43. Framing of pictures and mirrors.
44. Fountain pens, ball pens and felt pens.
45. Gold and Silver thread, kalabattu.
46. Hosiery products (without dyeing and bleaching).
47. Hats, caps, turbans including embroideries.
48. Information Technology enabled services
49. Ink making for fountain pens.

50. Interlocking and buttoning.
51. Jewellery items.
52. Khadi and handloom.
53. Khus tattis.
54. Knitting works.
55. Lace products.
56. Leather footwear.
57. Leather belts and assembly of buckles (by hand)
58. Leather and rexine made ups.
59. Milk Cream Separation.
60. Manufacture of Jute products.
61. Manufacture of Bindi.
62. Name plate making.
63. Production of following items.
    (i) Blanco cakes
    (ii) Brushes
    (iii) Kulfi and confectionery.
    (iv) Crayons.
    (v) Jam, jellies and fruit preserves.
    (vi) Musical instruments (including repairs).
    (vii) Lace work and like.
    (viii) Ornamental leather goods like purses, handbags.
    (ix) Small electronic components.
64. Paper stationery items and book binding.
65. Pith hat, garlands of flowers and pitch.
66. P.V.C. products (maximum one moulding machine).
67. Paper machine.
68. Perfumery and cosmetics
69. Photosetting.
70. Photostat and cyclostyling.
71. Photo copying of drawings including enlargement of drawings.
72. Packaging of Shampoos.
73. Packaging of Hair Oil.
74. Preparation of Vadi, Papad etc.
75. Processing of condiments, spices, groundnuts and dal etc.
76. Pan masala.
77. Production of Sweets and Namkeens (less than one ton/day)
78. Paper Mache
79. Paper cup, Plates, files cover and letter pads (without printing).
80. Photography (developing and printing).
81. Repair of watches and clocks.
82. Rakhee making
83. Repair of domestic electrical appliances.

84. Readymade garments (without washing).
85. Repair of bicycles.
86. Repair and assembly of computer hardware.
87. Repair of bags, brief cases, suitcases, except use of leather and PVC material.
88. Repairing of Water meters, stabilizer, UPS, etc.
89. Rubber Stamps.
90. Stone engraving.
91. Sports goods/Sports Nets.
92. Surgical bandage rolling and cutting.
93. Stove pipe, safety pins and aluminium buttons (by hand press).
94. Silver foil making.
95. Saree fall making.
96. Shoe laces.
97. Stamp pads.
98. Screen Printing.
99. Tailoring.
100. Thread balls and cotton fillings.
101. Toys and dolls.
102. Ties.
103. Tomato Ketchup.
104. Umbrella assembly.
105. Utensil washing powder (only mixing and packaging).
106. Velvet embroidered shoes/shawls.
107. Vermicelli and macaroni.
108. Wood carving and decorative wood wares.
109. Wool balling and lachee making.
110. Wooden/cardboard jewellery boxes (subject to no objection certificate from the department).
111. Wool knitting (with machine).
112. Zari Zardozi.

GROUP A - 1

HOUSEHOLD INDUSTRIES PERMISSIBLE IN VILLAGES (ABADI)

1. Black smithy.
2. Cane and bamboo products.
3. Clay and modelling with / without Plaster of Paris.
4. Dari/Carpet / Sari weaving (except dying & bleaching)
5. Ice cream and water-cooling by Refrigeration. (without cold storage)
6. Stone engraving.
7. Village pottery Industry (without bhatti).
8. Village oil ghani.
9. Wood carving and decorative wood wares.

None of the industries mentioned in Group A and A-1 shall carry out the following processes:

(i) Anodising
(ii) Bleaching

(iii) Burning of coal

(iv) Canning Facility

(v) Dyeing

(vi) Electroplating

(vii) Moulding works

(viii) Use of CFC gases

(ix) Varnishing

(x) Washing

Notes :

(i) Storing of chemicals listed under schedule I and/ or II of the Manufacture, Storage and import of hazardous Chemical Rules, 1989 and Public Liability Insurance Act, 1990 shall be prohibited.

(ii) No effluent / emissions shall be allowed to be generated by the units and these shall adhere to the noise standards as stipulated by Ministry of Environment and Forests, Government of India.

ANNEXURE II

GROUP-B

INDUSTRIES PERMISSIBLE IN COMMERCIAL CENTRES

1. Air Conditioner Parts.
2. Aluminium doors/windows/fittings/furniture.
3. Assembly and repair of Cycles.
4. Auto Parts.
5. Belts and Buckles.
6. Bulbs (battery).
7. Cloth Dyeing.
8. Cotton ginning.
9. Cycle Chain/Locks.
10. Diamond Cutting and Polishing work.
11. Electric fittings (switch, plug pin etc.)
12. Elastic products.
13. Engineering works.
14. Foundry (small job works as per prescribed limits of Industries Department/DPCC).
15. Ice-cream and water cooling by Refrigeration. (without cold storage)
16. Ice boxes and cooler bodies.
17. Iron grills and door making.
18. Jute products.
19. Key Rings.
20. Knife making.
21. Marble stone items.
22. Metal lathe cutting.
23. Motor winding works.
24. Printing Press.
25. Screws and nails.
26. Scissors making.
27. Spectacles and Optical frames.

28. Steel Furniture/Almirah.
29. Steel lockers
30. Steel Springs.
31. Surgical instruments and equipments.
32. Table lamps and shades.
33. Tin box making.
34. Transformer covers.
35. TV, Radio, Cassette recorders etc.
36. TV/Radio/Transistor cabinets.
37. Typewriter parts manufacturing and assembly.
38. Water meter repairing.
39. Water tanks.
40. Welding works.
41. Wire Knitting.
42. Wooden furniture works.
43. Information Technology enabled Services.

ANNEXURE III

PROHIBITED / NEGATIVE LIST OF INDUSTRIES

Industries manufacturing the following shall be prohibited within National Capital Territory of Delhi.

1. Arc/induction furnace
2. Acids
3. Alkalis
4. Animal & fish oils
5. Aldehydes
6. Acid slurry
7. Acetylides, phridines, iodoform, chloroform, E-nepthol, etc.
8. Ammonium sulphoajanide, arsenic and its compounds, barium carbonate, barium cyanide, barium ethyle sulphate, barium acetate cinnabar, copper sulphocyanide, ferrocyanide, hydro cyanide, hydro cyanic acid, potassium biocalate, potassium, cyanide, prussiate of potash, phynigallc acid, silver cyanide
9. Aircraft building.
10. Abattoirs, animal blood processing.(except existing and relocation)
11. Bitumen blowing (hot)
12. Brick kiln (using fresh earth as raw material, coal as fuel)
13 B-nepthol
14. Bakelite powder (starting from formaldehyde)
15. Barely malt and extract
16. Bone-grist, bone-meal, salting of bones, storages of bones in open, bone drying
17. Bone charcoal manufacturing
18. Blast furnaces - coal fired
19. Bicycles (integrated plant)
20. Brewery and potable spirits
21. Chlorinated paraffin wax purification

22. Carbon black
23. Cement industry
24. Calcium carbide, phosphorous, aluminum dust paste and powder, copper, zinc, etc. (electrothermal industries)
25. Cranes, hoists and lifts (excluding assembly)
26. General industrial machinery (such as hydraulic equipments, drilling equipments, boilers, etc.)
27. DOP (Dioctyl Phthalate), DBP & Plasticizer
28. Dry cell battery
29. Dye & dye intermediates
30. Distillation of wood, chemical seasoning of wood (excluding natural seasoning)
31. Explosives, i.e., Fireworks, Gunpowder, Guncotton, etc.
32. Earth moving machinery/equipment (manufacturing of assembly)
33. Electric wires and cables (more than 100 workers, 2000 sqm plot)
34. Fatty acids
35. Fungicides & pesticides
36. Flexographic ink
37. Fuel oils, illuminating oils and other oils such as stchetic oil, shoal oil, lubricants
38. Foundries (except Pit Furnace)
39. Gas compressors
40. Graphite production
41. Glass furnace (more than 1 ton/day capacity)
42. Gases-carbon-disulphide, ultramarine blue, chlorine, hydrogen, sulphur dioxide, acetylene, etc. (other than LPG/ CNG/Oxygen/medical gases)
43. Glandular/glandes extraction
44. Glue and gelatine from bones and flesh
45. Hot mix plant (except those approved by DPCC / CPCB)
46. Hazardous waste processing viz. hospital/medical/industrial waste
47. Polyurethene foam
48. Industrial gelatine, nitro glycerine and fulminate
49. Iron / steel metal forging (using pneumatic hammer).
50. Industrial gelatine, nitro glycerine and fulminate
51. Industrial trucks, trailers, etc.
52. Linear alkyd benzene
53. Lead manufacturing including secondary lead industry (recovery of lead from waste scrap)
54. Lime kiln.
55. Leather tanning and dyeing (raw hides/skins to semi finish)
56. Locomotives and wagons
57. Methanol
58. Methylated spirit
59. Mechanical stone crushers & washing of coarse sand
60. Manufacturing of pulp & paper
61. Melamine resin
62. Mineral salts (which involve use of acids: CuSO4, FESO4, alum, etc.)

63. Manufacturing of diesel engines, generators except assembly
64. Motor cycles, scooters, cars, tempos, trucks, etc.
65. News print manufacturing, pulping, fresh paper making
66. Nitrogeneors and phosphatic fertilizers, except mixing of fertilizers for compounding (large scale)
67. Organic solvent, chlorinated minerals, methanol, aldehydes, methylated spirits
68. Petroleum coke processing, not as fuel
69. Potteries/refractories (using coal or furnace oil)
70. Polyethylene polymers including resins
71. Paint industry (nitro Cellulose & Alkyd resin based)
72. Plasticisers manufacturing
73. Pyridines
74. Phenol formaldehyde resin and powder
75. Porcelain product potteries (using coal of production capacity more than 2 tonne per day)
76. Rubber solution and thinner (using naptha and rubber scrap)
77. Roasting of Ore Sulphide Oxides of mixtures
78. Rayon fibre manufacturing
79. Refractories
80. Reclamation of rubber.
81. Production of tyres and tubes (devulcanisation)
82. Saccharine
83. Secondary Zine industry
84. Synthetic rubber
85. Smelting
86. Sewing machines (integrated units) except assembly
87. Sluice gates and gears
88. Stainless Steel Pickling
89. Steam engines
90. Steel pipes and tubes (continuous welded/seamless)
91. Sugar, khand sari
92. Sodium silicate industry (more than 1 tonne/day)
93. Stone quarrying
94. Textile (more than 100 workers in all shifts, I acre of land, 100 LKD of water)
95. Thorium, radium and similar isotopes and recovery of rare earth
96. Turbines
97. Urea & Phenyl Formaldehyde resin
98. Vegetable oil hydrogenerated
99. Waste (crude / burnt) oil processing (refinery)

Notes :

(i) A public utility service involving any of the activities referred to above shall be permitted subject to environmental laws.

(ii) Further additions / alterations to the list of Prohibited Industries could be made if considered appropriate and in public interest by the Central Government to do so.

8.0 GOVERNMENT OFFICES

Delhi being the country's capital provides excellent opportunities in service sector. It has attracted people in government and quasi government sector from all parts of India. The growth in the sector was significant till 1981. However, as per the report on Economic Census, 2003, the employment in government sectors is on decline. The table below shows the growth of employment in different government sectors.

Table 8.1: Employment in Govt. and Quasi Govt. Sector (in lakh)

S.No.	Category	1981	1991	2000	2003
1.	Central Government	2.25 (6.64)	2.15 (-4.44)	2.13 (-0.93)	2.14
2.	Government of NCTD	0.58 (9.43)	1.04 (9.31)	1.13 (8.65)	1.21
3.	Quasi Government (Central + State)	1.41 (151.79)	2.14 (51.77)	2.04 (-4.67)	1.96
4.	Local Bodies	1.17 (30)	0.83 (-29.06)	0.95 (14.46)	0.93
	TOTAL	5.33 (30)	6.16 (15.57)	6.25 (1.46)	6.24

Figures in brackets indicate decadal growth rate in percentage.

Source: Directorate of Employment, GNCTD and MPD-2001

8.1 DECENTRALIZATION OF OFFICES

As per NCR Plan, no new Central Government and Public Sector Undertaking offices should be located in NCTD. However, the issue of shifting existing Government / PSU offices from Delhi as well as restricting the setting up of new offices would only be possible after a time bound action plan is prepared together with suitable incentives and disincentives.

8.2 OPTIMUM UTILIZATION OF GOVERNMENT LAND

Government of India, Govt. of NCTD and local bodies are occupying prime land in Delhi for their offices. Most of the offices have been setup immediately after Independence. Large areas are underutilized and have completed their economic life. Due to downsizing of government employment and need for generation of resources by the ministries, optimum utilization of existing government offices / land could be achieved by the following measures:

(i) Intensive utilization of existing government offices/land.

(ii) Utilization of Surplus land by the government for residential development.

(iii) Utilization of 10% of total FAR for commercial uses to make the restructuring process financially feasible. This shall be subject to approval of land owning agency and concerned local body.

Major GNCTD Offices, which were located in Old Secretariat building, have been shifted to the new premises at Indraprastha Estate. Old Secretariat is a historical building and needs to be conserved. Barracks area adjacent to the Old Secretariat could be redeveloped to accommodate additional GNCTD Offices.

Presently District courts are located at Tis Hazari, Karkarduma and Rohini Sub-city. Land has been earmarked at following locations to accommodate new District Courts.

(i) Near Saket District Centre -7 ha.

(ii) Narela Sub-City - 3ha.

(iii) Dwarka Sub-City- 3 ha.

Major employment of the Local Bodies and GNCTD should be accommodated in the public and semi-public facility areas such as health facilities, education etc. The head quarters of the Municipal Corporation of Delhi would be housed in the proposed Civic Centre under construction on Jawahar Lal Nehru Marg, which has been designated as Non-Hierarchical commercial centre.

In the Urban Extension as far as possible, the government offices should be provided along the MRTS corridor. Four sites (10-15 Ha. each) for the offices of the Govt. of NCT Delhi, Courts and Local Bodies, etc. should be provided.

Table 8.2: Development Controls - Govt. Offices

Use/ Use Premises.	Maximum			Parking Standard ECS/100 sq.m. of floor area	Definition	Activities permitted
	Ground	FAR	Height (m)			
(i) Integrated Office Complex	30	200	NR, subject to approval of AAI, Fire Department and other statutory bodies.	1.8	Premises used for the office of Central Government, Local Government and Local Bodies.	Government Offices, Watch and Ward Residence/ residential maintenance staff (maximum 5% of FAR), Retail shop of Chemist, Book and stationery, Consumer Store, Canteen, Post office, Bank Extension Counter etc. Public sector Undertaking/ Commercial offices (restricted to 10% of the total floor area)
(ii)District Court	30	200	NR, subject to approval of AAI, Fire Department and other statutory bodies.	1.8	Premises used for the offices of Judiciary.	Court, Residential maintenance staff (maximum 5% of FAR), Canteen, Restaurant, Ancillary services and Retail shop, Library, Dispensary, Administrative offices, Banks, Post offices, Police post, Fire post, Lawyer's chamber.

Notes:

(i) The norms for Local Government offices / Public Sector Undertakings under Government Land use shall be as per Integrated office complex.

(ii) The norms of Govt. use (undetermined) shall be as per approved layout / scheme, which development controls shall be as per respective use premises.

9. ENVIRONMENT

Creation of a sustainable physical and social environment for improving quality of life is one of the major objectives of the plan. The almost unprecedented scale and speed of urbanisation in Delhi has resulted in enormous pressures on the physical environment with a severe adverse impact in terms of pollution, and today Delhi is considered to be among the most polluted cities in the world.

The city's environment can essentially be seen in terms of two components of urban management- the environment per se, or the habitat, and services management. The former pertains to the natural features and resources including: the elements of air and noise, water (water bodies-river, lakes, drains and ponds and ground water) and land with reference to open spaces, green areas and other surface and sub-surface conditions. The latter is related to the built environment and includes the environmental infrastructure - water supply, sewerage, solid waste disposal, and the transportation network.

In the above stated background the following three fold approach and strategy will need to be adopted :

(i) Management of Natural Resources and the related environment infrastructure and services in a manner that would lead to optimisation of use of natural resources, and reduction/abatement of pollution.

(ii) Conservation and Development of the Natural features with a view to enhancing their environmental value; and

(iii) Development and preservation of open spaces, greens and landscape/ recreational areas.

A clear approach towards management of 4 types of wastes generated in Delhi, namely Solid Waste, Hazardous Waste, Bio-Medical Waste and Electronic Waste, should be adopted. The approach should take into account the need for adopting the Clean Development Mechanism (CDM) and the awareness of the carbon credits that can be earned and encashed through a planned and organized mechanism, to be developed for this purpose.

9.1 NATURAL RESOURCES

Natural Resource Conservation includes management of water (surface and ground), air and noise.

9.1.1 WATER (SURFACE AND GROUND)

(a) The surface water resources in Delhi are basically comprised of the river Yamuna, drains and the lakes/ ponds. The ground water in Delhi occurs in confined and semi-confined conditions, with depths varying from 1 m to 10 m below the ground level and in the alluvial terrain, several sandy aquifers occur at different levels upto a depth of 70 m.

Based on studies and statistics, some of the striking features that are revealed about the surface water resources in Delhi are :

i. The Yamuna river and the drains are highly polluted;

ii. The supply of water for human use is too much in absolute terms, but is characterized by iniquitous distribution in per capita terms in different areas, and significant wastage;

iii. Assuming that 80 percent of the water is converted into waste water, the capacity to treat waste water is grossly deficient; Various options for the re-use of treated waste water must be explored and implemented.

iv. The actual quantity of waste water treated is much below the installed capacity on account of missing links in sewer connectivity between the generation points and treatment plants and choking/silting of sewer lines, etc. The missing links in sewer connectivity must be covered for its continuity from the generation point to the treatment plant.

v. The planned re-use of treated waste water is minuscule;

vi. The treated wastewater is being largely put back into the drains and gets polluted again before flowing into the river Yamuna, which receives 70 percent of its waste from the 22 kms. of its flow through urban Delhi which, in turn, constitutes only 2 percent of the total length of the river basin stretching from its point of origin till its merger into the Ganga at Allahabad;

vii. A large number of the traditional water bodies in the form of ponds, etc. (excluding areas of unintended water logging along railway tracks, highways and canals etc.) have been encroached or have otherwise become defunct.

viii. The standards for STP / CETP developed by Central Pollution Control Board / Delhi Pollution Control Committee should be adhered to.

ix. The public participation and education programmes must be encouraged so that the sensitivity of the water resource is understood by the consumers, students and RWAs.

(b) Groundwater is one of the major sources for water supply in many parts of the country. In Delhi too, ground water contributes a substantial quantity of water supply. Especially in new development areas, groundwater is largely being used as drinking water resources. The Central Ground Water Board (CGWB) assessed the total groundwater potential to be 292 million cubic meters (MCM) in 2003 as compared to 428.07 MCM in

1983, showing an overdraft and reduction of around 130 MCM over the past 20 years. Out of the 6 blocks into which Delhi is divided, significant over drawl / reduction has been observed in the Najafgarh and Mehrauli blocks. Rapid urbanisation leading to reduction in recharge of aquifers, increasing demand in the agriculture, industrial and domestic sectors, stress put on groundwater resources in periods of drought/ deficient rainfall, and unplanned withdrawal from the sub soil aquifers, have been mainly responsible for decline in groundwater levels.

The average annual rainfall in Delhi is 611 mm. However, recharge of ground water gets limited due to decreased availability of permeable surfaces owing to urbanisation, and the runoff getting diverted into the sewers or storm water drains that convey the water into the river Yamuna. The annual rainwater harvesting potential has been assessed at 900 billion litres or 2500 million litres per day. If even 25% of this could be harvested it would imply availability of 625 mld, which would be nearly equivalent to the presently estimated deficiency. This is in addition to the potential for roof water harvesting assessed at around 27 mld.

The existing drainage basins shall have to be made self-sustainable in water management by integrating water-sewerage-drainage systems. New projects and upgradation of present infrastructure should be taken up in addition to promotion of water conservation through an integrated and a community driven model. Complimentary short term and long-term strategies as mentioned above will need to be initiated.

(c) Development of parks and green corridors along the Nallahs should incorporate conservation of ground water and water bodies. To recharge the ground water, conservation of water bodies and rainwater shall be essential. The area near Najafgarh Jheel and its surroundings and the Ridge can also be used as potential water conservation area.

(d) To increase sub-surface soil water through seepage of rain water, porous paving tiles should be used in the pavements and soft parking areas. All the new bridges / flyovers must have the provision for rain water harvesting.

Water bodies, having a minimum size of surface area of 1 ha., shall be preserved by the concerned authorities. Further efforts shall be made at the local level to retain smaller water bodies.

9.1.2 AIR

Despite various initiatives and measures taken over the past few years, like introduction of CNG and EURO II norms etc., the air quality in the city, in terms of pollution levels, has continued to be a matter of concern, and has been responsible for a number of respiratory diseases, heart ailments, eye irritation, asthma, etc. The three main sources of air pollution in Delhi are vehicular emission (around 70 percent) industrial emissions (around 20 percent) with a major element of this coming from the three thermal power plants, and from other sources such as diesel generator sets and domestic cooking, burning of biomass, etc.

Apart from the issue of pollution on account of industries, the major area of planning and intervention would relate to transportation planning. With the phenomenal growth in the number of vehicles, almost 8-10 times in the last two decades in absolute terms, the most significant aspect in the context of congestion and pollution, relates to the growth in personalised transport as compared to the availability of public transport. It has been estimated that buses, which constitute barely 1.2 percent of the total number of vehicles, cater to around 60 percent of the total transport load, while personal vehicles -cars and scooters, though almost 93 percent of the total number of vehicles, cater to around only 30 percent of the travel demand. Such a huge share of private vehicles in Delhi, while serving a relatively limited purpose in terms of the transportation modal split, obviously creates tremendous pressure on road space, parking, and pollution directly and through congestion.

Public transportation planning must, therefore, drive the future policy. So far public transport is largely seen as the transport mode for the not so well off and poorer sections of the community, who cannot afford to own/use personal transport. An important element of policy would now also have to aim to make public transport a mode for personal vehicle owners and users through a mix of incentives and disincentives. Apart from aspects like frequency, inter-modal integration, a possible single ticketing system, use of parking policy as a means to influence vehicle use, etc., the quality of public transport, particularly buses, would need to be significantly upgraded, inter-alia, keeping the element of clean transport in view.

Another issue which has been raised in the context of vehicular congestion and pollution relates to the policy of mixed land use, which will also have to be carefully considered.

The other elements which would need carefully thought out policy measures would relate to the operation of existing Power plants to significantly reduce the pollution arising from them, and industries, both in terms of pollution control in designated industrial areas, and relocation of non-conforming industries.

As per the Government of India Notification, it is mandatory for all construction agencies to use Fly Ash bricks or tiles or clay fly ash bricks along with pond ash in the construction of roads / flyovers embankments and reclamation of low-lying areas. To control the ambient air quality of Delhi, it may be made mandatory that all commercial vehicles (like trucks and tempos) are converted into CNG. All Thermal Power plants located in the NCT of Delhi should be gradually converted to gas based plants.

9.1.3 NOISE

Noise is emerging as a major pollutant and irritant as well as a constant source of disturbance and health hazards. Against a permissible level of 50-60 dB (A), the sound level in Indian cities often exceeds 80 dB (A). Faulty and leaking silencers, over-use of horns and vehicles plying on roads accentuate noise level, besides the noise from commercial and industrial activities, unabated use of sound amplifiers, generator sets and fire- crackers etc.

The Noise Pollution (Regulation & Control) Rules 2000 specify the noise levels in the industrial area, commercial area, residential area and silence zone. It also specifies banning of all noise creating activities between 10 PM to 6 AM, which may be adhered to by the concerned agencies.

By proper land use planning, such as location of public, semi-public and commercial activities along major transport arteries, a buffer can be created for residential zones. Green buffer through thin leaved trees, land formations, mounds, embankments, etc. along major roads could also provide effective barriers to transmission of noise. It is also necessary to improve monitoring and effective implementation of the Noise Pollution (Level) Rules 2000 and, to notify certain areas as 'No Horn Zones'. The design and surface material of roads and pavements should also ensure reduction of noise. The concerned authorities should prepare area wise traffic calming schemes and a Noise Monitoring and Control Plan (NMCP).

Working in night shifts for household industries or non-conforming industries in the residential areas should be prohibited. Areas located within the air funnel should be planned with due consideration of noise generated from the aeroplanes.

Environmentally stressed zones in Delhi should be identified and local area environment management plans should be prepared for such areas, together with regular monitoring.

9.2 NATURAL FEATURES

The major natural features and eco-systems of Delhi are the river Yamuna, together with a network of streams/ drains that empty into the river, and the Aravalli Range. Both of these are in a state of considerable degradation, and it is of vital importance to conserve and rejuvenate these ecosystems. This has regional bearing, therefore, surrounding states also have to contribute towards their conservation and rejuvenation.

9.2.1 RIVER YAMUNA

Once the lifeline, which spawned the many civilisations and Cities that grew in the area of the present NCT of Delhi, the River Yamuna today suffers from inadequate flow and quantum of water and an extremely high degree of pollution. The length of the river in the NCT of Delhi is 48 kms from Palla in the North to Okhla in the South, with a total river bed/flood plane area of around 97 sq.kms. which is about 7 percent of the total area of Delhi. A little over 50 percent of the river lies North of Wazirabad and the rest, around 22 kms., to its South, in the Urban area of Delhi. Apart from being the main sources of water supply for Delhi, it is one of the major sources of ground water recharge. However, over the years, rapid urbanisation, encroachments on the river banks, over exploitation of natural resources/water, and serious deficiencies and backlog in sanitation and waste water management services, have resulted in the dwindling of water flow in the river and extremely high levels of pollution in the form of BOD and Coliforms, etc. As against the stipulated 3mg./1, the designated water quality for bathing purposes, the water quality data for 2003-04 suggests that the BOD values range from 1-3 mg/1 at Palla, 5.56 mg/1 at Nizamuddin and nearly 7 mg/l at Okhla. Similarly, at all locations, except Palla, the total coliform levels are many times higher than the minimum tolerable standards for drinking and bathing purposes.

The major source of pollution in the river to the extent of about 80%, is the discharge of treated and untreated waste water through the 22 major drains, which flow into the river(Annexure-I). The CPCB data shows that six of these drains viz. the Najafgarh and the Supplementary Drain, the Shahdara Drain, the Drain near Sarita Vihar, the Maharani Bagh Drain, the Barapulla drain and the Sen Nursing Home Drain contribute almost 90 percent of the flow and 80 percent BOD load levels respectively.

The concerned agencies must ensure that through public awareness campaigns, people are discouraged from throwing garbage into the river or the drains and measures are taken to prevent throwing of garbage by the habitations along side. Regular de-silting of the drains should also be undertaken.

1. Measures for rejuvenation of River Yamuna

(a) The issue of pollution in the river Yamuna has engaged the attention of the Supreme Court for the last several years, and it constituted a Committee with Secretary, Ministry of Urban Development as a Member, to draw up an Action plan for the cleaning/rejuvenation of the Yamuna River. A summary of the recommendations of the Committee is given in Annexure II.

(b) Apart from the above measures, steps would also need to be taken to augment ground recharge from the river and decentralised wastewater treatment system. The creation of 'regulated flood plane reservoirs', for storing the excess monsoon overflow at suitable locations would augment the water retention capacity of the riverbed. The upstream of Wazirabad Barrage and some other areas offer such a potential. To facilitate ground water recharge it may also be ensured that minimum required flow in the river during lean season exists. The reservoirs may be created in low-lying areas.

(c) At another level, a strategy for the conservation/development of the Yamuna River Bed area needs to be developed and implemented in a systematic manner. This issue is sensitive both in terms of the environment and public perceptions. Any such strategy will need to take into account the cycle of flood occurrences and flood zones, the ground water recharge potentials and requirements, potential for reclamation derived from the foregoing considerations, designation and delineation of appropriate land uses and aesthetics of the River Front which should be more fully integrated with the city and made more accessible-physically, functionally and visually.

(d) Environmental study of the existing major drains should be conducted before their covering.

9.2.2 REGIONAL PARK

The Aravalli Range in the NCT of Delhi comprises of the rocky outcrop stretching from the University in the North to the NCT Border in the South and beyond, and sizeable areas of the same have been designated as the Ridge. This is not a continuum as various intervening stretches have, over a period of time, been brought under urbanisation - for example the Central Ridge area was planned as an integral part of New Delhi, at the time of the development of New Delhi as the Capital in the early part of the twentieth century. The Master Plan of Delhi - 2001 identified the Regional Park into four parts as below :

1.	Northern Ridge	87 ha.
2.	Central Ridge	864 ha.
3.	South Central Ridge (Mehrauli)	626 ha.
4.	Southern Ridge	6200 ha.

Subject to verification, the area of Regional Park is 7777 hectares. Part of this has been notified as Reserve Forest under the Indian Forest Act, 1927 vide Notification dated 24.5.94 and 02.04.96. There are discrepancies between the area notified and the physical boundaries of the total area owned by various agencies - DDA, CPWD, NDMC, MCD, Forest Department and the Ministry of Defence. Till the exact boundaries are identified by the Forest Department, the boundary indicated in the Master Plan for Delhi (land use plan) as Regional Park shall continue.

9.3 GREEN / RECREATIONAL AREAS

Delhi has a much larger green cover than any of the other metropolitan city in the country, and could well be called a "Green City". The green / recreational use constitutes 8,722 ha of land as per MPD 2001, which is around 19% of the total urban land area of 44,777 ha. This includes 1577 ha. under the Northern, Central and South Central Ridge (the remaining area of the Ridge is in the rural area). The balance area under recreational/ green use i.e. 7145 ha. is in the form of District Parks, City Parks, Community Parks etc. comprising around 15% of the total urban land area. In addition to this, a large chunk of green area is provided in the form of Neighborhood Parks / Tot lots in the gross residential use zones, plantations / greens in large campuses like President's Estate, JNU, IARI, Delhi University, plantations along drains and roadside plantations. In addition to above, two Bio-diversity parks are under development by the DDA.

In the Urban Extension the green cover is to be provided at the rate of 15% of the total land, excluding the Ridge/ Regional Park. Out of this, some area shall be developed in the form of formal parks for the community and the rest shall be developed as woodlands and incidental greens for balancing the environment. This will be in addition to the development of specialized parks like Bio-Diversity Parks, plantation along the roads, drains, riverbank, etc.,

Further, Sports Complexes, which were included in the green / recreational use category under the MPD-2001 will be seen under a separate category of sports. One of the main reasons for this modification is that, Delhi is emerging as an important centre for National and International sports events. Sports facilities are being developed by various agencies besides DDA in Delhi, mostly as a part of recreational activity/ facility. As a result there is still a need for planned and structured sports infrastructure which can take care of training needs of sportsmen and also act as integrated sports complexes for national and international events. This will not disturb the green areas, which are meant for recreational purposes. Keeping this in mind, sports facilities have been included as a part of social infrastructure, which in turn may help to develop better sports infrastructure for training needs, related logistics and sports medicine etc. This will also facilitate private participation. Integrated sports complexes are envisaged under one roof to accommodate variety of sports and related functions, by way of facilitating wide-range of permissibility, ground coverage and FAR.

Table 9.1: Planning Norms, Standards for Recreational Areas/ Parks at Sub-City Level

Sl. No	Category	Planning Norms & Standards	
		Population/Unit (Approx.)	Plot Area (Ha)
1.	City Park	10 lakh	100
2.	District Park	5 lakh	25
3.	Community Park	1 lakh	5

Note: 5 to 10 % of the area will be under use for rainwater harvesting / water body.

Table 9.2: Planning Norms, Standards for Recreational Areas/ Parks at Neighbourhood Level

Sl. No	Category	Planning Norms & Standards	
		Population/Unit (Approx.)	Plot Area (Ha)
1.	Neighbourhood Park	10000	1.0
2.	Housing Area Park	5000	0.5
3.	Tot lot at Housing Cluster Level	250	0.0125

9.4 MULTIPURPOSE GROUNDS

Experience shows that formal parks are fouled if used for marriages/ public functions etc. Therefore, a special category is proposed to take care of the same at three levels in the following manner :

Table 9.3: Planning Norms, Standards for Multipurpose Grounds

Sl. No	Category	Planning Norms & Standards	
		Population/Unit (Approx.)	Plot Area (Ha)
1.	City Multipurpose Ground	10 lakh	8
2.	District Multipurpose Ground	5 lakh	4
3.	Community Multipurpose Ground	1 lakh	2

Other Controls :

(i) Minimum 50% of total area shall be under Soft Parking and remaining 50% shall be utilized for activities.

(ii) Minimum 3% of the remaining area (excluding Soft Parking area) shall be utilized for Electric Sub Station, Toilets, Security and other marriage related activities etc.

(iii) Multipurpose Ground can be sub-divided suitably with minimum of 0.5 ha of plot area to accommodate number of functions at one time.

(iv) Park / multipurpose ground shall have provisions for rainwater harvesting

9.5 AMUSEMENT PARK

Amusement Park up to 10 Ha. may be permitted in District Park. Following development controls shall be applicable:

(i) Max Ground Coverage- 5%

(ii) Max. FAR- 7.5

(iii) Max. Height- 8 mt

(iv) Parking- 3 ECS/100 sqm. of floor area with the stipulation to provide min. parking for 100 cars.

9.6 GREEN BELT

The Plan provides for agricultural land as Green Belt along the border of NCT of Delhi, in synergy with the provisions of Regional Plan 2021 of NCR. The belt extends from the NCTD boundary up to a depth of one peripheral revenue village boundary, wherever possible.

Table 9.4: Permission of Use Premises in Sub Use Zones

Sl. No	Use Zone	Activities Permitted
1.	Green Belt	Forest, Agriculture use, Vegetation belt, Dairy Farms, Piggery, Poultry farms, Farm house, Wild life sanctuary, Bird sanctuary, Biodiversity Park, Veterinary Centre, Police Post, Fire Post, Smriti Van, Plant Nursery, Orchard, Area for water-harvesting, Floriculture farm, Open Playground, Agro forestry, Amenity structures (List given in note). Existing village Abadis, already Regularised Unauthorised colonies and already approved Motels may continue.
2.	Regional Park	Ridge, Residential Flat (For watch & ward), Picnic Hut, Park, Shooting Range, Zoological Garden, Bird Sanctuary, Botanical Garden, Local Government Office (Maintenance), Open Air Theatre, Police Post, Fire Post, Orchard, Plant Nursery and Forest. Approved Farm Houses sanctioned prior to 01.08.90 may continue.
3.	City park	Aqua park/water sports park, Arboretum, Botanical Garden, National Memorial (approved by Cabinet/ Govt. of India), Amphitheatre, Open Playground, Aquarium, Other activities same as permitted in District Park. 30% of the area shall be developed with plantation of native species.
4.	District Park	District Park, Theme park, Recreational Club, National Memorial, Open-air food court, Children Park, Orchard, Plant Nursery, Area for water harvesting, Archaeological Park, Specialized Park, Amusement Park, Children Traffic Park, Sports activity, Playground, Amenity structures. Restaurant in a District Park having an area above 25 Ha. subject to following : a. Area of the restaurant plot shall not be more than 0.8 Ha or 1% of the District Park, whichever is less. b. Restaurant plot shall have no physical segregation from the rest of the District Park area. c. The building shall be a single storey structure with max. FAR of 5 and height not more than 4m. without any residential facility and to harmonize with the surroundings. d. In case there is no parking lot in the vicinity, parking should be provided at a reasonable distance from the restaurants. Parking area should not form part of the restaurant complex / greens. e. 30% of the area shall be developed as dense plantation.
5.	Community Park	Park, Children Park, Open-air food court, Playground etc.
6.	Multipurpose Ground	Public meeting ground, Public address podium, Social functions, Soft drink and snack stalls etc.

Notes:

i) The following amenity structures are permissible in the above use premises except in Central Vista and Heritage areas : Toilet blocks, Pump Room, Electric Room, Guard Room, Equipment Room.

ii) Interpretation Centre and Administrative office is permissible only in Heritage Areas.

ANNEXURE I

LIST OF DRAINS OUT FALLING INTO RIVER YAMUNA :

1. **Najafgarh drain**
2. **Magazine Road drain**
3. **Sweeper Colony drain**
4. **Khyber pass drain**
5. **Metcalfe drain**
6. **Kudsia Bagh drain**
7. **Moat drain**
8. **Trans Yamuna MCD drain**
9. **Mori Gate drain**
10. **Civil Mili Drain**
11. **Power House drain**
12. **Sen Nursing Home drain**
13. **Drain No. 14**
14. **Barapullah Drain**
15. **Maharani Bagh drain**
16. **Kalkaji drain**
17. **Okhla drain**
18. **Tughlakabad drain**
19. **Shahdara drain**
20. **Sarita Vihar Drain**
21. **LPG Bottling Plant Drain**
22. **Tehkhand Drain**

ANNEXURE II

RECOMMENDATIONS OF THE COMMITTEE UNDER SECRETARY (UD) MOUD, GOVT. OF INDIA, FOR YAMUNA ACTION PLAN (2004)

1. Minimum flow in river Yamuna to be ensured by Riparian states by releasing adequate water

2. Refurbishment of Trunk Sewerage System

DJB has a network of approx. 130 Kms. length of trunk sewerage system to convey the collected sewage to different STPs for treatment. Nearly 91 Km of sewer lines are in highly dilapidated condition and have been silted to the extent of 50% to 70% at different stretches. Therefore, rehabilitation of following three major trunk sewers is proposed to be taken up under the Yamuna Action Plan.

(a) **Rehabilitation of Ring Road trunk sewer under Yamuna Action Plan-II (YAP-II)**

(b) **Rehabilitation of Bela Road trunk sewer under YAP-II**

(c) **Rehabilitation of West Delhi trunk sewer under YAP-III**

3. Treatment of the flows in Najafgarh and Shahdara drains

The drains contributing maximum to the pollution load in the river water are Najafgarh and Shahdara drains. Action plan to check flows in Najafgarh Drain and Shahdara drain is recommended. The untreated sewage results in pollution of the water flowing in the drain and affects its quality by increasing BOD level and suspended solid. Majority of the untreated

sewage is contributed by unauthorised colonies. It would be possible to treat this sewage only after laying of internal sewerage system or installation of decentralized treatment plants, which are proposed to be attempted by MCD on pilot basis.

4. Laying of Sewer Lines in the un-sewered areas of Delhi

DJB has pointed that it has laid internal sewerage system in 482 unauthorized / regularised colonies and in 98 urban villages of Delhi. The sewerage systems in 496 unauthorized / regularised colonies and 103 urban villages are likely to be laid by December 2005. In 516 unauthorized / regularised colonies and 105 urban villages, sewerage systems are expected to be completed by May 2006.

5. Slum Cluster and Yamuna River Bed

One of the contributory factors to the flow of untreated sewage into river Yamuna is the slum clusters that have come up unauthorisedly on both eastern and western bank of river Yamuna. Local bodies have already removed several JJ Clusters existing on the Western Bank. Slum clusters need to be cleared from riverbed.

6. Treatment of Industrial Effluent

Delhi Small Industries Development Corporation has constructed 10 Common Effluent Treatment Plants (CETPs) having an installed capacity of 133 mld for treating the industrial effluent before they are discharged into the drains/river. Better capacity utilisation and laying of conveyance system wherever required is needed.

7. Utilisation of Treated Effluent

Currently 109.5 MGD of treated effluent is being supplied by DJB to CPWD, DDA, Pragati Power Plant and Minor Irrigation Department. Additional 241 MGD is available for other user agencies. The issue of utilising the additional treated water is being deliberated by CPWD.

8. Removal of Coliform at STPs

The task force has set up a Committee to determine the permissible level of coliform in the treated wastewater and the process required for achieving the same keeping in view its techno-economic feasibility.

10. CONSERVATION OF BUILT HERITAGE

10.1 CONSERVATION OF BUILT HERITAGE

Delhi is a historical city, whose remnants are spread right from Mehrauli to Shahjahanabad having large number of monuments scattered all over Delhi. The built heritage of Delhi is an irreplaceable and non-renewable cultural resource. Besides being part of life for many, it has educational, recreational and major tourism potential. It enhances Delhi's environment, giving it identity and character. It encompasses culture, lifestyles, design, materials, engineering and architecture.

The Heritage Resources include symbols of successive civilizations and cities that came up over the millennia, historic buildings and complexes, historical gardens, water engineering structures and their catchments, the remains of fortified citadels, places for worship and for the deceased, historic cities and villages, unearthed heritage and their components.

The surveys conducted by the DDA & INTACH identify 1208 historical monuments in Delhi of which the Archeological Survey of India has declared 170 monuments as protected. In addition to these MCD, NDMC and the State Archaeological Department have published lists of Heritage Buildings.

10.2 CONSERVATION STRATEGY

The agencies concerned with the protection of Delhi's Built Heritage are ASI, GNCTD, State Archaeology Department, NDMC, MCD, Cantonment Board and DDA.

Built heritage of Delhi needs to be protected, nourished and nurtured by all citizens and passed on to the coming generations. It is suggested that with the aim of framing policies and strategies for conservation, appropriate action plans may be prepared by all the agencies. These should include promotion of conservation of the civic and urban heritage, architecturally significant historical landmarks, living monuments, memorials and historical gardens, riverfront, city wall, gates, bridges, vistas, public places, edicts and the ridge.

It is recommended that these should be suitably incorporated while preparing layout plans / schemes. In case of major monuments it is necessary that the surrounding area should be identified in the layout / detail plan, and should have building controls in relation to height, material and spread of the monuments.

It will also be necessary to maintain close interaction and coordination between all these agencies keeping in view the following objectives and requirements.

i. Maintain and update a database.

ii. Develop organizational capacity for heritage management.

iii. Define all the applicable terms.

iv. Listing of Heritage Buildings based on the following criteria:

(a) The age of the building;

(b) Its special value for architectural or cultural reasons or historical periods;

(c) Its relevance to history;

(d) Its association with a well-known character or event;

(e) Its value as part of a group of buildings;

(f) The uniqueness of the building or any object or structures fixed to the building or forming part of the land and comprised within the curtilage of the building.

v. Prepare guidelines for development, redevelopment, additions alterations, repairs, renovations and reuse of the heritage buildings.

vi. Implementing programmes for education and awareness.

10.3 HERITAGE ZONES

Heritage Zone is an area, which has significant concentration, linkage or continuity of buildings, structures, groups or complexes united historically or aesthetically by plan or physical development. The following areas have been identified as Heritage Zones as indicated in the Zonal Plan:

i. Specific heritage complex within Walled City of Delhi, Shahjahanabad

ii. Specific heritage complex within Lutyens Bungalow Zone

iii. Specific heritage complex within Nizamuddin and Humayun's Tomb Complex.

iv. Specific heritage complex within Mehrauli area.

v. Specific heritage complex within Vijay Mandal - Begumpur - Sarai Shahji - Lal Gumbad.

vi. Specific heritage complex within Chirag Delhi.

However more areas can be added to this list based on studies by concerned agencies.

10.4 ARCHAEOLOGICAL PARK

Archaeological Park is an area distinguishable by heritage resource and land related to such resources, which has potential to become an interpretive and educational resource for the public in addition to the value as a tourist attraction.

All decisions regarding Built Heritage in general and Archeological Parks in particular should be based on evaluation of the pertinent aspects like form and design, materials and substance, use and function, traditions and techniques, location and setting, spirit and feeling and other internal and external factors.

The following areas have been designated as Archaeological Parks :

i. Mehrauli Archaeological Park.

ii. Tughlaquabad Archaeological Park.

iii. Sultan Garhi Archaeological Park.

Qther areas can be added to the list on the basis of studies.

10.5 SPECIAL CONSERVATION PLANS

Each local body/ land owning agency should formulate "Special Development Plans" for the conservation and improvement of listed heritage complexes and their appurtenant areas. Alteration or demolition of any listed heritage building is prohibited without the prior approval of the Competent Authority.

The development plans/schemes for such areas shall conform to the provisions, in respect of Conservation of Heritage Sites including Heritage Buildings, Heritage Precincts and Natural Feature Areas.

11. URBAN DESIGN

A city is an assemblage of buildings and streets, system of communication and utilities, places of work, transportation, leisure and meeting places. The process of arranging these elements both functionally and beautifully is the essence of Urban Design. Delhi had a traditional Urban Design, which is reflected in the glory of 17th century Shahajahanabad and New Delhi. In the course of time Delhi has been becoming amorphous aggregate of masses and voids.

The Walled City of Shahjahanabad has certain urban form characteristics. The Jama Masjid is a dominating feature located on hilltop and is different, both in form and scale from the other developments of the city. The boulevard of Chandni Chowk was its commercial centerpiece, with certain visual character terminating at two landmarks viz. Red Fort and Fatehpuri Mosque at its ends.

In the planning of New Delhi in 1916, the Central Vista was conceived as a landscaped stretch to form continuity between the ridge and the river Yamuna. The stretch with the Rashtrapati Bhawan and the India Gate at two ends has tremendous visual quality and is one of the finest examples of Urban Design and monumentality in planning in the world. The Jama Masjid was visually linked with Parliament House and Connaught Place.

The following aspects need to be considered to arrive at the basis for policies affecting the urban fabric:

(i) Areas of significance in built environment.

(ii) Visual integration of the city.

(iii) Policy for tall buildings.

(iv) Policy on unhindered access movement, parking and pedestrian realm.

(v) Policy on Hoardings, Street furniture and Signage.

(vi) Urban Design Scheme.

(vii) Policy for design of pedestrian realm.

(viii) City structure plan and Urban Design objective.

(ix) Policy for conservation of Heritage precincts Buildings and Zones.

11.1 SIGNIFICANT AREAS OF BUILT ENVIRONMENT

The areas identified for Urban Design guidelines are as given below:

11.1.1 METROPOLITAN CITY CENTRE

1. Connaught Place and Extensions

The various proposals are:

(i) Detailed Urban Design and Landscape Schemes should be prepared to integrate MRTS stations, safe pedestrian walkways, parking areas, recreational and cultural areas, etc.

(ii) The intermediate public transport such as monorail, battery operated / high capacity buses, sky buses should be introduced to increase the mobility within the City Centre.

(iii) Activities such as viewing gallery, open-air theatres, amusement parks, mini-golf courses/sports activities, food plazas etc. should be introduced to make them more attractive even after working hours.

(iv) The envelope, FAR, architectural features of the buildings in the Connaught Circus - Connaught Place should be retained as existing.

(v) Continuity of the sidewalks should be maintained in terms of the width, surface treatment, curb cuts, tree and street furniture locations, for the pedestrians and disabled.

(vi) Use of alternative renewable sources of energy should be encouraged for new buildings (especially those of commercial or institutional nature), traffic signals and public signage, etc

2. Walled City and Extensions

The various proposals for revitalizing the glory of Walled City are:

(i) Conservation approach to retain the overall traditional character of the Walled City.

(ii) Visual integration of major landmarks to revitalise the past glory.

(iii) Many areas in Shahjahanabad should be pedestrianised and made completely free of vehicular traffic so as to restore the human scale and convenient living.

(iv) Judicious use of existing spaces for development of recreational uses.

(v) MRTS station areas should be dealt as per specific Urban Design schemes and be declared as pedestrian zones.

(vi) Introduction of activities such as traditional / craft bazaar / heritage walk / rides to attract tourists. Generation of urban culture at neighbourhood level such as festivals/fairs, kite flying etc.

(vii) Environmental up-gradation to reduce degenerative effects of traffic congestion.

(viii) Rejuvenation and conservation through management options, financing incentives, innovative development controls.

11.1.2 DISTRICT CENTRES

A District Centre should have all the components to create a pleasant environment with easy accessibility from the major transport nodes and surrounding residential areas through pedestrian approach or by subways etc. Planned District Centres can be best utilized for creating public spaces.

11.1.3 OTHER AREAS

Other areas of Urban Design importance are as follows:

a. Central Vista and the areas in its North and South, Lutyen's Bungalow Zone.

b. Ancient settlements.

c. Historical Monuments and Gardens.

d. Exhibition grounds, Zoo etc.

e. Areas along entry routes and other important routes in Delhi.

f. Republic day parade route.

g. Road and Rail, MRTS corridors, entries, and terminals.

h. City as a whole for aerial view.

11.2 VISUAL INTEGRATION

Delhi has a tremendous diversity of built form, color, scale and texture with a heterogeneous end product from aesthetic point of view. Visual integration can possibly be achieved by identifying features such as appropriately conserved historic buildings and heritage zones, which integrate and provide strong visual identity.

The important mass movement corridors i.e., Ring road/Outer ring road and major radials are used by city dwellers for internal city commuting. These corridors along with newly introduced MRTS corridors have potential to acquire an additional dimension of visual quality and integration. The studies and proposals for ring road and MRTS corridors should be formulated to improve, geometry, landscaping, street furniture, signage, introduction of urban forms at selected points and clearance of unsightly developments.

Other important elements for the integration of different parts of the city, planned at different times are (i) flora i.e. tree plantation, (ii) linking open spaces and (iii) harmonious treatment for major ecological features i.e. the Ridge and the River Yamuna.

11.3 TALL BUILDINGS

The height of buildings (above and below the ground) needs to be seen in the light of modern technology with due consideration for natural disasters like earthquakes, floods etc.

Restrictions on tall buildings would be necessary in important areas like Lutyen's Bungalow Zone, Civil lines and North Delhi campus. In case of Urban Extension, areas for specific Urban Design projects and tall buildings should be identified.

11.4 URBAN CORRIDORS

Delhi with huge intra city trip lengths and increasing number of personalized vehicles, few imperatives cannot be ignored for its sustainable and healthy growth, such as more dependency on efficient, convenient and safe modes of public transport, linking large number of work centres with residential areas and overall disincentives for the private vehicle ownership.

11.4.1 CITY GATEWAYS

1. Road:

i) Non-residential public buildings with pleasing appearance should be located on entry corridors.

ii) Attractive landscape should be developed in accordance with the highway landscape norms.

iii) Segregation of goods and passenger vehicles at the entry point through separate lanes to improve the visual environment.

2. Rail:

i) Enhancing visual experience for commuters through appropriate landscape along railway tracks.

ii) Reconstruction / redevelopment of existing stations should be undertaken through comprehensive Urban Design schemes.

iii) Attractive designs should be evolved for new stations.

3. Air:

i) Natural and built environment should be revitalized to give an impression of global city.

ii) The overall green cover in this zone should be enhanced and protected.

11.4.2 MRTS CORRIDOR

City structure of Delhi had been conceived in terms of hierarchies with CBD, District Centres and Community Centres in descending order of importance. With the development and introduction of MRTS, need is felt to connect these scattered districts with more imageable components. These components with enhanced built up areas and activities, form a network by which the experience of various District and commercial centres becomes a part of continued urban experience.

11.5 SERVICES

The organization of services makes the city to work along with the buildings and the open spaces. Services and public amenities should, therefore, be provided in a coordinated way, conforming to the National Building Code, wherever applicable.

11.5.1 PUBLIC AMENITIES

The clean, litter free public spaces add to the pleasant built environment. Thus the design, location and maintenance of public amenities such as public toilets, garbage bins, bus stops, etc. determine the quality of public spaces. These should be located appropriately while formulating the schemes.

11.5.2 PARKING

Access to the parking should be well defined and conducive to its usage, whether at the surface or underground. Basement parking lots need to be structured legibly and access to vertical cores clearly defined. Surface parking should be located in a manner that does not diminish or hinder the continuity and homogeneity of the spatial and pedestrian movement.

11.6 HOARDINGS, STREET FURNITURE & SIGNAGE

Hoardings, sign boards, directional boards, bill boards, neon sign bards, balloons, banners etc. have become symbols of present day urban scape and important instruments of outdoor publicity and public information. These, if located properly and aesthetically, may enhance the visual quality of the city. Otherwise, these may cause hazards, obstruction and visual pollution etc.

11.6.1 STREET FURNITURE & SIGNAGE

Public art is an important part of the urban spatial experience, which can be incorporated in the form of functional objects such as street furniture and paving designs.

Street furniture and signage should be designed sensitively considering the land use, intensity of activity and other identified design districts. Their design must also reflect respect to pedestrians and physically challenged people.

Access provisions for the physically challenged should be made from the street to overcome curb heights, rain water gratings etc. Parking spaces close to the entrance should be reserved for physically challenged. Exclusive parking bays are proposed near major intersections as part of road R/W with adequate landscaping to provide for parking of mobile repair vans, PCR vans, ambulances, cranes, fire tenders and other public utility vehicles.

11.6.2 ROAD SIGNAGE & SAFETY

Safety of road users shall be one of the prime consideration while planning / designing of road network and infrastructure. A major cause for present day chaos on the roads is that the road infrastructure, signage and road markings are not in accordance to the standards laid down by the Motor Vehicle Rules and Highway Code.

Appropriate road signage and markings are excellent means of educating road users about road safety rules and road discipline and add to the road beautification. These prevent the deviant behaviour of motorists and at the same time provide useful route related information. Concerned road owning agencies shall be responsible for installing the appropriate road signage and markings on regular basis.

Few other measures by the concerned agencies shall be:

i. Provision of adequate pedestrian facilities.

ii. Removal of encroachments from footpaths.

iii. Improvement in accident handling and reporting.

11.7 PEDESTRIAN FRIENDLY CITY

Major work centres, where large number of pedestrian networks emerge and culminate, should have enhanced facilities for the pedestrians. This will lead to more sensitive and intricate design of street furniture, making major image able components part of daily urban experience.

Pedestrian networks affect spaces in a very distinctive way. Establishment of pedestrian networks in any area reveals its vitality. They provide richness in terms of spatial experience and community interaction etc.

11.8 URBAN DESIGN SCHEME

In case of development / redevelopment of an area of around 4 ha., an Urban Design scheme shall be prepared for approval by the Competent Authority.

12.0 TRANSPORTATION

The period between 1981 and 2001 has seen a phenomenal increase in the growth of vehicles and traffic in Delhi. There has been a rise in per capita trip rate (excluding walk trips) from 0.72 in 1981 to 0.87 in 2001. Keeping in view the population growth, this translates into an increase from 45 lakh trips to around 118 lakh trips. The population of motor vehicles has increased from 5.13 lakh in 1981 to 32.38 lakh in 2001, and the number of buses has increased from 8,600 to 41,483 during this period.

Besides the above, Delhi has developed as a borderless city and an urban continuum comprising of a number of rapidly growing towns in Haryana and UP. This has added to the flow and movement of traffic within Delhi.

Despite measures by way of increasing the length of the road network and road surface space through widening, construction of a number of flyovers/grade separators and, launching of the Metro, the traffic congestion has continued to increase unabated. This has its inevitable consequences in terms of accidents, pollution, commuting time, and wasteful energy / fuel consumption.

Based on the rate of increase in the number of trips between 1981 and 2001, it is estimated that the total trips would rise to 280 lakh by the year 2021, including 257 lakh motorized trips and 23 lakh non-motorized trips. In this context, it needs to be noted that roads already occupy 21 percent of the total area of the city, which clearly limits the potential for increase in road length.

Apart from the problems and requirements of transportation at the macro level, there are special problems in specific areas, particularly the old city, which deserve special attention. Special requirements will also arise from the mega events such as the Commonwealth Games.

The plan and strategy for transportation will have to be worked out in this background. The broad aim of this would be to ensure safe and economical commuting between place of origin and destination, convenient and quick access to all areas for all sections of the society, reduction of pollution and congestion, energy efficiency and conservation, safety for all sections of the road and transport users and, towards meeting these objectives, providing a significant increase in efficient rapid public transport systems and facilities with a corresponding reduction in individual private transport usage. This is in addition to pedestrianisation and properly planned use of non-motorised transport systems in specific areas.

The following strategy is proposed in order to meet these objectives: -

i. Preparation and operationalisation of an integrated and mutually complementary multi-modal transportation and traffic plan comprising the Road, Rail and Metro-rail network, so that work centers / residences are within a walkable distance.

ii. The multimodal system will be integrated with safe facilities for pedestrians, bicyclists, disabled persons and Intelligent Transport System (ITS) enabled taxis and three-wheeled scooter rickshaws (TSR).

iii. Optimal use and utilisation of the existing road network and full development of ROW by removing all impediments. All arterial roads will be restructured to allow for smooth and safe flow of buses and non-motorised transport to minimize pollution and congestion.

iv. Expansion and restructuring of the existing network through expressways, arterial roads, elevated distributors and relief roads with a view to creating alternate access ways and reducing congestion on the existing roads to the extent possible. Urban Relief Roads should also be identified as additional or alternative link roads, wherever possible, to reduce congestion.

v. Planning of new road network in such a manner as to prevent possibilities of future congestion by modifying road sections to promote use of public transport, which would reduce use of private transport modes.

vi. Planned and targeted expansion of the Metro-rail network.

vii. Expansion and strengthening / restructuring of the Ring Rail System and sub-urban rail system.

viii. Developing an integrated relationship between the bus, rail and metro-system to provide for seamless multi-modal transport, through provision of additional stations, park and ride facilities, introduction of single multi-modal ticketing, etc. The choice of technology for the multimodal public transport system (Bus Rapid Transit System, Metro, Mono-Rail, Light Rail) be based on comparative cost effectiveness analysis studies to ensure rapid development of public transport and to ensure judicious use of public funds.

ix. Development of a comprehensive parking policy in line with the broad aims of the Plan for transportation mentioned earlier, including measures for linking new vehicle registration with owner parking facilities.

x. Establishment of a quick and efficient transport network between the NCR and the NCT of Delhi.

xi. Provision of directional Goods and Passenger Terminals with adequate infrastructure.

xii. Review of the licensing policy and systems, and effective arrangements for training of drivers / transport operators.

It is proposed that unrestricted movement of buses, taxis and auto rickshaws be permitted within the National Capital Region by developing a consensus amongst the constituents of the NCR.

12.1 INTEGRATED MULTI-MODAL TRANSPORT SYSTEM

Keeping in view the diverse built up physical forms within the city, it is logical to state that a single mode of transport cannot practically and effectively, serve the needs of the city. Accordingly, an Integrated Multi Modal Transport System suitable for the overall structure of the city and at the same time interlinking the various sub-structures is necessary. It is envisaged that the future transport system shall consist of a mix of rail and road based systems which may include Metro Rail, ring rail, dedicated rail corridors for daily commuters, (IRBT/RRTS corridors as identified in NCR Plan 2021), Bus Rapid Transit System (BRTS), other mass transit modes as technologies become available and Intermediate Passenger Transport (IPT) and private modes on selected corridors to be identified as per the needs from time to time. All roads should be made pedestrian, disabled and bicycle friendly as far as possible.

12.2 METROPOLITAN TRANSPORT AUTHORITY

Establishment of a single authority is the need of the hour for planning/development of an integrated system, implementation and enforcement of the policies, which may be framed in that context. Inter alia, this would help to avoid wasteful expenditure and other problems that could arise from duplication, overlap and even mutually exclusive/and contradictory facilities. Therefore, a single unified Metropolitan Transport Authority, on the lines recommended by the National Transport Policy Committee, needs to be established on priority.

12.3 ROADS

Delhi is planned on a ring - radial pattern with a hierarchical road network. Broadly, the road network is designed for regional, intra - city and local traffic. The proposed roads are classified taking into account the land use pattern and road system hierarchy with recommended right of ways as follows:

1. National Highways

The recommended minimum right of way (ROW) is 90 meters, wherever possible. However, within the city it shall not be less than 60meters. All the National Highways within the NCTD shall be access controlled upto the Delhi Border.

2. Arterial Roads

These include primary roads with access control and other primary roads.

i) Primary Roads: Vehicular routes carrying heavy volumes of traffic will generally have free / stable flow conditions with controlled access. The recommended ROW in existing urban area is 60-80 m. and minimum 80 m. in the proposed urban extension. While designing roads with 30m. ROW and above, provision should also be made for public mass rapid transport system, which may include BRT. Present ring road and outer ring road to be converted to access controlled arterial roads. Cycle tracks should also be constructed along all arterial roads wherever possible.

ii) Other Primary roads: Vehicular routes carrying heavy volumes of traffic, BRT route may also be allowed on these roads. The recommended ROW in existing urban area is 45-60 m. and minimum 60 m. in the proposed urban extension. Cycle tracks should also be constructed along all other primary roads wherever possible.

3. Sub Arterial Roads

These include primary and secondary collector streets.

(i) Primary Collector: These roads will connect major arterial roads and inter residential district collectors. The recommended ROW in existing urban area is 30-40 m. and minimum 45 m. in the proposed urban extension. In addition to this, a separate cycle track should be provided wherever possible.

(ii) Secondary Collector: These roads are intended to collect traffic from local streets within one residential district. The recommended R/W in existing urban area is 18-24 m. and minimum 30 m. in the proposed urban extension.

4. Local Streets

These are intended for neighbourhood (or local) use on which through traffic is to be discouraged. The suggested ROW is 12 to 20 m. in the existing and proposed urban area. These roads should be made pedestrian and bicycle friendly by using modern traffic calming designs to keep the speeds within limits as per design. A special cell should be set up within Transport Deptt. for developing standards and guidelines for traffic calming designs and for their implementation in the whole city in a phased manner. In existing areas like Rohini project, having plot sizes below 90 sq.m., minimum ROW of 9 m. may continue.

As a matter of general policy, it is proposed that for all categories of roads, the full cross section should be developed in future and no encroachments will be permitted on the existing road network. Further, the development of roads should start from the extremes of the designated ROW.

12.3.1 URBAN RELIEF ROADS

In order to reduce congestion on the existing roads, it is proposed to identify additional/alternative links and access corridors. Such links termed as Urban Relief Roads, may be proposed subject to feasibility, along drains (including their covering), identification of new alignment, or upgradation/strengthening of an existing road/alignment or in the form of elevated roads/grade separators etc. All the options should be exercised for restoration of full ROW, including relaying of services etc., if affecting ROW.

The following priority stretches for provision of Urban Relief Roads have been identified.

i. Shankar Road - alternative elevated road may be explored.

ii. Vikas Marg

iii. Extension of NH-24 to join Mathura Road (near Humayun's Tomb).

iv. Prem Bari Pul (Pitampura) to Outer Ring Road along disused Western Yamuna Canal.

v. Road between Nehru Place and Hotel Park Royal to be extended up to Lotus Temple and towards East of Kailash, if feasible.

vi. Badarpur Border entry point.

vii. Karol Bagh (new Rohtak Road) -alternative alignment by extending Arya Samaj Road through Anand Parbat to connect existing roads leading to Patel Road and Shivaji Marg on ROB or RUB.

viii. More bridges on river Yamuna (at Geeta Colony, Mayur Vihar, etc. - alignments of Platoon Bridges can be considered.)

ix. Along drains passing through Lajpat Nagar, Defence Colony, Sarai Kale Khan, Lodhi Road, etc.

x. Sarita Vihar (Junction of Mathura Road and Road No. 13-A) to Okhla Industrial Areas (road between Ph I and Ph. II to be connected by ROB or RUB).

xi. Elevated road corridor between Connaught Place and East Delhi (Marginal Bundh Road).

xii. Missing link and Outer Ring Road from NH-8 to Najafgarh Road.

Additional stretches of missing links could be identified from time to time by the concerned agencies. Their project may be implemented after carrying out detailed studies.

12.3.2 UNDERGROUND ROADS

Vehicular traffic is a major contributor to the air pollution in Delhi. In order to reduce road congestion and the level of pollution, the possibility of having Underground Roads or Tube roads in critical areas needs to be considered. Such measures, together with provision of Metro Services, will also help to make historically important areas like Connaught Place, Chandni Chowk and Karol Bagh etc. pedestrian friendly. With advancement in technology, and a better climate for private participation and investment in infrastructure development, such proposals could be explored.

12.3.3 GRADE SEPARATORS

The Master Plan studies indicate the need for provision of intersections with grade separators. In case of existing grade separators the possibility of providing cloverleaves and direct interchanges, wherever necessary and feasible, may be examined in order to make the junctions signal free. To provide uninterrupted traffic movement various other options such as elevated roads with supporting infrastructure etc. will also need to be explored.

In the proposed urban extension, space reservation is to be kept for provision of grade separators, cloverleaves and Left Slip roads at intersections of all roads of 30 m. and above ROW. However, grade separated junctions shall be considered if there is no other possibility of including traffic flow. Further it should also be ensured that pedestrians and bicyclists continue to have safe and convenient access to the junction.

12.3.4 FREEWAYS

Freeways are defined as divided arterial highways for vehicular traffic with full access control and provided generally with grade separation at intersections. A freeway network in the NCR should be developed so that the cris-cross movement through Delhi is lessened.

With such a network of Freeways, Highways, MRTS and Electric Multiple Units (EMUs) a 2 to 3 hour movement network can be generated which will cover entire NCR. This will encourage interaction between Delhi and NCR towns.

12.4 MASS RAPID TRANSIT SYSTEM (MRTS)

The Metro Rail System the most important, component, of a Mass Rapid Transport System (MRTS) in the City. The Metro Rail network for the entire city has been identified in various phases, which comprises of a network of underground, elevated and surface corridors aggregating to approximately 250 Kms., and is expected to carry 108 lakh daily passengers with an average trip length of 15 Km. by 2021.

Phase I of the network is already implemented and operational.

Phase-II of the network covering a length of 56.76 km is likely to be completed by 2010 for the following stretches.

a. Vishwavidyalaya - Jahangir Puri.

b. Central Secretariat - Qutab Minar.

c. Indra Prastha - Yamuna Depot - New Ashok Nagar.

d. Yamuna Depot - Anand Vihar ISBT.

e. Shahdra - Seemapuri.

f. Kirti Nagar - Nangloi along Rohtak Road.

Subsequent phases shall be worked out in conjunction with the overall circulation plan for the city.

Rohini and Narela sub-city projects with population of more than 10 lakh each need to be connected to the MRTS. Following extensions of routes are proposed:

i. From existing Rithala Station upto Barwala (Rohini Ph.IV-V).

ii. From Sanjay Gandhi Transport Terminal to Narela.

Considering the future needs of the city additional links of MRTS may be identified by the DMRC.

It is expected that about 60% of the urban area will be within 15-minute walking distance from the proposed MRTS stations, after full development of the system. Additional areas could come within easy access and connectivity with the Metro Rail through inter-linkages with other transport modes. About 15% of urban area of Delhi is likely to be directly affected, and may undergo a dramatic impact and change. Further, due to development of economic activities along the Metro Corridors and optimization of connectivity provided by it, the rider ship on the Metro is expected to grow substantially over time. Correspondingly, it is expected that vehicular trips may also progressively shift from road-based transport to MRTS, particularly, with reference to the longer trip lengths (greater than 10 Kms) within the city.

To achieve the above potential impact of the Metro Rail System a number of measures will be necessary. These will include the following:

i. Preparation of detailed plans to facilitate and encourage direct pedestrian access to the Metro Rail System/ Station.

ii. Preparation of detailed multi-modal transport plans with reference to each major Metro Station, with particular reference to bus transport routes, which could provide inter-linkages and feeder arrangements.

iii. Parking arrangements at Metro Stations, both for short and medium period viz. for those who would travel for local level requirements such as shopping, etc. and those who would need parking by way of a Park and Ride facility.

iv. Provision of Park and Ride facilities at identified points from where feeder bus services would be available, or convenient direct pedestrian access would be feasible.

12.4.1 SYNERGY BETWEEN TRANSPORT AND LAND USE

The concept of the Master Plan for Delhi 1962 was based on a poly-nodal, polycentric, distribution of work centres, largely based on road transport nodes. A major fall-out of this has been distortion between infrastructure, transport and land use. To achieve spatial balance, development should take place according to new corridors of mass movement. This has implications in terms of land use planning along major transport corridors and the Mass Rapid Transport/Transit System. This would not only help to solve, to some extent, the enormous problems of mass transportation, but would also generate a dynamic potential for growth and employment. This is particularly true for the Metro Rail System. In this context the Metro corridors upto a certain depth would require selective re-development and re-densification/ intensification of existing land uses based on site conditions. It is proposed that comprehensive redevelopment schemes of the influence area of MRTS stations be prepared.

12.5 BUS

Apart from the Metro Rail System, buses will continue to be other major public transport in the city. The Bus Transport system is presently estimated to carry around 23.40 lakh passengers per day (2002). Even after the introduction/ expansion of the Metro, major dependence will continue to be on Bus Transport as a form of comfortable and convenient public movement within the city. However, keeping in view the extension of road network in Delhi on one hand and the existing/likely congestion on the roads on the other, it is necessary to take steps for rationalization of Bus Transport. This would entail action on the following fronts:-

i. Bus connectivity would need to be planned to a considerable extent in the form of feeder services to the Metro Rail Stations and the Ring Rail System.

ii. Park and ride facilities will have to be developed at important bus terminals.

iii. The quality and design of buses would have to be significantly upgraded with a view to providing comfort to the riders and thereby make bus travel a part of an efficient mass public transport system which could also help to reduce individualized / private vehicle usage.

iv. On all roads with ROW greater than 30 m exclusive bus lanes will be planned to implement the Bus Rapid Transit System (BRTS) in a phased manner to cover the whole city.

v. New bus terminals need to be planned and developed in strategic locations to make the use of BRTS and Metro Stations convenient for all commuters.

12.6 BICYCLE/ CYCLE-RICKSHAW

Bicycle/ Cycle-Rickshaw could be an important mode of travel, particularly with reference to short and medium trip lengths. To the extent that it meets individual or public transport requirements, it is a non-energy consuming and non-polluting mode of transport. However, there are several issues, which have to be kept in view while planning in respect of these modes.

With a mixed type of fast moving traffic on the roads, travel by bicycle and rickshaws is very unsafe.

In so far as rickshaws are concerned, apart from issues pertaining to the aspect of mixed traffic, this mode also provided employment to a very large number of unskilled workers residing in the city.

In view of the above, the following actions should be considered/ taken: -

i. On all arterial roads fully segregated cycle tracks should be provided with provision for safe parking in park and ride lots.

ii. In urban extension, cycle tracks should be provided at the sub-arterial and local level roads and streets.

iii. In specific areas, like the Walled City / Chandni Chowk / Sadar Bazar / Karol Bagh / Lajpat Nagar and Trans Yamuna Area, the use of cycles/rickshaw as a non-motorised mode of transport should be consciously planned along with pedestrianisation.

12.7 TRANSPORTATION FOR SPECIAL AREAS

Central congested areas of the Walled City, Sadar Bazar, Karol Bagh and other similar areas like certain Trans Yamuna areas are characterized by heavy traffic congestion. In order to address this problem a medium capacity Mass Transit system comprising of BRTS, Light Rail Transit System (LRT) and battery operated bus system may be considered on selected routes based on feasibility.

For proper functioning of above said systems a restraint on the use of private modes and provision of parking would be required. This would be necessary in order to revitalize the area and to improve its environment quality. This will also increase accessibility to such areas considerably.

In order to manage the additional traffic of Metro stations at Old Delhi, Chandni Chowk and Chawri Bazar, the following management measures are required to be taken:-

i. Need based Traffic circulation schemes integrating various modes.

ii. Improvement of major road stretches and intersections like Ajmeri Gate, Fountain Chowk. Fatehpuri Chowk, Kaudia Pul, Khari Baoli, etc.

iii. Removal of encroachments from footpaths to facilitate smooth movement.

iv. The movement of heavy vehicles will continue to be banned in the Walled City. However, for the services of this area Light Commercial goods vehicles may be allowed during the night.

12.8 RAIL

In the National Capital Territory of Delhi both intercity and intra city passenger movements are being catered to by the existing rail network comprising the Regional and Ring Rail Systems respectively.

In order to improve the rider-ship on Ring Rail, the following is proposed:

a) Intensive land use around the following:

   i. Anand Parbat

   ii. INA Colony

   iii. Pusa Institute

   iv. Kirti Nagar

b) Accessibility improvement and augmentation of infrastructure on ring rail stations:

   i. Shivaji Bridge

   ii. Bhairon Marg

iii. Kasturba Nagar (Sewa Nagar)

iv. Lajpat Nagar

v. Kirti Nagar

vi. Shakur Basti

c) Provision of Halt Stations on ring rail at the following locations:

i. Moti Bagh

ii. Bhairon Road

iii. Hans Bhawan (ITO)

iv. Ganesh Nagar

v. Preet Vihar

vi. Shyamlal College.

The interchange points of Regional Road, MRTS, Ring Rail and any other future rail network should be developed as interchange stations/convergence zone. The change over facilities should include approach roads, pedestrian walkways, shuttle services, wherever feasible parking, areas for various modes including feeder buses, and adequate public conveniences, etc.

12.9 MODAL SPLIT

The transport network is based on the modal split for Delhi to move 280 lakh trips by the year 2021 as given below:

1. Present Scenario

As per Modal Split (2001) among the vehicular trips, maximum 60% trips are being performed by buses, which include chartered and school buses. The personalised modes of transport are carrying about 35.9% of vehicular trips. The modal split projected for the years 2011 and 2021 is as follows:

Table 12.1 Modal Split Projections

Mode	Modal Split (%)	
	2011	2021
Public Transport (including Rail/ Light Rail/ MRTS/ IRBT/ Bus/ Tram)	70.25	80.0
Personal modes (including Personal Fast Modes / Hired Fast Modes/ Hired Slow Modes/ Bicycle)	29.75	20.0

12.10 INTERCITY PASSENGER MOVEMENT

In 2001, on a normal weekday 56.46% of the commuters visited Delhi by Road, 42.67% by Rail and 0.87% by Air.

Table 12.2: Passenger Trips at Outer Cordons per Day

Medium	Total Passengers	Commuters
Road	15.98 lakh (57.46%)	9.59 lakh
Rail	12.08 lakh (42.67%)	9.06 lakh
Air	0.22 lakh (0.87%)	N.A.

12.10.1 RAIL

At present there are 43 railway stations in Delhi. The total passengers catered to at these stations in 2001 are 12.08 lakh/day including about 9.06 lakh commuters. Out of these stations, major stations catering more than 1.0 lakh passengers per day are:

Delhi Junction	2.72 lakh
New Delhi	3.19 lakh
Nizamuddin	1.28 lakh
Sadar Bazar	1.00 lakh

Five directional Metropolitan Passenger Terminals (MPT) have been proposed to decongest the central area. These are:

i. Anand Vihar, East Delhi

ii. Bhartal in Dwarka, South-West Delhi

iii. Holumbi Kalan in Narela, North Delhi

iv. Tikri Kalan, West Delhi

v. Hazrat Nizammudin, South West Delhi

It is proposed to integrate the Inter State Bus Terminus with Delhi main railway station and the land should be made available by the shifting the IP University to the new campus.

Since about 75% of the total passengers are commuters, therefore in order to facilitate improvement in their movement between Delhi and surrounding towns either of the following is proposed based on the feasibility by the concerned authorities:

i. Extension of MRTS.

ii. Provision of dedicated railway corridor with supplementary feeder bus services for linking with other modes of transport (IRBT Corridors).

12.10.2 BUS

The total passenger trips per day catered by road-based transport are 15.97 lakh, out of which about 9.54 lakh (60%) are commuters. Majority of such trips are by bus.

Out of four new Interstate Bus Terminals (ISBT) as proposed in MPD-2001, only one at Anand Vihar in East Delhi has been developed as a part of Metropolitan Rail Terminal. The terminal at Dwarka (Bhartal) has also been included in Dwarka Project. The remaining two terminals at Okhla (Madanpur Khadar) and Narela (Holambikalan) have not been developed.

In order to cater to the additional passenger requirements, it is proposed to develop the following ISBTs (10 Ha each) along the Metropolitan Passenger Terminals:

i. At Bhartal, Dwarka.

ii. At Holambi Kalan, Narela Subcity.

iii. At Sarai Kale Khan. the existing Bus terminal should be upgraded and be linked to Hazrat Nizammudin Railway Station.

iv. At Tikri Kalan.

Apart from above ISBT, it is proposed to identify exclusive bus terminal sites at the intersection points of NH and outer ring road/ ring road to cater to the passenger movement.

These could be developed at:

i. Dhaula Kuan.

ii. IFC Madanpur Khadar to relieve Intercity Passenger congestion at Ashram Chowk.

iii. Tikri Kalan to relieve Intercity Passenger congestion at Peeragarhi Chowk.

iv. Narela to relieve Intercity Passenger congestion at Outer Ring Road and G.T. Karnal Road Junction-Jahangirpuri Byepass.

A smaller Terminal at Narela Railway Station and ISBT along G.T. Road may be considered. This concept can be applied wherever possible to intercept Intercity Passenger Traffic at Arterial roads.

12.10.3 AIR

The International and Domestic air passenger movement in Delhi is catered by Indira Gandhi International Airport and Palam Airport respectively. Both the Airports have been linked to other parts of the city and urban extension through the transport network to facilitate fast movement. The passenger movement by air in Delhi on an average day in 2001, was as under :

Table 12.3: Distribution of Daily Air Passengers

Airport	Number of Travelers (%)	Number of Visitors, Staff (%)	Total Nos., (%)
Domestic Airport	12450 (82.0)	2650 (18.0)	15100 (100.0)
International Airport	10120 (77.0)	3000 (23.0)	13120 (100.0)
Total	22570 (80.0)	5650 (20.0)	28220 (100.0)

A strong and vibrant economy of Delhi Metropolitan Area provides a backdrop to a healthy demand for air travel. IGI Airport, Delhi has witnessed a phenomenal growth of traffic during the last few years both on account of business travel and leisure trips. Total passenger traffic through Delhi Airport grew by 27.4% in 2005 -06 over the previous year and reached an annual figure of 162 lakh. According to the current forecasts, the passenger traffic through Delhi Airport is expected to increase to 290 lakh in 2010 and 370 lakh in 2012. In terms of air cargo traffic, Delhi airport handled 383,000 tons of cargo during 2005-06, and this is estimated to grow to 540,000 tons in 2010 and 638,000 tons during 2012. Long-term forecasts indicate that Delhi Airport would be handling over 1000 lakh passengers and 3.6 million tons of cargo in the year 2036.

In order to meet the requirements of growing traffic and to upgrade the facilities to world-class standards, phased development of the airport has been initiated according to a Master Plan. The first phase of development is scheduled to be completed in early 2010, in line with the Commonwealth Games being hosted in Delhi. The airport may be connected by an expanded NH-8, as well as the MRTS by providing a rail station close to the passenger terminal to shorten the journey time. The development of the airport will also require augmentation of utilities serving the airport, particularly power supply, water supply and drainage facilities.

12.10.4 GOODS MOVEMENT

With the expansion of commercial and industrial activities in Delhi Metropolitan Area, the goods movement within urban area and outside has grown considerably, leading to environmental deterioration in the city.

In 2001, on an average day, the goods movement by various modes at outer cordons in Delhi was as under:

Table 12.4: Goods Traffic at Outer Cordons

Mode	Traffic
Road	68808 vehicles/day
Rail	1463 wagons/ day
Air	644 tonnes/ day

1. Goods movement by Rail

Presently the goods are terminating as below: -

Commodity		Terminal
Iron and Steel	—	Tuglaqabad (Bahadurgarh) thereafter by road to Naraina
Food Grains	—	Delhi Cantt., Narela, Ghevra
Coal-		Badarpur Border, Rajghat, I.P.Thermal Power Station.
Fruits and Vegetables	—	Naya Azadpur
Fuel	—	Shakur Basti
Cement	—	Shakur Basti, Naya Azadpur, Safdarjung Rail siding.

2. Goods movement by Road

Out of the total Goods traffic volume, major share is handled by the points at NH-8, NH-1, NH-24 and Kalindi Kunj. On an average day in 2001, about 68,808 goods vehicles were entering and/or leaving Delhi.

Movement of incoming /outgoing goods traffic in 2001, on different highways and other major roads on average weekday, is given as under:

Table 12.5: Directional Distribution of Daily Goods Traffic in Delhi - 2001

Name of Location	No. of Goods Vehicles	Modal Share (%)
South and South East		
Kalindi Kunj	9948	14.46
Badarpur Border (NH-2)	5993	8.71
North and North East		
Singhu Border (NH-1)	8542	12.41
Loni Border	4881	7.10
West		
Tikri Border (NH-10)	4460	6.48
South West		
Sirhole Border (NH-8)	9139	13.28
Dundahera Border	4933	7.17
East		
Ghaziabad Border (NH-24)	7914	11.51
Chilla Check Post	2101	3.05
Jhundupura	1376	2.01
Gazipur	2220	3.22

12.11 INTEGRATED FREIGHT COMPLEXES

Integrated Freight Complexes have been recommended for the integration of goods movement by road and rail. These would consist of wholesale market, warehousing, road for trucks and rail transport terminals so as to curtail the movement of heavy vehicles within the complex. The freight complexes are to be located in the places where they intercept the maximum possible regional goods traffic entering Delhi.

Based on the pattern of goods traffic movement in Delhi, following four sites for Integrated Freight Complexes (IFC), are presently at various stages of planning and/ or development and one more new site is proposed in Urban Extension area. These freight complexes shall be dedicated to meet the demand of Delhi's needs and not cater to the distributive requirements of regional goods.

i. Madanpur Khadar (NH-2)

ii. Gazipur (NH-24)

iii. Narela (NH-1)

iv. Dwarka (NH-8)

v. New site in Urban Extension (Rohtak Road) Tikri Kalan

12.12 FUEL STATIONS

The environmental concerns have been constantly advocating identification of clean and environment friendly fuels. Presently, the main fuel types being used include: Petrol, Diesel and CNG. These fuels are being made available from Petrol Pumps and CNG stations. With the advancement of technology some new types of clean fuels may also be used in future. CNG stations may be permitted in all use zones except in Regional park / Ridge, developed District Parks. Petrol pumps are permissible in all use zones except in Recreational use zone.

12.12.1 FUEL STATIONS IN URBAN AREAS.

Fuel Stations are permissible on Master Plan / Zonal Plan roads and shall not be permitted in absence of an approved Zonal Plan of the area.

At the time of preparation of layout plans of various use zones namely, residential commercial, industrial, PSP facilities and other areas the location of Fuel Stations should be provided as per the norms given in Table 12.6.

12.12.2 DEVELOPMENT CONTROL NORMS AND PERMISSIBILITY

The regulations for locating the fuel stations -cum-service stations, the development control and permissibility shall be governed by the policy / decision by competent Authority / Government Notifications issued from time to time. New fuel stations shall be regulated by the following controls:

i. Fuel stations shall be located on roads of minimum 30m ROW.

ii. The plot size for fuel stations shall be minimum of 30m X 36m and maximum of 33m X 45m (75m X 40m for CNG mother station as per requirement).

iii. The minimum distance of plot from the road intersections shall be as follows:

  a. For minor roads having less than 30m ROW - 50m.

  b. For roads of ROW 30m or more - 100m

  c. Frontage of plots should not be less than 30m.

iv. Maximum Ground Coverage: 20%, Maximum FAR: 40

v. Maximum Height: 6m

vi. Canopy: equivalent to ground coverage within set back.

vii. Maximum 10 FAR permissible for non-inflammable, non-hazardous commercial activities subject to payment of conversion charges/ levies as may be prescribed.

Table 12.6: Norms for Fuel Stations

S. No	Land Use/Use Premises	Norms
1.	Residential Use Zone	Two Fuel Stations (One Petrol Pump + One CNG station) per 150 ha. Of gross residential area
2.	Industrial Use Zone	Two Fuel Stations (One Petrol Pump + One CNG station) per 40 ha of gross industrial area
3.	Freight Complexes	Four Fuel Stations (Two Petrol Pumps + Two CNG stations) in each
4.	District Centres	Four Fuel Stations (Two Petrol Pumps + Two CNG stations) in each district centre
5.	Community Centre	Two Fuel Stations (One Petrol Pump + One CNG station) in each
6.	Public & Semi Public use zone	Two Fuel Stations (One Petrol Pump + One CNG station) in each PSP area.
7.	Security Forces Campus / Police/ Hospitals/ Govt.	For captive use/ as per requirement.

12.12.3. CNG SERVICE STATIONS:

Already existing authorized CNG service stations for public transport vehicles may continue for this purpose alone, till regulations in this regard are notified or the Zonal Plans for such areas are finalized, whichever is earlier. While finalizing Zonal plans, efforts may be made to integrate such service stations in the Plan.

12.13 PARKING

With the phenomenal increase in personalized motor vehicles, one of the major problems being faced today is an acute shortage of parking space. In the absence of adequate organized parking space and facilities, valuable road space is being used for vehicular parking. The problem of parking in the city can be broadly divided into the following categories:

i) Along streets, which are commercialised.

ii) In planned commercial centres.

iii) In residential colonies.

iv) In the large institutional complexes.

The experience has shown that :—

(a) The provisions relating to parking within the plot area are normally not adhered resulting in vehicles spilling over on to the roads and adding to congestion; and

(b) The norms themselves appear to be considerably on the lower side keeping in view the actual vehicle use, both in terms of the multiple vehicle ownership in the same family and the pattern of individual private vehicle use.

In the above background, the whole subject of parking has become a matter of serious public concern and requires a carefully considered policy and planned measures to alleviate the problem to the maximum feasible extent in existing areas and for adequate provisioning with reference to future developments. As recommended by the Environment Pollution (Prevention & Control) Authority for the National Capital Region, the approach should be focused more on demand management (restricting vehicle numbers) through enforcement and pricing policy rather than only on increasing supply of parking. In this background, the following measures are proposed.

12.13.1 PARK AND RIDE

Apart from providing Park and Ride facilities with reference to integration between the Road and Metro Rail / Rail Transport systems, such facilities would also need to be provided to reduce the problem of parking on main arterial roads in the context of identified work and activity centres which may not be directly connected by the MRTS and to encourage use of public transport.

12.13.2 PUBLIC PARKING

The major efforts will have to come through the creation of public facilities in designated commercial/work centres and other areas and corridors where significant commercial activity has developed by way of mixed use. In the context of the latter, it would also need to be linked to pedestrianisation within the identified areas. In the above context following steps would be necessary :—

i. All existing areas of concentration of business / commercial activity, where absence of adequate parking and congestion is visible, should be identified and listed, and based on studies of vehicle volumes specific projects for multi level parking, using the latest available technologies should be formulated and implemented in a time bound manner.

ii. Major corridors along which commercial activity has grown over the years by way of mixed land use with/ without authorisation should be identified and taken up for redevelopment with a major objective being the identification and development of open areas for parking, green development and pedestrianisation.

iii. In all new Commercial / Business/ Industrial centres, adequate parking on the surface as well as below and above the ground must be provided. Revised norms in terms of Equivalent Car Space (ECS) are being provided and would need to be strictly adhered to and enforced.

iv. The development of multi level parking facilities may be taken up, wherever, feasible in a public private partnership framework, with private sector investment and involvement, for which incentives may be provided by way of land use and FAR etc.

v. The use of basement wherever provided for parking, must be strictly adhered to.

vi. Stringent provisions by way of fine and other penal actions need to be provided for violation of parking rules.

vii. A graded parking fees structure should be evolved as of measure of parking demand management, and encouraging use of public transport.

viii Serious consideration should be given to evolve a policy linking registration of new vehicles to availability of owner parking facilities.

ix. All encroachments on land earmarked for public parking should be removed. However, Public Parking Areas may be used for Second Hand Car Bazaar on payment basis, only during holidays subject to meeting requirement / conditions of the concerned authorities.

x. Wherever feasible, space on roofs, under stilts and basements should be exploited to the optimum for parking so as to reserve the max. ground space for landscape development, pedestrian movement etc.

12.13.3 PARKING FACILITIES IN DTC DEPOTS

The use of DTC terminals and depots for development of public parking alongwith parking of DTC buses, private buses and Chartered buses, should be explored and specific projects developed.

12.13.4 UNDERGROUND PARKING

Based on the site feasibility, parking facilities can be created under the open spaces without disturbing the green areas on the surface and surrounding environment. The approvals from the concerned agencies are mandatory before taking up such works.

12.13.5 PARKING IN RESIDENTIAL AREAS

Over the years a large number of the residential areas have been experiencing severe problems of vehicular congestion and shortage of parking space. Most of the parking is, in fact, being done on the road, which significantly reduces the carriageway width. The problem has been exacerbated by the traffic congestion generated by schools in gross residential use areas. Some measures required to alleviate the problem, to some extent, will be as under: -

i. All the encroachments on residential streets in the form of kitchen gardens/roadside private greens, large projections/ramps, etc. need to be removed.

ii. Road cross sections may be redesigned wherever possible to accommodate planned car parking along the residential streets, and also creating more surface movement space.

iii. Other options, in selected areas, such as creation of underground parking below parks and open spaces will also have to be considered.

iv. Resident Welfare Associations will have to be called upon to participate in this process by raising contributions from the residents on the basis of objective criteria such as number of cars owned, etc.

v. Problem of congestion arising on account of the traffic generated by schools have to be specifically addressed, and the main responsibility for putting up the required additional facilities has to be borne by the schools themselves. Policy guidelines will have to be evolved for this purpose.

12.13.6 PARKING STANDARDS

Parking is one of the utilities permitted in all use zones except in regional park / ridge, developed recreational areas and parks as per the approved layout plan. Parking standard have been prescribed in each use premises. However, where not prescribed, these will be followed as per standards given in Development Code section of the Master Plan. The standards given are in Equivalent Car Space (ECS) which include parking for all types of vehicles i.e. cars, scooters, cycles, light and heavy commercial vehicles, buses etc. Parking adequacy statement/study for large projects like Stadia, Shopping Malls, Multiplexes will be desirable.

12.13.7 MULTI LEVEL PARKING

Multi level parking facility should preferably be developed in the designated parking spaces or in the residential, public-semi-public facilities, commercial, transport node, DTC depot, etc. with the following Development Controls:

i. Minimum Plot Size - 1000 sqm.

ii. In order to compensate the cost of Multi-level parking and also to fulfill the growing need of parking spaces within urban area, a maximum of 25 % of gross floor area may be utilized as commercial / office space.

iii. In addition to the permissible parking spaces on max. FAR, 3 times additional space for parking component shall be provided.

iv. Maximum FAR permissible shall be 100 (excluding parking area) or as per the comprehensive scheme. However, no FAR shall be permissible in plots / existing buildings where 5% addl. ground coverage is permissible (Refer para 8 (4) i) Parking Standards, Chapter 17.0 Development Code).

v. Maximum ground coverage shall be 66.6%. The maximum height shall be restricted to permissible height of the land use in which the plot falls. There will be no restriction on the number of levels of basement subject to structural safety.

vi. In case of comprehensive schemes, development controls including height shall be as per approved scheme.

vii. Number of basements - No Limit, subject to adequate safety measures.

viii. For development of Multilevel Parking, models should be worked out to encourage the private sector initiative with restricted commercial component, not exceeding 10% limited to FAR 40 on the plot.

ix. Specific proposals requiring relaxation in above-mentioned norms would be referred to the Authority.

A number of multilevel parking sites have been identified by the local bodies / agencies. (List given in the Annexure I).

12.14 REGISTRATION AND LICENSING

The aspects of registration and training of transport operators / drivers needs to be viewed as an important element of the overall transport plan and policy. Licensing system should be made strict to create awareness about traffic rules and regulations among road users.

12.15 BARRIER FREE ENVIRONMENT

A major consideration in the planning and design of outdoor and indoor movement should be that people with disability, older persons and people in wheel chairs could move about without help from others. This requires that:

i) Paths and pavements shall be flat, uniform, slip-free and free from unnecessary obstacles.

ii) Orientation points and guide routes may be provided for visually disabled people;

iii) Information and warning signs must be understandable, clear and well lit.

Table 12.7: Development Controls for Transportation

S. No	Use Premises	Activities Permitted	Development Controls (4)			
			Area under Operation (%)	Area under building (%)	FAR *	Floor area that can be utilised for passenger accommodation
1.	Airport	All facilities related to Airport/Aviation Passengers as decided by Airport authority of India including watch & ward	-NA-			
2.	Rail Terminal/ Integrated Passenger Terminal Metropolitan Passenger Terminal	All facilities related to Railway, Passengers, operations, goods handling, passengers change over facilities, including watch & ward, Hotel.	70	30	100	15%
3.	Rail Circulation	All facilities related to Railway Tracks, operational areas including watch & ward.	-NA-			
4.	Bus Terminal/ Bus Depot	All facilities related to Bus & Passengers, parking including watch & ward. Soft Drink & Snack Stall, Administrative Office, Other Offices, and Hotel.	50	50	100	25%
5.	ISBT	All facilities related to Bus & Passengers, parking including watch & ward, Bus Terminal, Soft Drink & Snack Stall, Administrative Office, hotel.	a. Ground coverage: 25% b. FAR: 100, subject to the following: (i)FAR shall be available on a maximum area of 10 ha. or area of site whichever is less. (ii)ISBT, including operational structures Maximum FAR 70 (iii) Hotel/passenger accommodation and facilities Maximum FAR 30. c. Parking: In addition to the requirement of parking for ISBT/buses, parking for Hotel/ passenger accommodation and facilities shall be at the rate of 2 ECS per 100 sq.m. of floor area. d. The development shall be undertaken in a composite manner.			
6.	Toll Plaza	Toll collection booth, utilities, facilities and required infrastructure.	-NA-			
7.	Road Circulation	All types of road, street furniture, bus shelters, under ground & over ground services utilities, signals, metro tracks as part of r/w, sub-ways, under-passes, ROB & RUB including watch & ward.	-NA-			
8.	Metro Yards	Idle parking of coaches, washing and cleaning facilities, maintenance related facilities, watch & ward and staff related facilities.	80%	20%	100	15%

* The F.A.R. is to be calculated on the Building Plot. Area under Bus Shelter not to be included in FAR.

Development Controls for Metro Stations :

1. Metro Stations along with property development (composite development) up to a maximum area of 3.0 ha shall be permitted in all Use Zones, except in Recreational and Regional Park / Ridge Use Zone, Lutyens' Bungalow Zone and Heritage Zones, subject to approval of Technical Committee of DDA.

2. This enabling provision of property development would have the following broad development controls:

i. 25% ground coverage and 100 FAR, including area under Metro Station with no height restrictions and subject to approval of the statutory bodies such as ASI, Airport Authority, DUAC etc.

ii. In addition to the requirement of parking for Metro Stations, parking for the commercial component will be @ 2 ECS per 100 sq.m.

iii. The development shall be undertaken in a composite manner and DMRC shall obtain approval of all the concerned local bodies/ agencies.

3. The following structures shall be treated as operational structures:

i) All Metro Stations and tracks supporting at grade, elevated and underground including entry structures, ancillary buildings to house DG sets, chilling plants and electric sub station, supply exhaust and tunnel ventilation shafts etc.

ii) Depots and maintenance workshops.

iii) Traction sub-stations.

iv) Operational Control Centers

v) Police Station.

ANNEXURE I

Proposed Multi-Level Parking Sites

NDMC:

1. Baba Kharak Singh Marg
2. Behind Hindustan Times Building, Kasturba Gandhi Marg
3. Sarojini Nagar

MCD :

1. Hamilton Road
2. Lajpat Nagar
3. Bahadur Shah Zafar Marg
4. Green Park
5. Rajinder Nagar
6. Anupam PVR, Saket
7. Rajouri Garden
8. Sant Nagar, Ravi Bagh Market
9. Parade Ground
10. Kamla Nagar
11. Ramlila Ground
12. South Extension Part - I
13. South Extension Part - II
14. Mehrauli
15. Greater Kailash
16. Shastri Park, Karol Bagh

DDA :

1. Nehru Place District Centre
2. Mangalam Place District Centre

Note : In addition to above, the concerned agencies shall finalise other sites from time to time.

13. SOCIAL INFRASTRUCTURE

The quality of life in any urban centre depends upon the availability of and accessibility to quality social infrastructure. Social infrastructure can be looked at in terms of the facilities indicated in the City Level Master Plan, and Community Facilities, which are indicated at the layout plan level in various use zones. Together, these include social infrastructure facilities pertaining to health, education, sports facilities, socio-cultural activities, communications, security and safety, and other community facilities pertaining to recreation, religious activities, social congregations and community events, cremation / burial grounds etc. These are generally planned in terms of population norms with stipulated permissibility conditions and development controls.

13.1 HEALTH

The capital city is strategically located and has many specialised health facilities, which serve the city population as well as that of the region, and in many respects the country as a whole. As per available statistics, there are 23 types of health units (facilities) in Delhi. The total numbers of health units are 1914 and the number of beds is 30,667. The existing bed density per thousand population in Delhi works out to only 2.2. The World Health Organization (WHO) has recommended a norm of 5 beds per thousand population. It is estimated that the total number of beds required in the year 2021 will be about 1,15,000.

The following broad strategies are proposed in order to meet the requirements of health related infrastructure:

i. Shortfall in the availability of number of beds per 1000 population is proposed to be met through-
   (a) Enhancement in FAR for various levels of health facilities;
   (b) Promoting rebuilding of the existing old hospitals and;
   (c) Shifting of contagious diseases hospitals from existing urban areas to the proposed urban extension with proper seclusion facilities and connectivity, and using the space thus made available for general hospitals.

ii. Essential provisions shall be made for Old Age Home-cum-Care Centres for Senior Citizens and Mentally Challenged by way of specialised / target group oriented facilities, which will also relieve the pressure on general hospitals to some extent.

iii. Premises earmarked for health facilities should also include other medical streams like Ayurvedic/omeopathic medicine, governed by any statutory code/body.

iv. Complementary health facilities at par should be developed in the NCR to reduce burden on Delhi.

There shall be following 5-tiers health facilities for the city population:

i. Hospitals category:
   (a) Category A- 501 beds and above;
   (b) Category B- 201 beds to 500 beds;
   (c) Category C- 101 beds to 200 beds;
   (d) Category D- Upto 100 beds
   (e) Other health facilities, which include maternity home, nursing home, family welfare centre, polyclinic, pediatrics centre, geriatric centre, diagnostic centre, etc.

ii. For health care of animals and pets the following 3 tier of health facilities has been proposed :
   (a) Veterinary Hospitals for pet/ domestic animals and birds shall be provided as per need.
   (b) Dispensary for pet animals and birds shall be provided in all the zones at Community Level.
   (c) Pet clinic is permitted in all landuse zones except in Recreational use zone.

Table 13.1: Planning Norms and Standards for Health Facilities

Sl. No.	Category	Population / Unit (approx.)	Plot Area
1	Hospital A (501 beds & above)	5.0 lakh	2.5 ha to 4.5 ha
2	Hospital B (201 beds to 500 beds)	2.5 lakh	1.5 ha to 2.5 ha
3	Hospital C (101 beds to 200 beds)	1.00 lakh	0.5 ha to 1.0 ha

Sl. No.	Category	Population / Unit (approx.)	Plot Area
4	Hospital D (Upto 100 beds)	1.00 lakh	0.25 ha to 0.5 ha
5	Other Health Facilities a. i) Maternity Home	1 per 50000	1000 sqm to 2000 sqm
	ii) Nursing Home/ Polyclinic iii) Dispensary	1 per 50000 1 per 10000	1000 sqm to 2000 sqm 800 sqm to 1200 sqm
	b. i) Family Welfare Centre ii) Pediatric Centre iii) Geriatric Centre iv) Diagnostic Centre.	1 each per 50000	500 sqm to 800 sqm each
6	a. Veterinary Hospital for pet animals and birds	1 per 5.0 lakh	2000 sq m. (Subject to availability of land)
	b. Dispensary for pet animals and birds	1 per 1.0 lakh	300 sq m.
7	a. Medical College	1 per 10 lakh	As per norms of Medical Council of India/Regulatory Body (subject to availability of land)
	b. Nursing and Paramedic Institute	1 per 10 lakh	2000 sqm (Subject to Nursing Council of India/ Ministry of Health norms).
	c. Veterinary Institute	As per requirement	As per the Veterinary Council of India / Ministry norms (subject to availability of land)

Table 13.2: Development Controls for Health Facilities

Sl. No.	Category	Maximum Ground Coverage	Maximum FAR	Maximum Height	Other Controls
1	Hospital A (501 & above)	30% + additional 5% for multi level parking (not to be included in FAR)	200	37 m.	1. Upto 15% of max. FAR can be utilized for residential use of essential staff. 2. Upto 10% of max. FAR to be kept for dormitory/ hostel for attendants of the patients, Crèche etc. 3. Parking standard @ 2.0 ECS/100 sq m of floor area.
2	Hospital B (201 to 500)				
3	Hospital C (101 to 200)				
4	Hospital D (Upto 100)				
5	Other Health Facilities a. i) Maternity Home ii) Nursing Home/ Polyclinic/ Dispensary b. i) Family Welfare Centre ii) Pediatric Centre iii) Geriatric Centre iv) Diagnostic Centre.	30%	150	26 m	Parking Standard @ 2.0 ECS/ 100 sqm of floor area.

Sl. No.	Category	Maximum			Other Controls
		Ground Coverage	FAR	Height	
6	a. Veterinary Hospital for pet animals and birds	30%	150	26m	Parking standard @ 1.33 ECS/ 100 sq m of floor area.
	b. Dispensary for pet animals and birds	35%	100	26m	Parking standard @ 1.33 ECS / 100 sq m of floor area.
7.	a. Medical College	As per norms of Medical Council of India/Regulatory Body			
	b. Nursing and Paramedic Institute	30%	150	26m	Parking standard @ 2 ECS/100 sqm. of floor area.
	c. Veterinary Institute	As per the Veterinary Council of India / Ministry norms			

Notes:

1. Plot area for all hospitals would be worked out @ 100 sqm of gross floor area per bed. However, for other health facilities like Maternity/ Nursing homes, family Welfare and other centres, the plot area would be worked out @ 60 sqm of gross floor area per bed.
2. Max. upto 300 sqm of floor area shall be allowed to be used for community space/ religious shrine/ crèche/ chemist shop/bank counter on Hospital sites and also Medical College/ Nursing and Paramedic Institutes sites.

Other controls:

a. In case of super specialty medical facilities/ hospitals duly certified as such by the competent authority, the gross area shall be worked out @ upto 125 sqm per bed.

b. In case of existing premises / sites, the enhanced FAR shall be permitted, subject to payment of charges as may be prescribed by the Authority/ land owning agency and other clearances.

c. In case of hospitals, service floor is exempted from FAR calculation. Basement if utilized for Hospital purpose shall be counted in FAR.

d. Other controls related to basements etc. are given in the Development Code chapter.

13.2 EDUCATION

The literacy rate in Delhi has increased from 75.3% in the year 1991 to 81.82% in the year 2001. In overall terms Delhi has a fairly elaborate network of educational institutions from the pre-primary/ primary to the higher education and professional education levels. . At present there are 2416 primary schools, 755 middle schools, and 1576 secondary/senior secondary schools. At the higher/ professional education levels, there are 114 colleges for general education, 8 engineering colleges, 4 universities, 7 deemed universities and one Open University.

However, there is a deficiency in few planning zones, particularly in the field of school education. Further, keeping in view the fast changing national and global economic scenario, the employment and educational requirements are also undergoing a rapid change involving the development of new professional and vocational avenues for specialised education. A number of coaching centres, computer training institutes and language / training classes are opening up. However, these are mainly operated by the private sector. Suitable provision for such centres in commercial areas is desirable with a view to enhancing the financial resources of the concerned land owning agency.

With the consequent potential for availability of financial resources for this purpose, involvement of the private sector in the development of educational facilities is growing.

Keeping the need for expansion and diversification as brought out above, the availability of land could become a major constraining factor. It has, therefore, become necessary to develop policies and norms, which would enable optimal utilisation of land and available educational infrastructure. As far as school education is concerned, the policy should be geared to encourage integrated schools from the pre-primary to the higher secondary level, rather than allocating space separately for Nursery Schools, Primary Schools and Middle Schools. Primary Schools may specifically be set up by the Delhi Government or the Local Civic Bodies.

Following planning policy parameters are proposed:

(i) Differential norms and standards for various educational institutes/ institutions shall be applicable in the light of the norms of the concerned controlling authorities e.g. University Grants Commission (UGC) / All India Council for Technical Education (AICTE) / Directorate of Education, GNCTD / Central Board of Secondary Education (CBSE) etc.

(ii) Coaching centres/vocational training centres would be permissible in school classes after school hours with (a) prior approval of Competent Authority in the case of schools run by GNCTD or local body and (b) with prior intimation to lessor and payment of fee to be prescribed in the case of schools run privately on leased land. Structured courses leading directly to degree / diploma shall however not be permitted.

(iii) The educational institution premises may be permitted to function in two shifts, subject to statutory approvals and any other conditions that may be stipulated by the relevant competent authority.

(iv) Nursery School may function as part of Primary School / Secondary School / Senior Secondary School, wherever needed. Separate / exclusive Nursery Schools are permitted in residential premises as per the Mixed-use policy.

(v) Requirement of schools and training centres for mentally and physically challenged with differential development norms are given.

Table 13.3: Planning Norms and Standards for Education Facilities

Sl. No.	Category	Population / unit (approx.)	Plot Area
1.	Primary School	10,000	0.2 - 0.4 ha
2.	Sr. Secondary School	10,000	0.6 - 0.8 ha
3.	School for Mentally challenged	10.0 lakh	0.2 ha
4.	School for Physically challenged	10.0 lakh	0.2 ha

Table 13.4: Development Controls for Education Facilities

Sl. No		Maximum			Other Controls
		Gr. Cov.	FAR	Height	
1	Play School, Coaching Centre, Computer-Training Institute, physical Education Centre etc.	N.A.	N.A.	N.A.	1. Practice of providing dedicated Nursery School plots in the layout plan discontinued as same is permissible in Mixed use. Parking standard @ 1.33 ECS/ 100 sq m of floor area.
2	Nursery School	33.33%	100	15 m	2. In case of schools for mentally/ physically challenged, 20% of max. FAR can be utilized for residential use of essential staff and student accommodation. Parking standard:— Primary School / Middle School @ 1.33 ECS / 100 sq m of floor area.-Sr. Sec. School @ 2.00 ECS / 100 sq m of floor area. The areas earmarked for parking if misused, liable to be municipalized/ taken over. 3. Other controls related to basements etc. are given in the Development Code chapter.
3	Primary school	30%	120	18 m	
4	Sr. Secondary School	35%	150	18 m	
5	School for Mentally challenged	50%	120	18 m	
6	School for Physically challenged	50%	120	18 m	

Notes:

Pre-Primary Schools/ Nursery Schools/ Montessary Schools/ Creche, Play Schools, are permissible in residential use premises as per Mixed use policy.

Other Controls :

1. **In case of new schools, the front boundary wall shall be recessed by 6 m to accommodate visitors parking within setback area.**
2. **Upto 10% variation in plot size is permitted. Differential norms will be applicable to Special Area, Regularized Unauthorized Colonies, Urban Villages and Resettlement Colonies.**
3. **Playground shall be developed on pool basis in different areas at neighborhood level.**

Table 13.5: Planning Norms and Standards for Education Facilities (Higher Education)

Sl. No.	Category	Pop./ unit (approx.)	Plot Area
1	Vocational Training Centre(ITI/ Polytechnic/ Vocational Training Institute/ Management Institute/ Teacher Training Institute etc.), Research and Development centre	5.0 lakh	0.4 ha
2	General College	5.0 lakh	As per UGC norms
3	Professional College (Technical)	5.0 lakh	As per the AICTE norms.
4	University Campus including International Education Centre (IEC) - Large campus (10 ha and above) will be divided into following four parts: (a) Academic including Administration (45% of total land area). (b) Residential (25% of total land area). (c) Sports and Cultural activities (15% of total land area). d) Parks and Landscape (15% of total land area).	4 sites in urban extension.	Upto 20.0 ha

Upto 10% variation in plot size is permitted.

Table 13.6: Development Controls for Education Facilities (Higher Education)

Sl. No.	Category	Maximum			Other Controls
		Ground Coverage	FAR	Height	
1	Vocational Training Centre (ITI/Polytechnic / Vocational/ Training Institute/ Management Institute/ Teacher Training Institutes etc.) / Research and Development centre.	35%	150	37 m	1. Upto 15% of max. FAR can be utilized for residential use of essential staff and student accommodation. 2. Parking standard @ 1.33 ECS / 100 sq m of floor area. The areas earmarked for parking if misused liable to be municipalized / taken over by the authority. 3. Other controls related to basements etc. are given in the Development Code chapter.
2	General College				
3	Professional College (Technical)				
4	University Campus including International Education Centre (IEC) - Large campus (10 ha and above) will be divided into following four parts:				1. Parking standard @ 1.33 ECS / 100 sq m of floor area. 2. Other controls related to basements etc. are given in the Development Code chapter. 3. Landscape plan to be prepared.
	(a) Academic including Administration (45% of total land area)	30%	120	37 m	
	(b) Residential (25% of total land area)	1. Regulations for group housing shall apply. 2. The land shall be reserved for facilities as per residential norms.			
	(c) Sports and Cultural activities (15%)	10%	15	26 m	
	(d) Parks and Landscape (15%)	N. A.			

13.3 SPORTS FACILITIES

Delhi is emerging as an important centre for National and International Sports events.

Sizeable sports facilities have been developed in the City by various agencies like the Sports Authority of India (SAI), Delhi Development Authority (DDA), GNCTD, etc. However, sports activities, so far, been dealt with as a part of Recreational use. It is also felt that many of the facilities, which have been developed, could actually be seen as recreation and/or club type of facilities. As a result, even though the DDA has developed a large network of excellent sports facilities, over and above the facilities developed by the SAI, etc. there is an evident need for a properly planned and structured sports infrastructure in the city which, inter alia, should also be able to take care of mega/international sporting events, such as the forthcoming Commonwealth Games in 2010.

Even the various facilities, which have been developed as pure sports facilities, suffer from lack of full and proper utilisation, and there are issues related to maintenance and resources for the same. With reference to the latter, for example, the Jawahar Lal Nehru Stadium premises are, on the one hand, presently under use for a variety of non-sports related activities and on the other hand, the Stadium itself cannot be used for anything but sports activities. The latter aspect, in turn, is characterised by gross under utilisation. This also brings out the need for developing and prescribing planning and development control norms geared to planned, practical and proper development of sports facilities as an important component of social development and optimum utilisation of the facilities to be developed.

In addition to the above, there is a trend for development of gyms, spas, bowling alleys etc. at neighbourhood level. Since these are mostly being established as commercial ventures, provision of land / space for these should be made in commercial premises.

13.3.1 PROVISION OF SPORTS FACILITIES

Sports activities are an important part of physical and social development of an individual and, at another level sports activities have a significant aspect of, and potential in the form of congregational and competitive events at the community, city, national and international levels. Keeping this in view norms and space standards separately for sports facilities at neighbourhood level and city level have been proposed with the aim of development of sports and play areas for all age groups at appropriate levels.

Table 13.7: Planning Norms and Standards for Sports Facilities

Sl.No.	Category	Pop. / Unit (Approx.)	Plot Area (Ha.)*
1.	Divisional Sports Centre/ Golf Course	10 lakh	10 to 30 & above
2.	District Sports Centre	5 lakh	3 to 10
3.	Community Sports Centre	1 lakh	1 to 3
4.	Neighborhood Play area	10,000	0.5 to 1
5.	Housing Area Play Ground	5,000	0.5

* Subject to availability of land.

Notes:

(i) The sports facilities shall be developed according to proper layout plan and landscape plan with adequate parking facility.

(ii) The existing sports infrastructure shall be upgraded and efficiently re-planned to provide better facilities.

(iii) New play fields shall be preferably provided/ developed in the vicinity of educational institutions and landscape areas.

(iv) The playground and sports facilities should be accessible by a network of pedestrian and cycle tracks wherever feasible.

13.3.2 INTERNATIONAL SPORTS EVENTS

Suitable area of about 200 ha. shall be reserved for International Sports events wherever possible.

13.3.3 DEVELOPMENT CONTROLS

The development controls for the various sports facilities will be as indicated below :

Maximum ground coverage	20% including amenity structures
Max. FAR Height	40
	NR (Subject to clearance from AAI, Fire Dept. and other statutory bodies).
Parking	2 ECS/ 100 sqm of floor area.

Other Development Controls :

i To incentivise development of sports facilities and swimming pool (upto maximum 100 sqm) within the group housing areas, schools, clubs, etc. shall not be counted towards ground coverage and FAR.

(ii) All these various sports facilities shall have layout plan, landscape plan, and parking plan, etc.

13.4 COMMUNICATIONS - POST/TELEGRAPH/TELEPHONE FACILITY

With liberalisation and technological advancement, communication has become very important medium of accessibility. Following means of communication are available:

13.4.1 POST AND TELEGRAPH

Post and Telegraph is one of the most popular means of communication. The provision and management of Post and Telegraph facility in Delhi is the responsibility of Post Master General of Delhi Circle. At present Delhi has 553 post offices and 36 telegraph offices. Although, the number of telegraph offices is decreasing due to availability of other easier, cheaper and faster modes of communication these facilities still serve considerable population both at the city level and National level. The future space norms have been worked out accordingly.

13.4.2 TELEPHONE

With privatisation of tele-communication sector most of the space requirement is expected to be satisfied in private sector. There are 267 telephone exchanges in Delhi with provision of 140 lakh connections, which works out to be 145 connections per thousand population. The introduction of mobile telephony has completely transformed the telecommunication system in the city. Therefore, the future space requirement for telephone network has been worked out accordingly.

Table 13.8: Planning Norms and Standards for Communication Facilities

Sl. No.		Category	Population / Unit (approx)	Plot Area
A.		POST & TELEGRAPH		
	1	(a) Post Office Counter (without delivery)	1. No specific site reservation to be kept in the layout plan.	
		(b) Courier Service Office	2. Permitted in all use/zones/under mixed use as per requirement except in Recreational use zone.	
	2	Telegraph office (Booking & Delivery)		
	3	Head Post Office with Administrative office & with / without delivery office.	10.0 lakh	2500 sq m.
B		TELEPHONE		
	4	(a) Telephone Exchange	10.0 lakh	2500 sq m.
		(b) RSU (Remote Subscriber Units)	1 for 3 Km radius	300 sqm.

Upto 10% variation in plot size is permitted.

Table 13.9: Development Controls for Communication Facilities

Sl. No.		Category	Maximum Ground Coverage	Maximum FAR	Maximum Height	Other Controls
A.		POST & TELEGRAPH				
	1	a. Post Office Counter (without delivery) b. Courier Service Office	No specific site reservation to be kept in the layout plan since permitted in all use zones / under mixed use as per requirement, except in Recreational use zone.			
	2	Telegraph office (Booking & Delivery)				
	3	Head Post Office with Administrative office & with / without delivery office	30%	120	26 m.	1. Upto 15% of max. FAR can be utilized for residential use of essential staff. 2. Parking standard @ 1.33 ECS/100 sq m of floor area. 3. Other controls related to basements etc. are given in the Development Code chapter.

B	TELEPHONE			
4	a. Telephone Exchange	30%	120	26m
	b. RSU (Remote Subscriber Units)	30%	100	15 m

13.5. SECURITY- POLICE

Law and order are increasingly becoming a matter of concern in Delhi. For maintenance of proper law and order, the security force must keep pace with the growth and development of an area. The main agency looking after security aspect in the city is Delhi Police. At present, there are 123 police stations, 80 police posts, 10 Delhi Armed Police battalions, 9 District offices of DCPs and 9 District Lines.

Table 13.10: Planning Norms and Standards for Security (Police) Facilities

Sl. No.	Category	Pop./ unit (approx.)	Plot Area
1	Police Post	1.0 lakh	1000 sqm.
2	Police Station	2.5 lakh	1.0 ha
3	District Office and Battalion	One for each administrative zone.	1.0 ha
4	Police Lines		2.0 ha
5	District Jail	25.0 lakh	5.0 ha
6	Police Training Institute / College*	City level (to be located in fringe area)	5.0 ha
7	Police Firing Range		Upto 10.0 ha
8	Police camp including Central Police Organization /Security Forces*		Upto 10.0 ha
9	Traffic and police control room	As per requirement	

*Including Central Security Forces

Table 13.11: Development Controls for Security (Police) Facilities

Sl. No.	Category	Maximum Ground Coverage	Maximum FAR	Maximum Height	Other Controls
1	Police Post	35%	150	15 m.	1. Upto 30% of max. FAR can be utilized for residential use of essential staff. 2. Parking standard @ 2.00 ECS/ 100 sq m of floor area. 3. Additional space available in police station due to increased development controls shall be used for locating Civil Defence and Home Guards etc. 4. Upto 15% of max. FAR can be utilized for residential use/ hostel for essential staff and student accommodation, in Police Training Institute/ college. 5. Other controls related to basements etc. are given in the Development Code chapter.
2	Police Station	30%	150	26 m.	
3	District Office and Battalion	30%	120	26 m.	
4	Police Line	Land Distributio.ı			
	i) Administration	- 20%			
	ii) Residential	- 30%			
	iii) Sports & Facilities	- 10%			
	iv) Open Spaces	- 40%			
5	District Jail	30%	120	26 m	
6	Police Training Institute/ College*	30%	120	26 m.	
7	Police Firing Range	12.5%	25	9 m.	
8	Police camp including Central Police Organization /Security Forces*	12.5%	25	9 m.	
9	Traffic and police control room	1. As per requirement on major road junctions / stretches etc. as part of road right of way based on site feasibility. 2. Maximum area = 25 sq m.			

*Including Central Security Forces

13.6 SAFETY

13.6.1 FIRE

Fire services have to play pivotal role and be fully prepared in protecting people from fire hazards, building collapses, road accidents and other unforeseen emergencies etc. At present, there are 36 fire stations in Delhi.

Table 13.12: Planning Norms and Standards for Safety / Fire Facilities

Sl. No	Category	Population / Unit (approx.)	Plot Area
1	Fire Post	3 to 4 km radius	2000 sqm
2	Fire Station	5 to 7 km radius	1.0 Ha.
3	Disaster Management Centre	One in each Administrative Zone	1.0 Ha. along with suitable open area (2Ha) for soft parking, temporary shelter, parade ground etc.
4	Fire Training Institute / College	City level (one site in urban extension)	3.0 Ha.

Table 13.13: Development Controls for Safety / Fire Facilities

Sl. No.	Category	Maximum			Other Controls
		Ground Coverage	FAR	Height	
1	Fire Post	30%	120	26 m.	1. Upto 25% of max. FAR can be utilized for residential use of essential staff in fire station. 2. Parking standard @ 1.33 ECS/ 100 sq m of floor area. 3. Upto 15% of max. FAR can be utilized for residential use/hostel for essential staff and student accommodation, in Fire Training Institute / college. 4. Other controls related to basements etc. are given in the Development Code chapter.
2	Fire Station	30%	120	26 m.	
3	Disaster Management Centre	30% (on building area only)	120	26 m.	
4	Fire Training Institute/College	30%	120	26 m.	

13.6.2 GUIDELINES FOR LOCATING FIRE STATIONS & OTHER FIRE FIGHTING FACILITIES IN URBAN EXTENSION:

(i) Fire stations should be located so that the fire tenders are able to reach any disaster site within 3-5 minutes.

(ii) Fire Stations shall be located on corner plots as far as possible and on main roads with minimum two entries.

(iii) In the new layouts, concept of under ground pipelines for fire hydrants on the periphery, exclusively for fire fighting services should be considered.

(iv) Fire stations are permitted in all land use zones except in Recreational use zone.

(v) Necessary provisions for laying underground / over ground fire fighting measures, water lines, hydrants etc. may be kept wherever provision of fire station is not possible.

(vi) The concerned agencies shall take approval from Fire Department for fire fighting measures while laying the services for an area.

13.6.3 DISASTER MANAGEMENT CENTRE

According to the Indian Seismic Zone map, Delhi is placed in Seismic Zone IV, which means high damage risk zone. In the past, several earthquakes of Richter magnitude 5.5 to 6.7 have occurred in the National Capital Territory of Delhi. Two major lineaments, namely Delhi-Haridwar ridge and Delhi-Muradabad faults pass through the territory, both having potential of generating earthquakes of the magnitude upto 6.5 to 6.7 in future. Such natural and man made disasters neither can be prevented nor predicted. However, with the technological advancement to some extent mechanism can be developed to mitigate the after effects of the disaster. Areas of vulnerability can be identified and necessary measures can be proposed by the concerned agencies. The concerned local bodies should keep updating the building bye-laws to safeguard against disasters and ensure effective and impartial enforcement. Following policies and strategies for disaster management are proposed :

1. Pre-Disaster Preparedness

(i) a) Micro-zonation surveys should be referred for land use planning and be considered while preparing the Zonal Plans and Layout Plans.

- Seismic micro-zonation for selected areas having high growth rates should be taken up on priority.
- On the basis of vulnerability studies and hazard identification, which includes soil conditions, probable intensity of earthquake, physiographic conditions of the area, fault traces, etc., local level land use zoning and planning should be undertaken.

(b) Building bye-laws should incorporate the aspects of Multi Hazard Safety, and Retrofitting.

- Priority should be given to public buildings (such as hospitals, educational, institutional, power stations, infrastructure, heritage monuments, lifeline structures and those which are likely to attract large congregation) for their ability to withstand earthquake of the defined intensity.
- Suitable action should be taken for retrofitting and strengthening of structures identified as vulnerable as per earthquake manuals and National Building Code. A techno-legal regime has to be adopted for provisions on Multi Hazard Safety aspects.

(ii) Delhi Fire Services being the nodal agency for disaster management should identify vulnerable areas such as areas with high density and poor accessibility in the city and propose suitable measures. Proposed Disaster Management Centres should be established in every zone to deal with the disasters, including bio-chemical and nuclear disasters.

(iii) Sensitize people, particularly school children, about after effects of disaster.

(iv) Make people aware through media campaigns and advertisements about emergency procedures and location of emergency shelters etc.

2. Post Disaster Management

(i) It has been observed that any disaster is generally followed by break down of communication lines and disruption of essential services. Therefore, the key communication centres should be protected from natural disasters i.e. flood, fire and earthquake etc. and services restoration should be taken up on top most priority. Necessary setup should be created in each of the concerned department for such eventualities.

(ii) Standard type designs and layout should be prepared by the local bodies and made available to the people so that crucial time is not lost in approval of layout plans and building plans after disaster.

Disaster Management Centres have been proposed to serve people in the case of disaster and provide emergency shelters.

13.7 DISTRIBUTIVE FACILITIES

Milk, Fruit, vegetable and LPG are the basic requirements of the day-to-day life, and should have proper distribution set-up.

PDS facilities/ fair price shops may be provided in close proximity to EWS/LIG housing/ resettlement colonies at the same standard as the milk/ vegetable booths.

Table 13.14: Planning Norms and Standards for Distributive Services

Sl. No	Category	Population / unit
1	Milk Booth /Milk and Fruit & Vegetable Booth	One per 5000 population. As per standard design of the concerned department.
2	LPG godown including booking office.	3 LPG godowns per one lakh population.
3	SKO / LDO outlets	As per standard design of the concerned department.

Table 13.15: Development Controls for Distributive Services

Sl. No.	Category	Maximum			Other Controls
		Ground Coverage	FAR	Height	
1	Milk Booth /Milk and Fruit & Vegetable Booth	Permitted in all zones as per approved layout plan.			
2	LPG godown including booking office	i. Plot size - upto 600 sqm including booking office and security hut. ii. Permitted in all use zones except in residential and recreational use zones subject to statutory clearances.			
3	SKO / LDO outlets	i. Permitted in all use zones except in residential and recreational use zones subject to statutory clearances.			

13.8 SOCIO-CULTURAL FACILITIES

Table 13.16: Planning Norms and Standards for Socio-Cultural Facilities

Sl. No.	Category	Population / unit (approx.)	Plot Area
1	a. Banquet Hall	10000	800-2000 sqm
	b. Multipurpose Community Hall which may include provision for marriages, small public gathering, function, eating joint, and library etc.	1.0 lakh	2000 sqm
2	a. Community Recreational Club	1.0 lakh	2000 sqm
	b. Recreational Club	5.0 lakh	5000 sqm
3	Socio-cultural activities such as auditorium, music, dance & drama centre/ meditation & spiritual centre etc.	1.0 lakh	1000 sqm
4	Exhibition -cum-Fair Ground	2 sites in new urban extension	Upto 40 ha. Each
5	Science Centre	10.0 lakh	As per requirement
6	International Convention Centre	City Level	As per requiremen

Table 13.17: Development Controls for Socio-Cultural Facilities

Sl. No.	Category	Maximum			Other Controls
		Ground Coverage	FAR	Height	
1	a. Multipurpose Community Hall.	30%	120	26 m	1. Parking standard @ 3.0 ECS / 100 sq m of floor area.
	b. Banquet Hall.	30%	120	26 m	2. Other controls related to basements etc. are given in the Development Code chapter.
2	a. Community Recreational Club b. Recreational Club	25%	100	26 m	Parking standard @ 2 ECS / 100 sq m of floor area
3	Socio-cultural activities such as auditorium, music, dance & drama centre/ meditation & spiritual centre etc.	35%	120	26 m	1. Parking standard @ 2 ECS / 100 sq m of floor area. 2. A proper scheme for visitors parking and parking adequacy statement shall be prepared taking into consideration large number of visitors.
4	Exhibition-cum-Fair Ground	20%	20	Subject to statutory clearances	
5	Science Centre	30%	120	26 m	Parking standard @ 2 ECS
6	International Convention centre	30%	120	NR, subject to approval of AAI, Fire Department and other statutory bodies	Parking standard @2 ECS

Notes:

(i) In case of Community Recreational Clubs, 50 FAR shall be admissible on the area beyond 2000 sqm. and below 5000 sqm.

(ii) In case of Recreational Club, 50 FAR shall be admissible on the area beyond 5000 sqm. and upto 10,000 sqm.

(iii) In the open area apart from outdoor games / sport facilities, swimming pool would be permissible upto a area of 300 sqm. free from ground coverage.

(iv) In case of Banquet Hall,

a. Basements within the ground envelope shall be allowed for parking. Stilt floor for parking is permissible.

b. 30% of basement area for services/ storage shall not be counted in FAR.

13.9 OTHER COMMUNITY FACILITIES

The Planning Norms, Standards and Development Controls for other facilities such as old age homes, religious facilities, etc. are as given in Table 13.18.

Table 13.18: Planning Norms and Standards for Other Community Facilities

Sl. No	Category	Population / Unit (approx)	Max. Plot Area
1	(a) Old Age Home (b) Care Centre for Physically- Mentally challenged (c) Working women- men hostel (d) Adult Education Centre (e) Orphanage/ Children's centre. (One each) (f) Night shelter	5 lakh Each category for 10 lakh	1000 sqm, subject to availability of land.
2	Religious Facilities		
	(a) At neighbourhood level	5000	400 sqm
	(b) At sub city level in urban extension	10 lakh	4.0 Ha.
3	Anganwari		
	(a) Housing area /cluster	5000	200-300 sqm

Upto 10% variation in plot size is permitted.

Table 13.19: Development Controls for Other Community Facilities

Sl. No.	Category	Maximum			Other Controls
		Ground Coverage	FAR	Height	
1	Old Age Home/Care Centre for Physically/ Mentally challenged/ Working women/ men hostel/Adult Education Centre/ Orphanage/Children's Centre/ Night Shelter.	30%	120	26m.	1. Parking standard @ 1.8 ECS / 100 sqm of floor area. 2. Other controls related to basements etc. are given in the Development Code chapter.
2	Religious				
	(a) At neighbourhood level	35%	70	15m. including shikhara	
	(b) At sub city level in urban extension*	25%	50	26m.	
3	Anganwari				
	(a) At Housing area/ cluster level	30%	60	15m.	

* These facilities should be developed in a composite manner to accommodate a number of religious institutes / premises with common facilities.

Note: Sites for Dhobi ghats / laundry shall be provided in Residential use zone / PSP facility areas as per the norms of local body.

13.10 CREMATION GROUND, BURIAL GROUND & CEMETERY

At present there are 59 cremation grounds and 4 graveyards (qabristans) of the MCD and Delhi Waqf Board has 53 burial grounds.

(i) In the existing cremation grounds, provision of crematorium is to be made.

(ii) In proposed urban extension new burial grounds / crematorium / cremation grounds / cemetery etc. are to be planned with proper parking and landscape provisions. The plot area to be about 0.4 Ha. per 5.0 lakh population for a cremation ground and upto 1.0 Ha. per 10 lakh population for a cemetery and burial ground subject to availability of land.

13.11 PUBLIC & SEMI-PUBLIC FACILITIES/PREMISES

The following norms shall be applicable in case of PSP facilities / premises, for which specific development controls have not been specified.

1. Max. Ground Coverage 30%
2. Max. Floor Area Ratio 120
3. Max. Height 26 m.

Other controls:-

Parking @ 2ECS/100 sqm. of floor area. Other controls as given in Development Code chapter.

DEFINITIONS AND PERMISSIBLE USE PREMISES IN SUB USE ZONES

Table 13.20: Health Facilities

S. No.	Use Premises	Definitions	Activities Permitted
1.	Hospital	A premise providing medical facilities of general or specialised nature for treatment of indoor and outdoor patients. It may be managed by public, private or charitable institution.	Hospital, Staff accommodation, patient attendant accommodation, Institutional Hostel, Medical College, Parking, Retail Shop. (canteen, confectionery, grocery & general merchandise, books and stationery, chemist, barber, launderer, vegetable), Bank extension counter.
2.	Primary Health Centre/Family Welfare Centre/ Pediatric Centre/ Geriatric Centre/ Diagnostic Centre	A premise having facilities for treating indoor and outdoor patients having upto 10-15 beds. It may be managed by a public or charitable institution on non-commercial basis. It includes family welfare centre & maternity home.	Health Facility Watch & Ward Residence (Upto 20 sqm), Chemist Shop (Upto 20 sqm), Soft Drink & Snack Stall.
3.	Dispensary	A premise having facilities for medical advice and provision of medicine, managed by public or charitable institutions.	Dispensary, Watch & Ward Residence (Upto 20 sqm), Chemist Shop (Upto 20 sqm), Soft Drink & Snack Stall.
4.	Nursing Home/ Maternity Home / Polyclinic	A premise having medical facilities for indoor and outdoor patients having upto 50 beds. It may be managed by a doctor or a group of doctors. In case of polyclinic, it shall be managed by a group of doctors.	Nursing Home, Watch &Ward Residence (Upto 20 sqm), Chemist Shop (Upto 20 sqm), Soft Drink & Snack Stall.
5.	Clinic	A premise with facilities for treatment of outdoor patients by a doctor.	Clinic
6.	Clinical Laboratory	A premise with facilities for carrying out various tests for confirmation of symptoms of a disease.	Clinical Laboratory, Watch &Ward Residence (Upto 20 sqm), Chemist Shop (Upto 20sqm), Soft Drink & Snack Stall.
7.	Veterinary Hospital for pet animals and birds	A premise having medical facilities for indoor and outdoor treatment of pets animals and birds. It may be managed by a public or charitable institution or on community basis.	Hospital with Surgeon's lab, office, operation theater, examination room, X-ray rooms, wards, reception, store, kitchen, etc; staff accommodation, Watch & Ward Residence (Upto 20 sqm), Chemist Shop (Upto 20 sqm), Diagnostic Centre.

8.	Dispensary for pet animals and birds	Premises having facilities for medical advice and provision of medicines, managed by public/private or charitable institutions.	Surgeon's lab, office, Operation Theater, examination room, wards, reception, store, kitchen, etc
9.	Voluntary Health Service	A premise having medical facilities for treatment of outdoor patients and other like blood bank etc. by voluntary institutions. This service may also take the form of temporary camp with charitable motive.	Voluntary Health Service, Watch & Ward Residence (upto 20 sqm), Administrative Office, Dispensary, Canteen.
10.	Veterinary Institute	A premise having educational and playing facilities for students of under-graduate & post-graduate courses along with research facilities under a university.	College, Residential Flat (For maintenance staff), Institutional Hostel, Retail Shops of area 20 sqm each (confectionery, grocery and general merchandise, books & stationery, chemist, barber, launderer, vegetable), Canteen, Bank Extension Counter, Auditorium, Indoor Games Hall, Swimming Pool, Play Ground, Post Office Counter Facility, Facilities for Indoor & Outdoor Treatment for Pets, Animals & Birds.

Table 13.21: Educational Facilities

S. No.	Use Premises	Definition	Activities Permitted
1.	Pre-Primary/ Nursery/ Montessary/ Creche & Day Care Centre	A premise having nursery facilities for infants during day time. The centre may be managed by an individual or an institution on commercial or non-commercial basis.	Creche & Day care Centre, Watch & Ward Residence (upto 20 sqm).
2.	Primary School	A premise having educational and playing facilities for students upto V standard.	Nursery School, Primary School, Watch & Ward Residence (Upto 20 sqm). Books & Stationery Shop (Upto 20 sqm.), Soft Drink & Snack Stall.
3.	Middle School	A premise having educational and playing facilities for students upto VIII standard.	Nursery School, Middle School, Watch & Ward Residence (Upto 20 sqm), Books & Stationery Shop (Upto 20 sqm.), Soft Drink and Snack Stall.
4.	Senior Secondary School	A premise having educational and playing facilities for students upto XII standard.	Nursery School, Sr. Secondary School, Watch & Ward Residence (Upto 20 sqm), Books and Stationery Shop, Uniform Shop (Upto 20 sqm each) Soft Drink & Snack Stall, Canteen, Bank Extension Counter, Auditorium, Indoor Games Hall, Swimming Pool, Post Office Counter Facility.
5.	School for Mentally / Physically challenged	A premise having educational (formal and vocational) and playing facilities for mentally & physically challenged.	School, Ward & Watch Residence (Upto 20 sqm), workshop, sale counter, hostel facility (15% of permissible built up area), Books & Stationery Shop (Upto 20 sqm), Canteen, Bank Extension Counter, Post Office Counter facility, Indoor Games Hall, Upto 20% of max. FAR can be utilized for residential use of essential staff and student accommodation, office, professional activity, rehabilitation centre.

6.	College (including Professional College)	A premise having educational and playing facilities for students of under-graduate & post-graduate courses under a university. It includes all professional disciplines.	College, Residential Flat (For maintenance staff), Hostel, Retail Shops of area 20 sqm each (confectionery, grocery and general merchandise, books & stationery, chemist, barber, launderer, vegetable), Canteen, Bank Extension Counter, Auditorium, Indoor Games Hall, Swimming Pool, Playground, Post Office Counter facility.
7.	Library	A premise having a large collection of books for reading and reference for general public or specific class.	Library, Watch & Ward Residence (upto 20 sqm.), canteen, exhibition and art gallery, auditorium.
8.	Technical Training centre / Institute, Nursing and Paramedic Institute	A premise with facilities for training in discipline of technical nature. It includes technical school and industrial training institute etc.	Technical Training Centre, Residential flat (for maintenance staff), Books and stationery and chemist shops (Upto 20 sqm each) Canteen, Bank Extension counter, Auditorium, Post Office Counter facility.
9.	Vocational Training Institute	A premise with training facilities for short term courses for discipline e.g. Commercial, Secretarial, Nursing training etc., preparatory to the employment in certain profession & trade. It shall be run by public or charitable institution on non-commercial basis. It includes training-cum-work centre.	Vocational Training Institute, Watch & Ward Residence (upto 20 sqm.), Hostel (only in case of Government Centres), Books & Stationery Shop (Upto 20 sqm.), Canteen, Library, Chemist Shop (Upto 20 sqm), Bank Extension Counter, Auditorium, Post Office Extension Counter Facility.
10.	Commercial and secretarial training centre	A premise having training facilities for stenography, correspondence, record keeping etc.	Commercial and secretarial training centre, Watch & Ward Residence (upto 20 sqm.), Canteen.
11.	Hotel Management Institute	A premise with training facilities for hotel management discipline. It shall be run by public/ private body. It includes training-cum-work-centre.	Hotel Management Institute, Watch & Ward Residence (Upto 20 sqm), Books and stationery and chemist shops (Upto 20 sqm each) Canteen, Bank Extension counter, Auditorium, Post Office Counter facility.
12.	Social Welfare Centre	A premise having facilities for welfare and promotion of community development. It shall be run by a public and charitable institution.	Social Welfare Centre, Watch & Ward Residence (upto 20 sqm.) canteen, Exhibition cum sale counter.
13.	Research and Development Centre	A premise providing facilities for research and development for any specific field.	Research and Development Centre, Watch & Ward Residence (upto 20 sqm.) residential flat,(For maintenance staff) Hostel, Canteen, Bank Extension counter, Library, Post Office counter facility.
14.	University Campus and International Education Centre	A premise having an educational institution designed for instruction, examination, or both, of students in many branches of advanced learning, conferring degrees in various faculties, and often embodying colleges and similar institutions.	Educational Institution, Colleges, Residential Flat (for maintenance staff), Institutional Hostel, Retail Shops of area 20 sqm each (confectionery, grocery and general merchandise, books & stationery, chemist, barber, launderer, vegetable), Residential, Library, Bank Extn. Counter, Auditorium, Post Office Extn. Counter Facility, Canteen, Indoor Games Hall.

Table 13.22: Sports Facilities

S. No.	Use Premises	Definition	Activities Permitted
1.	Divisional Sports Centre/ Golf Course	A premise for Outdoor and Indoor games with pavilion buildings, stadium structure for spectators and related facilities.	a. Sports related Commercial component - 5% of total floor area. b. Multiuse Stadium (Seating capacity 15,000). c. Multipurpose Hall (Seating capacity 4,000) for Exhibitions, Trade Shows, Banquets, Multiple sports & related events, d. Aquatic Centre (covered or otherwise with full size competition pool, a training / lap pool, diving pool which can also be used for Water Polo and Synchronized swimming as well as other aquatic recreational facilities like waterslides, wave pool, hydrotherapy pool, Akhara etc. e. Facilities for Outdoor Sports like Cricket, Football, Hockey Grounds etc including extreme sports & Golf Course/ Range. f. Sports academy for multiple sports events. g. Sports Medicine Centre. h. Residential accommodation/ Hostel, Watch & Ward Residence. i. Playground.
2.	District Sports Centre	A premise for Outdoor and Indoor games with pavilion buildings, stadium structure for spectators and related facilities.	a. Indoor Stadium with ancillary halls for basket ball, badminton, table-tennis, volley ball, swimming pool. b. Facilities like open Cricket, Football and Hockey grounds, Skating Rinks, Jogging track, Cricket practice nets, children's' corner, etc. c. Provision for extreme sports like skate boarding, etc., can also be made. d. At least one of these can be designed for a sports academy/ sports training centre for multiple sports events with residential accommodation/ hostel. Retail shops, bank, post office & sports related commercial component - 5% of total FAR. e. Playgrounds.
3.	Community Sports Centre	A premise used for Outdoor Games. It may have landscaping, parking facility, public toilets etc.	These can have facilities like open Cricket, Football and Hockey grounds, Volleyball courts, Skating Rinks, Jogging track, Cricket practice nets, children's' corner, etc. Besides, amenities for small change rooms, offices, lavatories and store rooms should be provided. In these some provision for extreme sports like skate boarding, etc., can also be provided, Playgrounds, sports centre related component maximum 5% of FAR for sports, retail shops, cafeteria/ snack bar.

Table 13.23: Communication Facilities

S. No.	Use Premises	Definition	Activities Permitted
	Post Office		
1.	Post office Counter (without delivery)	A premise with facilities of post office counter only (without post delivery)	Post office counter, watch and ward residence (upto 20 sq mt).
2.	Post and Telegraph office (Booking & Delivery)	A premise with facility for postal and telegraphic communication.	Telegraph office, watch and ward residence (upto 20 sq mt).
3.	General and Head Post Office with Administrative office with/without delivery office	A premise with facility for postal and telecommunication to and from a number of post offices attached to it.	Head post office, general post office, watch and ward residence (upto 20 sq.mt), canteen.
	Telephone		
4.	Telephone Exchange/ RSU	A premise having central facilities for operation of telephone system for a designated area.	Telephone Exchange/RSU, Logistics, Watch & Ward Residence (upto 20 sqm.) canteen.
5.	Radio & Television Station	A premise with facilities for recording, broadcast and transmission of news and other programmes through the respective medium. It may include some hostel accommodation for artists, transmission facilities like towers.	Radio and television station, watch and ward residence (upto 20 sqm) hostel, library and canteen.
6.	Transmission Tower and wireless station	A premise used for installation of a tower for communication purposes.	Transmission tower, watch and ward residence (upto 20 sqm).
7.	Satellite and Tele-Communication Centre	A premise with facilities for research & development of satellite & telecommunication technology.	Satellite and telecommunication centre, residential flat (for maintenance staff), watch and ward residence (upto 20 sqm) research laboratory, canteen.
8.	Observatory & Weather Office	A premise with facilities for research and development of data relating to weather and forecasting thereof.	Observatory and weather office, residential flat (for maintenance staff), watch and ward residence (upto 20sqm).

Table 13.24: Security Facilities

S. No.	Use Premises	Definitions	Activities Permitted
1.	Police post	A premise having facility for a local police post of a temporary nature or on smaller scale as compared to a police station.	Police Post, essential staff housing.
2.	Police station	A premise having facilities for offices of local police post.	Police Station, essential staff housing, canteen, bank extension counter.
3.	District Police Office and Battalion	A premise having facilities for the offices and paramilitary forces.	District Police Office and Civil Defence & Home Guard residential flat (For maintenance staff) Hostel Play Ground, canteen, bank extension counter.

4.	Police Line	An area having facilities for work and residential accommodation of paramilitary forces.	Police line and related facilities.
5.	Jail	A premise with facilities for detention, confinement and reform of criminals under the law	Jail and related facilities.
6.	Police Training Institute/ College	A premise having facilities for training of paramilitary forces.	Training institute/college, residential flat (for maintenance staff), hostel, retail shops of area 20 sqm each, confectionery, grocery, merchandise, books and stationary, chemist, barber, laundry, vegetable, canteen, bank extension counter, auditorium, indoor, outdoor games, swimming pool, playground, post office counter facility.
7.	Police Firing Range	A premise having facilities for firing practice of the paramilitary forces.	Police firing range (Temporary Structure only).
8.	Traffic and Police Control Room	A premise of temporary structures having facilities for the managing of traffic, & law and order related issues.	Temporary traffic and police control room.
9.	Civil defense and home guards etc.	A premise having facilities for offices and other functions of civil organization for internal defence.	Civil Defence & Home guard residential flat (for maintenance staff) hostel play ground, canteen, bank counter.
10.	Forensic science laboratory	A premise having facility for application of medical knowledge.	Forensic science laboratory and related facilities.

Table 13.25: Safety – Fire

S. No.	Use Premises	Definitions	Activities Permitted
1.	Fire post	Premises with lesser degree of facilities for fire fighting. The post may be attached to specific premises with fire prone activities.	Fire post with residential flat for staff.
2.	Fire station	A premise having facility for fire fighting for a catchment area assigned to it. It may include residence of essential staff.	Fire station, residential flat, service workshop.
3.	Fire station with essential residential accommodation	A premise having facility for fire fighting for a catchment area assigned to it. It includes residence of essential staff.	Fire station residential flat (for maintenance staff), hostel (for employees), service workshop.
4.	Fire Training Institute	A premise having facilities of training for emergency times in case of fire, building collapse etc.	Fire training centre, hostels, staff residences, open practice grounds, fire station, watch and ward residence (upto 20 sq m) etc.
5.	Disaster Management Centre	A premise having facility of disaster emergency backup, hospital facility, training centre for disaster preparedness, wireless communication etc.	Disaster management training centre, hospital, open grounds for practice and relief camps, communication centre, hostels, staff residences, fire station, watch and ward residence (upto 20 sq m) etc.

Table 13.26: Distributive Services

S. No.	Use Premises	Definitions	Activities Permitted
1.	Milk Booth/Milk and Fruit & Vegetable Booth/Delhi Milk Supply Booth	A premise with basic facility for the supply of daily groceries to the local population.	Booth/ built structure for display and sale of dairy products/ fruits and vegetables etc.
2.	Dairy Farm	A premise with facility for rearing and processing of dairy products. It may have temporary structures for sheds of animals.	Dairy farm, watch & ward residence (upto 20 sqm.) All structures shall be temporary in nature.
3.	Poultry Farm	A premise with facility for rearing and processing of poultry products. It may have temporary structures for sheds of birds.	Poultry farm, watch & ward residence (upto 20 sqm.) All structures shall be temporary in nature.
4.	Piggery	A premise with facility for rearing and processing of piggery products. It may have temporary structures for sheds of pigs.	Piggery shed, watch & ward residence (upto 20 sqm.). All structures shall be temporary in nature.
5.	LPG godown including booking office	A premise for the booking, storing and supply of LPG to local population.	Booking office, store/ godown, watch & ward residence (upto 20 sqm.).
6.	SKO/LDO outlets	A premise with facility of retail storage of SKO/LDO for supply to local population.	Booking office, store/ godown, watch & ward residence (upto 20 sqm.).
7.	Gas godown	A premise having the facility of wholesale storage of LPG, godown, etc.	Gas godown, watch & ward residence (upto 20 sqm.) Care taker office.

Table 13.27: Socio-Cultural and Community Facilities

S. No.	Use Premises	Definitions	Activities Permitted
1.	Multipurpose Community Hall, Barat ghar	A premise having an enclosed space for various social and cultural activities.	Community Hall, Watch & Ward Residence (upto 20 sqm.) Soft Drink and Snack Stall and library etc.
2.	Music Dance and Drama Training Centre	A premise having facilities for imparting training and coaching for music, dance and dramatics.	Music, dance and drama training centre, watch and ward residence (up to 20 sq m.), canteen, auditorium.
3.	Yoga Meditation, Spiritual and Religious Discourse Centre	A premise having facilities for self attainment, achieving higher quality of mind and body, spiritual and religious discourse etc.	Yoga centre, meditation, spiritual and religious discourse centre, watch and ward residence (up to 20 sq mt), hostel, soft drink and snack stall.
4.	Recreational Club	A premise having the facility for recreation with indoor sports, swimming pool, outdoor sports, socializing and gathering space for small functions with restaurant.	Recreational club, watch & ward residence (upto 20 sqm.) Residential Component upto 15% total floor area subject to maximum of 300 sqm., library, swimming pool, indoor and outdoor games facilities club.
5.	Banquet Hall	A premise to hold small public gatherings, community functions, marriages, etc.	Hall for public gatherings, marriages, cooking facilities and other logistics.
6.	Open air theater	A premise having facilities for audience seating and a stage for performance and open to sky.	Open Air theatre, Watch & Ward Residence (upto 20 sqm.) canteen.

7.	Auditorium	A premise having an enclosed space to seat audience and stage for various performances like concerts, play, recitals, functions etc.	Auditorium, Watch & Ward Residence (upto 20 sqm.) canteen.
8.	Museum	A premise with facilities for storage and exhibition of objects illustrating antiques, natural history, art etc.	Museum, Watch & Ward Residence (upto 20 sqm.) canteen.
9.	Exhibition-cum-Fair Ground	A premise having facilities for the exhibition and display and other cultural activities for a group of participants.	Fair Ground, Residential Flat (for maintenance staff) Exhibition Centre (Temporary in nature) Restaurant, Soft Drink & snack Stall, Police Post, Fire Post, bank Extension counter facility, Post Office counter facility.
10.	Museum, exhibition centre and art gallery, auditorium and open air theatre	Combination of Museum, exhibition centre and art gallery, auditorium and open air theatre.	Museum, Exhibition Centre and Art Gallery Auditorium and Open Air theatre, Watch & Ward Residence (upto 20 sqm.)
11.	Cultural and Information Centre	A premise with facility for cultural and information services for an institution, state, and country.	Cultural and Information Centre, Watch & Ward Residence (up to 20 sqm.) Hostel, Canteen, Bank Extension Counter Facility, Auditorium (Up to 500 seating capacity) Library, Exhibition and Art Gallery.
12.	Social and Cultural Institute	A premise with facilities for activities of socio-cultural nature run by a public, voluntary or individual on primarily non commercial basis.	Social and Cultural Institute, Watch & Ward Residence (upto 20 sqm.) Soft Drink & Snack Stall, Restaurant, Canteen, Bank Extension Counter Facility Auditorium, Library, Music, Dance, and Drama Training Centre, Museum, Exhibition Centre and Art Gallery.
13.	International Convention Centre	A premise having all facilities for international / national conferences, meetings, symposium. etc..	International Convention Centre, watch and ward residence (up to 20 sq mt), residential flat (for maintenance staff), restaurant, bank, post and telegraph office, library, exhibition centre.
14.	Planetarium	A premise having the facility of watching and observing the sky and universe and information dissemination.	Planetarium, watch & ward residence (upto 20 sqm.), cafeteria.
15.	Rain Basera (Night Shelter)	A premise having the facility for providing the night accommodation to individuals without any charges or with token charges. It may run by local government or voluntary agencies.	Night Shelter and related facilities.
16.	Anganwari	Anganwari as a space provision at residential housing / neighbourhood level is a centre to provide service for children of 0 to 6 years age, pregnant women, feeding mothers, etc. under the Integrated Child Development Scheme (ICDS).	Kitchen, Toilet & Hall.
17.	Dharamshala and its equivalent	A premise providing temporary accommodation for short duration on no profit basis.	Dharmshala, personnel service shops of barber and launderer, soft drinks and snack bar (upto 20 sq m).

18.	Adult Education Centre	A premise having the facility of formal education and training to adults with flexible timings.	Flexible use given to a primary school, community centre or any such community building.
19.	Reformatory	A premise with facilities for behavioural reforms.	Reformatory and Orphanage, Residential Flat (For maintenance staff), Hostel, Personnel Service shop (upto 20 sqm.).
20.	Orphanage	A premise having the facility of boarding of children who are bereaved of parents. It may or may not have educational facilities.	Hostels, residence (for management and maintenance staff), primary school, watch and ward residence (upto 20 sq m).
21.	Reformatory and Orphanage	A premise with facilities for confinement and behavioural reform, boarding of children who are bereaved of parents. It may or may not have educational facilities.	Reformatory and Orphanage, Residential Flat (For maintenance staff), Hostel, Personnel Service shop (upto 20 sqm.).
22.	Old Age Home/Care Centre for Physically / Mentally challenged / Working women/ Men Hostel	A premise having the facility of caring and training boarding & lodging of the elderly / physically / mentally challenged / working women / men.	Care home with residential facility, residence (for management and maintenance staff), primary school, recreational, library, health, gym, canteen, dining facility.
23.	Religious Premises/Building	A premise dedicated to the service of the objects of religious nature. It may have different nomenclature in different religions / faiths.	Temple, Mosque, Church, Gurdwara, Synagogue, Ashram, Bathing Ghat, Gaushala, Dargah, Charitable Dispensary, Library.
24.	Dhobi Ghat/ Machine Laundry - public utility premises	A premise used for cleaning and drying of clothes and linen.	Overhead tank, Underground Tank, Oxidation Pond, Septic Tank Sewerage Pumping station, Public Toilet & Urinal, Electric Sub-station, Dhallao and Dustbin, Dhobi Ghat, Machine Laundry.

Table 13.28: Cremation / Burial Ground and Cemetery

S. No.	Use Premises	Definitions	Activities Permitted
1.	Burial ground	A premise with facilities for burying of dead bodies.	Burial Ground, Cremation Ground Cemetery and Crematorium, retail shops of Wood, flowers and related materials, Watch & Ward Residence (upto 20 sqm.).
2.	Cremation ground	A premise with facilities of performing last rites of dead bodies by burning.	
3.	Cemetery	A premise with facilities for burying of dead bodies.	Facility for registration of deaths, sheds for performing rituals, drinking water, parking, etc.
4.	Crematorium	A premise with facilities for last rites of the deceased.	

14.0 PHYSICAL INFRASTRUCTURE

A key issue related to the sustainable development of Delhi, and a minimum quality and standard of living pertains to the availability of, and accessibility to basic infrastructure facilities viz. water, power, sewerage, drainage and solid waste management. The rapid and almost uncontrolled growth of population has put these facilities under severe pressure, and there are significant deficiencies. Even a cursory analysis of the present state of affairs, infrastructure problems could become a cause of crisis. Sewerage and solid waste management are GNCTD affairs but water supply, power and drainage are Inter-State issues. Thus critical need of advance action and arrangement is required for the adequate provision of physical infrastructure. For each component a broad augmentation plan is essential to meet the projected requirement. GNCTD should prepare a detailed and integrated plan in coordination with concerned authorities, NGOs and community groups.

The Master Plan envisages an integrated approach that packages mutually supportive infrastructure components i.e. water-sewerage-drainage for recycling, harvesting and optimal use of water; solid waste-sewerage-power for power generation, etc. Innovative techniques for the use of alternative technologies like solar energy, recycling, etc., are also to be encouraged. The Plan accepts the need for institutional capacity building, "User Pays" approach and public private partnership as tools for institutional strengthening. To improve the efficiency and to boost the performance, more community participation and decentralised management is required. Technical feasibility of rehabilitation/ augmentation network of sewerage, water supply and drainage is required on priority for old built up areas and the areas identified for redevelopment.

14.1 PROJECTED REQUIREMENTS FOR THE YEAR 2021

The existing availability and projected requirement for physical infrastructure components as indicated by the agencies concerned are given in the Annexure I to IV.

14.2 WATER

Delhi depends largely on river Yamuna and partially on river Ganga for its share of raw water. For sustainable development of Delhi, it is essential to ensure adequate supply of water in terms of reliability, quality and quantity. Although, Delhi has an average water availability of 225 lpcd, the distribution of the same is not uniform. Some areas get 24 hrs water supply, whereas some get hardly 1-2 hr water in a day. In line with the norms laid down in CPHEEO Manual 1999, in respect of mega cities, after taking into account 15% losses, the minimum water supply @ 172 lpcd will have to be ensured for domestic use for the projected population. The water requirement has to be made from river water allocation and ranney wells in Yamuna flood plains. The future supply crucially depends on the progress of the proposed dams in U.P, Uttranchal and H.P; Satluj Yamuna link canal and Sharda Yamuna link canal. Further it will also depend upon the conveyance system, which should be in place before the release of allocated water to Delhi. However to some extent localised ground water extraction and its supply after treatment to prescribed level of quality may also be required to meet up the demands. In addition, promotion of recycled wastewater based on techno economic feasibility is also to be done by the concerned agencies for water augmentation.

To improve the water supply in accordance with the projected requirement upto the year 2021 Inter-State river water allocation is required to be worked out. All measures are to be taken to reduce unaccounted flow of water (UFW) and production losses at existing water treatment plants. The drainage basins shall be made self-sustainable in water management by integrating water-sewerage-drainage systems. It is imperative to not only initiate new projects and upgrade present infrastructure, but also to promote water conservation through an integrated and a community driven model, comprising of complimentary short term and long term measures as given below:

1. Towns/cities have so far been planned by their respective authorities for their individual needs. There has been total lack of regional approach for sustainable use of available water and its conveyance from areas of plenty to scarcity. The raw water augmentation should not be territory specific but it should be on regional basis irrespective of State boundaries.

2. Recycling of treated wastewater with separate lines for potable water and recycled water. For this, dual pipeline system has to be introduced in a phased manner in all the areas.

3. Ground water recharging through rain water harvesting, conserving water bodies and controlling groundwater extraction:

i) Groundwater extraction is to be controlled through registering boreholes and recharging according to test yields. Ground water management is to be enforced by concerned agency.

ii) Focused planning and action will be required to be taken to prepare and implement rain water as roof water harvesting schemes both with the aim of optimizing water use and ground water recharge. For this suitable mandatory provision should be made for planning and construction of various schemes.

iii) Blue print is required to be prepared for Integrated Water Management of all the water resources in the NCR as well as potential for water reservoirs in Himachal Pradesh and Uttaranchal. Further it is vital to identify all the potential surface water sources, ground water aquifers and inter-basin opportunities for transfer of water to the region. This should include water mapping, desilting of existing lakes/depressions for augmentation of storage of rain/flood water, capturing the monsoon run off, rain water harvesting, reuse and recycling of waste water and measures for conservation of water, inter-basin transfer of water. It should also ensure the conservation of natural depressions, water bodies, flood plains and aquifers. Major water bodies can be developed as places of tourist interest/picnic spots to make them sources of revenue as well as to ensure their protection. The concepts of 'zero run-off drainage', with retention ponds, sediments traps and balancing lakes should be adopted, with a segregated wastewater disposal system. A green network overlapping the blue network would protect the ecology of aquifers, and also provide a pleasant environment. Simple methods of site planning, which incorporate porous/semi permeable paving, drop inlet/down pipe, sediment trap, retention ponds, etc. will contribute in maintaining ground water table.

iv) Yamuna River, major drains and canals, with indiscriminate dumping of wastes, have become polluted and foul. These need strict pollution control measures and eco-sensitive land use controls. Water flow needs to be controlled and stabilized and marked at each kilometer station. The valleys should be zoned as water portals, so that these are flanked with greenery, farmlands and forests.

v) One of the prime objectives of development should be to live in harmony with the environment. Efforts should be made to improve the quality of river-water, to secure its continuous flow and to encourage the return of aquatic life. This needs improvement of drainage, waste water treatment and pollution abatement by sewerage improvement. The surplus water during the monsoons should be retained in balancing ponds along the riverbed rather than allowing it to the downstream areas.

vi) The drains and waterfront can be landscaped in the form of interconnected parkways. There is no need for elaborate gardening of the greenways, but wild, simple and natural stretch by itself would be ecologically important. Such trails could be one of the cheapest forms of drainage and recreation.

vii) Water supply in new areas should incorporate separate lines - one for washing, water coolers and garden taps, the second for supplying potable water. All non-residential buildings having a discharge of over 10,000 litres a day should incorporate a wastewater recycling. The capacity of the sewage treatment plants / recycling plants would be equal to or more than the water inflow requirements so that it may be possible to treat major part of the discharge excepting toilets and kitchen discharge. Keeping in view the uses of recycled water, a policy shall be formulated for determining the optimum water requirements for various uses.

viii) The wasteful practice of 'drill, pump, and spill' has to be replaced by efficient methods of water conservation, use, and recycling as standard and mandatory procedures. There is a need to incorporate the mandatory stipulation of water saving/waterless flushing system in the Building Bye-laws.

ix) At the time of preparation of zonal Development Plans, water bodies, large depressions and other ground water recharging areas will be identified and protected from unintentional filling and encroachments.

At the time of preparation of Zonal Development Plans, appropriate areas should be identified and earmarked for utilities pertaining to Power (Power Plants and Substations), Water (Sewage Treatment Plants and Sewage Pumping Stations) and Solid Waste management (Solid Waste Treatment Plants and Sanitary landfill sites). Appropriate land should accordingly be earmarked for solid waste management keeping in view a long term perspective.

4. Where the hazard of pollution exists, the minimum charge for operating permits should cover the expenses of adequate policing and controls. Mandatory performance bonds and liability insurance should pay for all damages plus any corrective measures, which might be needed. As a governing rule, no new development, manufacturing, process or operation of any polluting activity should be permitted, which may result in the significant degradation of any water resource.

5. About half of the water that is treated and distributed at public expense is non-revenue water. This is due to unrecorded usage or illegal taps and water connections. Reducing water losses is cheaper than augmenting water capacity for such losses.

To provide additional supply of water, augmentation of existing water treatment plants is proposed as given in Table 14.1. The actual provision of water treatment plants should be monitored depending on availability of raw water and need of potable water.

Corresponding requirement of land shall be kept in view.

Table 14.1. Water Augmentation Plan

S.No	Water Treatment Plants	Capacity 2001 (in mgd)	Capacity* 2021 (in mgd)
1.	Chandrawal I & II	90	100
2.	Wazirabad	120	130
3.	Haiderpur I & II	200	216
4.	Bhagirathi	100	110
5.	Dwarka	-	40
6.	Sonia Vihar	-	140
7.	Nangloi	40	40
8.	Bawana	-	20
9.	Okhla	-	20
10.	Ranney wells at Okhla	100	12
11.	Palla and other ground water sources	-	91
	Total	650	919

* Capacity 2021 is as proposed by DJB.

In addition, new water treatment plants may be identified for potable water requirement.

14.3 SEWERAGE

Sewerage is the core element of physical infrastructure that determines the environmental status of any city and requires minute planning, development and management. Development of appropriate sewerage system with efficient sewage treatment is vital to facilitate balanced and harmonized development. Augmentation of existing inadequate systems / treatment facilities as well as adoption of new technologies of waste treatment demands special efforts. Further, it is pertinent to point-out that the existing capacity of sewerage system in Delhi is grossly inadequate, as only about 55% of the population is covered under organised sewerage system and about 15% under on-site sanitation systems. Rest of the population does not have proper access to sanitation facilities. The sewage treatment facility is also inadequate. The increasing pollution in the river Yamuna is a major indicator of lack of sewage treatment facilities.

By the year 2021 entire Delhi should be served by regular sewerage system. It should be developed in a phased manner. The areas where immediate regular sewerage system is not available, low cost sanitation system by individual families could be adopted as a short-range provision. These should be planned in such a way that in the long term regular sewerage could be provided. To improve the sewerage and sanitation, the surface drainage and sewerage systems would have to be developed in an integrated manner.

Planning of the city must incorporate land at appropriate locations for sewage treatment plants (STPs), sewage pumping stations, recycling plants for waste water, sewage treatment plants, common effluent treatment plants (CETPs) with supportive distributive infrastructure i.e. conveyance system to be laid to carry treated wastewater from STPs to the areas for alternative uses. Decentralised STPs with smaller capacities are to be provided at the community / subcity level. Possibility of recovering energy/ gas as fuel from sewage shall be explored.

The liquid waste would be taken care of by augmenting the capacity of existing treatment plants as well as through new sewerage treatment plants. The sewerage system is designed to handle domestic liquid waste @ 80 % of the water supply, which has to cater to 1100 mgd (4950 mld) of waste water by the year 2021. The wastewater is also generated due to the use of ground water drawn from the boreholes installed by the public. The needed capacity has to be monitored with provision of water recycling infrastructure and mini/decentralised treatments. The treated sewage effluent should be recycled for non-potable uses like gardening, cooling towers, etc. The sewerage augmentation plan is given in Table 14.2.

Table 14. 2: Sewerage Augmentation Plan

S. No.	Treatment Plant	Capacity 2001 (in mgd)	Capacity* 2021 (in mgd)
1.	Okhla	140	170
2.	Keshav Pur	72	72
3.	Nilothi	40	70
4.	Coronation pillar	40	50
5.	Rithala	80	110
6.	Kondli	45	90
7.	Others		
a)	Sen Nursing Home Nalla STP	2.2	2.2
b)	Delhi Gate Nalla STP	2.2	17
c)	Yamuna Vihar	20	45
d)	Timarpur	6	6
e)	Mehrauli	5	5
8.	New plants in North Delhi		
a)	Narela / Alipur	10	50
b)	Rohini	15	55
9.	New plants in West Delhi		
a)	Dwarka/Pappankalan	20	40
b)	Najafgarh	5	5
10.	New plants in South Delhi		
a)	Vasant Kunj	5	5
b)	Ghitorni	5	5
c)	Badarpur		8
	Total	**512.4**	**805.2**

* Total sewerage treatment capacity based on 80% of water supply of 2011. Capacity 2021 is as proposed by DJB.

In addition, new sewerage treatment plants may be identified as per requirement.

14.4 DRAINAGE

Drainage has two aspects: flood protection and storm water discharge, which are interrelated. The storm water and flood protection in Delhi are not local but have regional bearing including areas of Haryana and Rajasthan. The main drainage system of Delhi is such that all water,collected through main drains, link drains and small rivulets is discharged into Yamuna. On the basis of topographical characteristics and existing drainage network, NCT of Delhi has been divided into five drainage basins namely Najafgarh, Alipur, Shahdara, Khushak nallah and Mehrauli. The blockage of natural channel is a matter of concern. It is mainly because of the encroachment by slum dwellers along the drains which causes choking of drains and flooding in the upstream areas due to reduced carrying capacity. The other major reason is dumping of solid waste in the drains causing blockage. The blockage of natural depressions and drainage channels must be prohibited.

To improve the drainage system of Delhi, effluent treatment plants should be provided at outfall of drains and aeration units at interceptions with advanced techniques for maintenance of drains. A time bound action program for augmentation and capacity revision of existing and new drains (due to increase in run off from urban extensions) is also vital. Check dams and depression/ lakes may be designed for increasing ground water table and as storm water holding points wherever needed. The design shall preserve the natural drainage pattern after the development of an area.

Drainage should be linked with the ecology and green networks, by adopting the concept of "bio-drainage".

Regular desilting of drains and control of dumping of solid waste / malba into the drains should be taken up. Public awareness program need to be taken up in association with NGOs and RWAs to make the people aware about the consequences of dumping malba in the drains.

Other measures essential for proper drainage are the following:

1) Drainage to be integral part of Road Development Plans / flyover / Grade Separators.

2) A proper database should be prepared and GIS based drainage mapping and planning should be promoted.

3) Sub-wells need to be developed under flyovers for trapping rainwater.

4) Pump houses in low-lying areas should be provided with back-up power.

5) Remodelling of selected drains may also be required considering the upstream flow in the region.

14.5 POWER

The present total availability of power is 3170 MW. The existing power generation stations within Delhi and their capacity are given:

Table 14.3: Existing Power generation Stations in Delhi

Station	Installed Capacity (MW)	Present Generation (Max) (MW)
Rajghat Power Station	135	105
IP Power Station	247.5	160
GT Power Station	282	210
Pragati Power Station	330	330
Badarpur Thermal Power Station	705	630
Total	1699.5	1435

Source: GNCT-Delhi

Based on the 17th Electricity Power Survey of India, Central Electricity Authority (CEA), requirement of power for Delhi in the year 2021, as tentatively estimated by the Delhi Transco Ltd. is 11000 MW. To meet the additional requirement of 7830 MW, the concerned agencies need to augment the power supply and improve the transmission and distribution system. The additional power requirement would be met from allocated share from the grid system and local generation for which required land component will be identified. Further, land for transmission network and grid stations will be identified in the Zonal Development Plans / Urban Extension Plans as per requirement. A 400 KV ring has been established around Delhi to draw power from northern regional grid.

A detailed Sectoral Plan for power development in NCT-Delhi may be prepared by the concerned agencies in consultation with DDA within one year after the approval of the MPD-2021.

Table 14.4: Proposed Power Plants

In NCTD

1.	Pragati-II	330.0
2.	Pragati-III	1000.0
3.	I.P.	700.0
4.	Total	2030

Outside NCTD

Location	Generation	For Delhi	Year of Commissioning
Jhajjar (Haryana)	1500 MW	750 MW	2010
DVC (West Bengal)	2600 MW	2600 MW	2007-11

THDC (Uttranchal)	1000MW	600 MW	2010
TOTAL		3950 MW	2011

The remaining power requirements are proposed to be met from the power projects proposed to be taken up during the 11th Plan period. The Government of NCT of Delhi should enter into power purchase agreements with power generating companies for effectively meeting Delhi's power demand within a perspective plan framework.

Following critical areas need to be attended for energy efficiency:

i) The concept of energy efficiency should begin with the idea of Zero-fossil Energy Development (ZED) which envisages an urban form and design of passive building envelope that reduce the demand for power to the point where it becomes economically viable to use energy from renewable resources. This involves a holistic approach combining the issues and actions at various levels of planning, design, construction and maintenance leading to a sustainable and energy efficient regime. The city geometry, restructuring and zoning with self-contained neighbourhoods could minimise the need to travel and substantial saving of recurring energy/ fuel consumption. Integrated mass transport system, traffic and transit operation and management; better tele-communications, promoting bicycles and NMV transport, is another major area of energy efficient habitat. The introduction of energy audit and design of energy efficient buildings by site planning, heights, form, construction and materials and reducing energy demand by passive micro-climatic design approach, intelligent energy controls, heat recovery, landscape, opening design, furnishings, etc., are the critical considerations. The key to future is a cybernetic form of sustainable energy, which integrates symbosis, recycling and energy chains.

ii) Load management techniques and energy accounting should be adopted. Schemes to minimise power thefts/ losses by improved metering arrangements should be enforced.

iii) Non-conventional energy sources like recovering energy from sewerage, solar energy, etc. should be used for street lighting, lighting at public spaces, open areas, traffic signals, hoardings, etc.

iv) To supplement part of the estimated growing power requirement, non-conventional sources / solar energy and other actions proposed are as follows:

1. Solar energy should be encouraged for all establishments with floor area of more than 300 sqm.
2. Solar Panels for public advertising, lighting in open areas, public utilities, streets, etc.
3. As alternate mandatory arrangement during power cuts to replace generators/inverters etc.
4. Adoption of Load Management Technique.
5. Tariff restructuring and improved metering arrangement to minimize power thefts/losses.
6. Interim solutions of single point connection in unauthorized colonies and jhuggies.
7. Private Sector Participation in different stages of Power generation, transmission and distribution.
8. Incentivising energy savings and use of energy efficient gadgets.
9. Public awareness, capacity building and training.

v) As per Asian Development Bank's report (1997) potential in saving due to better overall efficiency in domestic sector is about 20% by adopting following measures:

a) Replacement of low efficiency incandescent lamp with high efficiency fluorescent tubes (CFLs) without compromising with the lumens output.

b) Similarly for refrigerators, which account for 30% of total electricity consumed, measures like increased thickness of foam insulation, use of high coefficient compressors increased evaporator surfaces, use of tighter door seals and through technical improvements can reduce consumption from 510 KWH/year to 300 KWH/year (for a 165 litre refrigerator).

c) Incandescent bulbs, neon tubes and fluorescent lamps are giving way to light-emitting microchips that work longer, use less power and allow the use of light in new ways. The chips, known as light emitting diodes, or LEDs have huge performance advantages in many mundane tasks (such as traffic lights). These consume 80 per cent less electricity than the bulbs and have longer life. Moreover, they have the safety advantage of gradually fading instead of burning out. This eventually results in huge savings in terms of energy and maintenance costs.

14.6 SOLID WASTE

The problem of solid waste management in Delhi is assuming serious proportions due to increasing population, urbanisation, changing lifestyles and consumption patterns. The garbage from unauthorised developments, slums, JJ settlements, etc is not collected which further adds to the environmental degradation. The projected average garbage generation upto the year 2021 is @ 0.68 kg per capita per day and total quantum of solid waste is 15750 tons/day as given in Table 14.5.

Table 14.5: Quantum of Municipal Solid Waste (Tons/Day)

Local body area	Existing capacity 2001	Projected generation for 2021
MCD	5250	15100
NDMC	245	550
Cantonment	48	100
Total	5543	15750

Management of solid waste involves waste generation, segregation and storage; waste collection; waste transfer/ transportation; treatment, recycle, reuse, recovery; and disposal. For effective waste management, its segregation at the community and neighbourhood level is imperative. The waste shall be segregated and collected, in separate chambers at dalaos. For this, involvement of rag pickers with RWAs, CBOs and NGOs is to be encouraged.

The projected composition of municipal waste for the Plan period is estimated as given in Table 14.6. For biodegradable and recyclable waste, which is segregated at the source, decentralised treatment at neighbourhood level may be adopted, while for non-biodegradable, centralised treatment may be followed.

Table 14.6: Projected Composition of Total Municipal Solid Waste for 2021

Constituents	Quantum (in tones)	Percentage to total waste
Bio-degradable	6000	38
Non Bio-degradable	6000	38
Recyclable	3750	24
Total	15750	100

Notes:

(i) Above figures are based on Report on Solid Waste Management in Delhi conducted by NEERI, Nagpur through DDA;

(ii) Figures of MCD are based on 'Feasibility study in Master Plan for Optimal Waste Treatment & Disposal for the entire State of Delhi' June, 2004 by COWI Consultants appointed by MCD.

The other type of specialised waste includes biomedical waste; hazardous waste from industries; construction debris and fly ash; meat processing centre etc. Disposal of bio-medial waste is to be as per bio-medical waste rules and hazardous waste requires special handling according to hazardous waste handling rules. Proper dumping, recycling and reuse of construction debris and fly ash have to be linked. Meat processing centre waste is to be recycled for chicken feed etc.

Considering the nature of solid waste and the economic aspects of its disposal, major part of solid waste especially non bio-degradable has to be disposed off in sanitary landfills. Recycling should be preferred than disposing off the waste in sanitary landfill sites' wherever possible. The segregation of solid waste should start at the point of generation of the waste. It should be collected in two separate bags of green and black colour. The involvement of RWAs and Rag pickers association will reduce the quantum of waste drastically. And it will also result in the reduction of area required for landfill sites.

Further, some more viable alternatives to landfills are vermiculture, fossilisation, composting etc. Waste Minimisation Circles (WMCs) should be constituted and made effective. Implementation and monitoring & Bio-Medical Wastes (Handling & Management) Rules, 1998, for hospitals, nursing homes, and clinics should be taken up. The sites, which are filled up or are in operation, are given in Table 14.7. The filled up sites may be reused for plantation or as recreational area. The proposed sites for sanitary landfill and compost plants are to be finalised by the MCD.

Table 14.7: Existing Landfill sites for Waste Management

S.No.	Location	Area (in ha.)	Remarks
1.	Kailash Nagar, East Delhi	1.8	Filled up
2.	Tilak Nagar, West Delhi	16.0	Filled up
3.	Subroto Park	-	Filled up
4.	Purana Qila/Bharion Road	2.7	Filled up
5.	Timarpur	16.0	Filled up
6.	Sarai Kale Khan	24.0	Filled up
7.	Gopal pur	4.0	Filled up
8.	Chhaterpur	1.7	Filled up
9.	S.G.T. Nagar	14.4	Filled up
10.	I.P. Deoit	1.8	Filled up
11.	Sunder Nagar	2.8	Filled up
12.	Tuglakabad Extension	2.4	Filled up
13.	Haider Pur	1.6	Filled up
14.	Mandawali Fazilpur	2.8	Filled up
15.	Rohini Phase III	4.8	Filled up
16.	Near Hastal Village in West Delhi	9.6	Filled up
17.	Site near Ghazipur Dairy Farm	28.0	In operation
18.	Site near Jhangipur / Bhalswa	16.0	In operation
19.	Okhla Phase I	12.8	In operation
20.	Crossing on G.T. Karnal Road	3.2	In operation
21.	Jaitpur / Tajpur	9.84	New
22.	Near Puthkhurd	55.0	New
23.	Bawana to Narela Road	28.0	New
24.	Sultanpur Dabas (Bawana)	16.0	New

Appropriate land should be earmarked for solid waste management keeping in view a long-term perspective.

The area required for solid waste disposal through various technologies including sanitary landfill sites shall be reserved in the Zonal Plans. This shall also include buffer zone of 'no development' around landfill sites. Keeping in view the fact that finding new sanitary landfill sites in Delhi is becoming extremely difficult, there is no option, but to resort to alternative and decentralised methods of waste treatment, reduction, recycle and use, which include vermiculture, fossilisation and composting. Pilot projects in this regard have been taken up by the MCD with the consultants.

15. MIXED USE REGLATIONS

The policy acknowledges the need for permitting use of land for purposes other than that for which it was originally envisaged and lays down the conditions under which this may be applied in different situations. The general procedure to be followed for implementation of the said policy, and mitigating measures to be taken to counter the effect of such non-intended use in such area also described.

15.1 GOVERNING PRINCIPLES FOR MIXED USE

i. Mixed use means the provision for non-residential activity in residential premises.

ii. The policy aims to balance the socio-economic need for such activity and the environmental impact of the said activity in residential areas.

iii. Mixed use allows access to commercial activities in the proximity of the residences and reduces the need for commuting across zones in the city. However, at the same time, it needs to be regulated in order to manage and mitigate the associated adverse impact related to congestion, increased traffic and increased pressure on civic amenities.

iv. The over-riding principles for permitting mixed use are the need to acknowledge and make adequate pr·vision for meeting community needs, mitigating environmental impact and providing for safe and convenient circulation and parking.

v. Mixed-use, (including small shops as per para 15.6.3.) shall not be permitted in the Lutyens' Bungalow Zone, Civil Lines bungalow zone. government housing, institutional/ staff housing of public and private agencies and buildings/ precincts listed by the Heritage Conservation Committee.

15.2 MIXED USE IN RESIDENTIAL AREAS

15.2.1. DIFFERENTIATED APPROACH

i) The need for differentiated approach to mixed use policy arises from the fact that Delhi, being the country's capital and an important centre of economic activity has a large diversity in the typology of residential areas. Apart from the planned residential colonies built as part of Lutyens' Delhi as well as through the process of planned development undertaken by the Delhi Development Authority, there are authorized residential areas in the Walled City, Special areas and urban villages. Other planned areas include resettlement colonies and pre-Delhi Development Act colonies, including post-partition rehabilitation colonies and pre-1962 residential colonies as per list given in Annexure I. There are also regularized-unauthorized colonies; unauthorized colonies as well as slums and jhuggi jhompri clusters in various parts of Delhi.

ii) Moreover, the extent of non-residential activity seen as being necessary or desirable by the residents themselves varies from area to area based on the socio-economic status of the residents as well as the past pattern of development in that area. While certain colonies may need non-residential activity as an integral part of their livelihood, some others may wish to preserve the residential character of their colonies and neighborhood.

iii) Hence, it is proposed to follow a differentiated approach in the application of the mixed-use policy in Delhi. The differentiated approach would be based on categorization of colonies from A to G as adopted by MCD for unit area method of property tax assessment as applicable on 7.9.2006. Any change in the categorization of these colonies shall not be made applicable for the purpose of this chapter without prior approval of Central Government.

15.2.2 TYPES OF MIXED USE

Subject to the provisions of this chapter, the following three broad types of mixed use shall be permissible, in residential premises:

i) Commercial activity in the form of retail shops as per conditions given in para 15.6 in plots abutting notified mixed use streets.

ii) "Other activity" broadly in the nature of 'Public and Semi-Public' facilities listed in para 15.7.1 and as per conditions specified in para 15.7, in plots abutting roads of minimum ROW prescribed in para 15.3.2.

iii) Professional activity as per conditions specified in para 15.8.

The above mentioned types of mixed use shall be subject to the general terms and conditions specified in the succeeding paragraphs.

15.3 IDENTIFICATION OF MIXED USE AREAS IN EXISTING URBAN AREAS AND URBANIZABLE AREAS

The identification of mixed use areas/ streets in both the urbanized / urban as well as urbanizable areas of Delhi would be as follows:

15.3.1. In already urbanized / urban areas, mixed use shall be permissible in the following areas:

i. On all streets/ stretches already notified by the competent authority.

ii. Residential areas and streets/ stretches earlier declared as commercial areas/ streets or where commercial use was allowed in MPD-1962 shall continue such use at least to the extent as permissible in MPD-1962.

iii. Commercial activity existing from prior to 1962 in residential areas, subject to documentary proof thereof.

iv. Identification and notification of mixed use streets in future shall be based on the criteria given in para 15.3.2 and as per procedure prescribed in para 15.3.3, and given wide publicity by the local bodies concerned.

v. Plotted development in pre-1962 colonies listed in Annexure I shall be treated as rehabilitation colonies in their respective categories (A to G) for the purpose of this Chapter.

15.3.2 The extent of mixed use permissible in various categories of colonies is further clarified as follows:

1. In colonies falling in categories A and B

No commercial activities will be permissible in the colonies of A & B categories except the following:

- Professional activity, subject to conditions given in para 15.8, mixed use and commercial activity up to one plot depth, in plots abutting Master Plan roads that are notified as mixed use streets, and commercial streets respectively, since such roads are not internal to the colonies (provided that the request of the RWA concerned shall not be necessary for notifying the Master Plan roads abutting the colonies, as mixed use streets on commercial streets).
- "Other activity" restricted to guest houses, nursing homes and pre-primary schools, as defined in para 15.7.1, subject to conditions contained in para 15.7, in plots abutting roads of minimum 18m ROW in regular plotted development, since these activities are in the nature of 'Public and Semi-Public' facilities. New Banks and Fitness Centres will not be permissible. Banks and Fitness Centres, which already exist, in accordance with notifications issued in this regard from time to time, and are on plots abutting roads of minimum 18m ROW, on the date of notification, shall, however, continue.
- Retail shops in terms of para 15.6 on such mixed use streets with a minimum 18m ROW, within the colony, in regular residential plotted development, as are notified in terms of para 15.3.3, if there is a specific request of the RWA concerned, in terms of para 15.10.

Note:

Commercial activity on mixed use streets, within A & B category colonies, earlier notified under MPD-2001 shall cease with immediate effect (other than in plots abutting Master Plan roads).

2. In colonies falling in categories C & D

- Mixed use in the form of Retail shops shall continue to be permissible as per conditions in para 15.6, in plots abutting notified mixed use streets.
- "Other activity" in terms of para 15.7 shall be permissible in plots abutting roads of minimum 18m ROW in regular plotted development, 13.5m ROW in rehabilitation colonies and 9m ROW in Walled City, regularized -unauthorized colonies, resettlement colonies, Special Areas, and urban villages, subject to conditions in para 15.7.
- Notification of mixed use streets in future, of minimum 18 m ROW in regular residential plotted development, 9 m ROW in rehabilitation colonies and any road in regularized- unauthorized colonies, resettlement colonies, Walled City, Special Area and urban villages in terms of para 15.3.3 shall be subject to consultation with RWAs concerned in terms of para 15.10.
- Mixed use shall be permissible in pedestrianized shopping streets as per para 15.3.3.
- Professional activities shall be permissible as per conditions laid down in para 15.8.

3. In colonies falling in categories E, F and G

- Retail shops shall continue to be permissible as per conditions in para 15.6., in plots abutting notified mixed use streets.
- "Other activity" in terms of para 15.7 shall continue to be permissible in plots abutting roads of minimum 13.5m ROW in regular plotted development, 9m ROW in rehabilitation colonies and any road in Walled City, regularized-unauthorized colonies, resettlement colonies, Special areas, and urban villages subject to conditions in para 15.7.
- Professional activities shall be permissible subject to conditions in para 15.8.
- Notification of mixed use streets in future, of minimum 13.5m ROW in regular residential plotted development, 9m ROW in rehabilitation colonies and any road in regularized-unauthorized colonies, resettlement colonies, Walled City, Special Area and urban villages shall be in terms of para 15.3.3

- Mixed use shall be permissible in pedestrianised shopping streets as per para 15.3.3.

4. Group housing in all categories of colonies

- Only professional activity, and small shops in terms of para 15.6.3 shall be permissible. Retail shops specifically provided for in the lay out plan of group housing would be permissible.

5. In respect of colonies falling in NDMC area

Excluding Lutyens' Bungalow Zone, government housing, institutional and staff housing of public and private agencies and buildings/ precincts listed by the Heritage Conservation Committee, existing mixed use streets/ stretches will be notified by NDMC. Future notification of mixed use streets/ stretches will be done on a field level survey to assess the community needs, environmental impact and traffic circulation/ adequate parking and in consultation with Residents Welfare Associations concerned.

15.3.3 NOTIFICATION OF MIXED USE STREETS IN URBAN AREAS

i) Where more than 50% of the plots in a stretch/ street, are having shops on ground floor, such streets/ stretches shall be eligible for notification as mixed use street.

ii) The minimum ROW for identification of a street or stretch of road as mixed use street would be follows*:

In A &B Colonies:	18m ROW in regular plotted development on the specific request of RWAs.
In C & D colonies:	18 m ROW in regular residential plotted development, 9 m ROW in rehabilitation colonies and any road in regularized-unauthorized colonies, resettlement colonies, Walled City, Special area and urban villages; in consultation with RWA concerned.
In E,F & G Colonies:	13.5m ROW in regular plotted development, 9m ROW in rehabilitation colonies and any road in Walled City, regularized-unauthorized colonies, resettlement colonies, Special Areas, and urban villages.

* Provided that consistency shall be maintained by the local body in determining the ROW whether the street is bordered by service road, green verge, park or not.

iii) Streets of less than 6 m ROW notified as mixed use streets or as commercial streets, in regularised-unauthorised colonies, resettlement colonies, Special Area, urban villages, will be declared as pedestrian shopping streets (PSS) and will not be open to motorized transport.

Note:

(a) Request of the RWA concerned or consultation with RWAs concerned, shall not be necessary for notifying the Master Plan roads abutting the colonies as mixed use streets, since such roads are not internal to the colonies.

(b) Specific request of or consultation with RWA concerned shall be governed by Para 15.10.

iv) For the notification of mixed use streets, in areas that have not been surveyed or have been surveyed but streets have not been notified pursuant to notification dated 7.9.2006, local bodies shall be required to carry out within a reasonable time of the notification coming into force, and with due expedition, and not later than 90 days, a survey of all streets of the above-mentioned width, if not already done, with a view to identifying stretches of such streets as mixed use streets.

v) The field survey shall assess the extent of existing non-residential use on the streets, the stretch of the street to be notified, the additional requirement of civic amenities and the provision for traffic circulation and parking.

vi) The notification shall be issued by the Urban Development Department, GNCTD immediately after the field survey is completed.

15.3.4 NOTIFICATION OF MIXED USE STREETS IN URBANISABLE AREAS IN FUTURE

In new urbanisable areas, mixed use shall be permissible in the following areas:

i) In newly developed residential areas, mixed use as specified above shall be permitted only on residential plots abutting 18m. ROW roads.

ii) The layout plan in newly developed urban extension shall earmark such stretches/ plots and notify them under the mixed use policy at the time of grant of permission for layout plan in the case of private development and at the time of disposal by allotment or auction in the case of areas developed by DDA.

iii) In the Abadi area of villages in urbanisable area, mixed use shall be permissible as per the provisions of urban villages and for this purpose, local bodies shall be required to carry out within a reasonable time of the notification coming into force, and with due expedition, and not later than 90 days, a survey of all streets of the above-mentioned width, if not already done, with a view to identifying stretches of such streets as mixed use streets

15.4 GENERAL TERMS AND CONDITIONS GOVERNING MIXED USE

In terms of the conditions prescribed for different categories of colonies, in para 15.3.2, and provided that the plot abuts a notified mixed use street (in the case of retail shops) or a road of prescribed minimum ROW (in the case of other mixed use activities), mixed use shall be permitted, subject to the following general terms and conditions:

In residential plotted development

(i) Where there is only one dwelling unit in a residential plot, only one type of mixed use (i.e. retail shop as per para 15.6 or professional activity or one of the other activities listed in para 15.7) shall be permissible in that unit.

(ii) Where there are more than one dwelling units in a residential plot, each of the dwelling units will be permitted to have only type of mixed use activity (either retail shop as per para 15.6. or professional activity or any one of the other activities listed in para 15.7).

In group housing

Only professional activity and small shops in terms of para 15.6.3 shall be permissible. Retail shops specifically provided for in the lay out plan of group housing would be permissible.

Other terms and conditions

(i) No encroachment shall be permitted on the streets or public land..

(ii) Development control norms as applicable for the particular residential use will continue to be applicable, even if the plot/ dwelling unit is put to mixed use.

(iii) If the notified street is a Master Plan road, and if a service road is available or provided for by local bodies, then, the mixed use premises should be approached from such service road and not directly from the main carriageway.

(iv) In plotted development, front setback should not have boundary wall, so that it can be used for additional parking.

(v) Parking @ 2.0 ECS per 100 sqm built up area shall be provided within the premises. Where this is not available, cost of development of parking, shall be payable by the plot allottee/ owner to the local body concerned. This condition shall apply even if residential premises are used only for professional activity.

(vi) Common parking areas would be earmarked on notified mixed use streets taking into account the additional load on traffic and parking consequent upon notification of the street under Mixed Use Policy. If no parking space is available, land/ plot on the said street may be made available by Traders association, wherever possible, or acquired for construction of parking facilities, preferably, multi level parking. Development of such parking facilities shall be done by either the traders Association or by local bodies and may include public-private partnership as model for implementation.

15.5 PERMISSIBLE AND NON-PERMISSIBLE USES

Any trade or activity involving any kind of obnoxious, hazardous, inflammable, non-compatible and polluting substance or process shall not be permitted.

15.6 RETAIL SHOPS

15.6.1. (i) Retail shops shall be permitted on plots abutting streets notified for mixed use only on the ground floor up to the maximum permissible ground floor coverage.

(ii) Shops operating from basement on such streets may continue, subject to relevant provisions of building bye laws, structural safety and fire safety clearance. However, if such use of basement leads to exceeding the permissible FAR on the plot, such FAR in excess shall be used, subject to payment of appropriate charges prescribed with the approval of Government.

15.6.2. The following activities shall not be allowed under Mixed Use:

a) Retail shops of building materials [timber, timber products (excluding furniture), marble1, iron and steel, (gravel, cement and sand2], firewood, coal and any fire hazardous and other bulky materials.

b) Repair shops / workshops of automobiles, tyre resoling and re-treading, and battery charging3.

c) Storage, go-down and warehousing.

d) Junk shop (except paper and glass waste)

e) Liquor shop

f) Printing, dyeing and varnishing

g) Any other activity that may be notified from time to time by Government.

Notes:

Will not include:

1. Business of finished marble products where cutting and polishing activity of marble is not undertaken.

2. Retail shops of gravel, sand and cement shall be permissible in residential plots of at least 50sq.m., in notified mixed use streets in E, F and G category colonies, provided that the material is kept entirely within the plot premises.

3. Repair shops and workshops in case of automobiles shall not be prohibited on plots abutting mixed-use streets or commercial streets of right of way (ROW) of 30m or more.

15.6.3 The small shops of maximum 20 sqm. area, trading in or dealing with the following items/ activities, may be allowed on ground floor only, in residential premises, including in A and B category colonies:

i) Vegetables / fruits / flowers

ii) Bakery items / Confectionary items;

iii) Kirana / General store;

iv) Dairy product;

v) Stationery / Books / Gifts / Book binding;

vi) Photostat / Fax / STD / PCO;

vii) Cyber café / Call phone booths;

viii) LPG booking office / Showroom without LPG cylinders;

ix) Atta Chakki;

x) Meat / Poultry and Fish shop;

xi) Pan shop;

xii) Barber shop / Hair dressing saloon / Beauty parlour;

xiii) Laundry / Dry cleaning / ironing;

xiv) Sweet shop / Tea stall without sitting arrangement;

xv) Chemist shop / Clinic / Dispensary / Pathology lab;

xvi) Optical shop;

xvii) Tailoring shop;

xviii) Electrical / Electronic repair shop; and

xix) Photo studio;

xx) Cable TV / DTH Operation;

xxi) Hosiery / Readymade Garments / Cloth shop;

xxii) ATM

xxiii) Cycle Repair Shop

xxiv) Ration shop & Kerosene Shop under PDS.

Any other item/ activity that may be notified by the Central Government.

15.7 OTHER ACTIVITY

15.7.1 Subject to the general conditions given in para 15.4 and additional conditions given in para 15.7.3, the following public and semi-public activities shall also be permitted in the residential plots abutting roads of minimum ROW prescribed in 15.7.2, whether or not the road is notified as mixed use street:

(a) Pre-primary school (including nursery / Montessori school, creche.)

(b) i. Nursing home

ii. Clinic, Dispensary, Pathology lab and Diagnostic center.

(c) Guest house (including lodging houses) irrespective of number of rooms.

(d) Bank

(e) Fitness Centre (including gymnasium, yoga/ meditation centre)

(f) Coaching centres /tuition centres other than those imparting structured courses leading directly to the award of a degree or diploma or conducting classes such as a regular school.

15.7.2. The minimum ROW of a street/or stretch of road on which the above-mentioned other activities are permissible is as follows:

In A & B Colonies*:	18m ROW in regular plotted development;

Notes

*Banks and fitness centers shall however, not be permissible, except those already operating as on 07.09.06.

In C & D colonies:	18 m ROW in regular residential plotted development, 13.5 m ROW in rehabilitation colonies and 9 m ROW in regularized- unauthorized colonies, resettlement colonies, Walled City, special area and urban villages; and in pedestrian shopping streets (of less than 6 m ROW).
In E,F &G Colonies:	13.5 m ROW in regular plotted development, 9 m ROW in rehabilitation colonies and 6m ROW in Walled City, regularized- unauthorised colonies, resettlement colonies, Special areas, and urban villages and in pedestrian shopping streets (of less than 6m ROW).

15.7.3 The above mentioned public and semi-public activities shall be subject to the following additional conditions in addition to general conditions prescribed in preceding paras:

i. Subject to the specific conditions mentioned in succeeding paras, the minimum size** of the plot on which these activities shall be permissible, on streets of prescribed minimum ROW, shall be 200 sqm in regular plotted development, 75 sqm in rehabilitation colonies, regularized -unauthorized colonies, resettlement colonies, Walled City, Special Area & urban villages subject to the following specific conditions.

ii. Banks shall be permissible on maximum 2/3rd of FAR subject to 600 sqm, while guesthouse and nursing homes will be permissible up to 3/4th of the floor area.

iii. Nursing Homes, dispensaries, clinics and pathology labs shall be permissible: on minimum plot size of 100 sqm in regular plotted development on 13.5 m ROW in C&D colonies and 9 m ROW in E, F& G colonies. However, the minimum plot size shall be 50 sqm for clinics, dispensaries and pathology labs running in these colonies and also in E, F and G category colonies. In Walled City, Walled city extension, villages and unauthorized-regularized colonies, conditions of plot size and minimum ROW shall not be applicable.

iv. Nursing Homes operating in plots abutting Master Plan roads and Zonal Plan roads shall be permissible up to 100% of built up area and the limit on the size of the plot would not apply.

v. Guest Houses operating in plots abutting streets of prescribed minimum ROW in Special Area and in plots abutting Master plan roads and zonal plan roads shall be permissible up to 100% of built up area and the limits on the size of the plot shall not apply. Provided that except in LBZ and Civil Line Bungalow Zone, Guest houses that were operating validly under provisions of MPD, prior to 7.9.2006 would continue to the extent as was permissible at that time.

vi. Pre-primary school and fitness center (other than those on plots abutting commercial streets) shall be restricted only to the ground floor up to the permissible ground coverage.

vii. Coaching centres and tuition centres referred to in para 15.7.1 (f) shall be permissible in up to 2/3 rd of the maximum permissible FAR in plots of less than 250 sqm. There shall be no restriction as to minimum size of plot. Other existing coaching/ tuition centers may be allowed to continue till end of May 2008 and shift to conforming locations by then.

viii. The above mentioned activities shall also be subject to any other specific terms and conditions, as may be prescribed in the relevant statutes/ acts applicable to them.

ix. It shall be the responsibility of the plot allottee/ owner to make arrangements for parking so that the parking does not encroach/ spill over on public land.

Note:

**Variation of ± 5% in plot size may be disregarded.

15.7.4 BANQUET HALL

Banquet Hall shall also be permissible in industrial and commercial areas including notified commercial streets under Mixed Use Regulations. Development control norms in respect of ground coverage, FAR, height and basement shall be applicable as per master plan norms for the specific land use for that premises till specific regulations are notified for this purpose.

15.8. PROFESSIONAL ACTIVITY

Subject to the general terms and conditions specified in para 15.4, professional activity is permissible in plotted development and group housing under the following specific conditions:

i. Professional activities shall mean those activities involving services based on professional skills namely Doctor, Lawyer, Architect, and Chartered Accountant, Company secretary, Cost and Works Accountant, Engineer, Town Planner, Media professionals and Documentary Film maker.

ii. In group housing, and plotted development with multiple dwelling units, professional activity shall be permitted on any floor subject to maximum of 50% of the permissible or sanctioned FAR, whichever is less, of each dwelling unit.

iii. In the case of plotted development with single dwelling unit, professional activity shall be permissible on any one floor only, but restricted to less than 50% of the permissible or sanctioned FAR whichever is less on that plot.

iv. Existing professional activity in basements may continue in plotted development, subject to relevant provisions of Building bye laws, structural safety norms and fire safety clearance. In case the use of Basement for professional activity leads to exceeding the permissible FAR on the plot, such FAR in excess shall be used subject to payment of appropriate charges prescribed with the approval of Government.

15.9 REGISTRATION OF MIXED USE PREMISES AND PAYMENT OF CHARGES

i) In respect of a residential premises already under mixed use or intended to be put to mixed use, the owner/ allottee/ resident of the plot/ dwelling unit, in case of plotted development and dwelling unit in the case of group housing, shall be required to declare such mixed-use by filling up a form in this respect and depositing it with the local body concerned any pay one-time registration charges at rates to be notified with the approval of the Central Government.

ii) The premises under mixed use shall also be liable for payment of mixed- use charges every Year to the local body concerned at the rates notified with the approval of Central Government, for the period during which the property is put to mixed use. Such payment will be made by the property owner/ allottee voluntarily before 30th June of every year in respect of the previous assessment year (April - March).

iii) No modification to the building for using residential premises for non-residential activities, under the mixed use policy, shall be permitted unless the allottee/ owner has obtained sanction of revised building plans and has paid necessary fees or charges.

iv) The local body concerned shall be responsible for the conduct of test check of properties under mixed use, whether registered with it or not.

v) In addition to other penal action available under the relevant act, properties found to be under mixed use, without registration or in violation of the terms of this notification shall be liable to pay, to the local body, a penalty amounting to 10 times the annual conversion charges for mixed use.

15.10 CONSULTATION WITH RWAs

i) The Residents Welfare Association (RWA) shall be a body registered before 21.07.06, or registered for at least three years under any statute, such as Societies Registration Act.

ii) Consultation with the RWA concerned for the purposes of declaring mixed use streets shall be done by the local bodies concerned.

iii) Genuine efforts for meaningful consultation with RWAs shall be made by the local bodies. Such efforts may include wide publicity to the proposed consultations, maintenance of record of consultation and providing access to those records to RWA concerned and public.

iv) Consultation with the RWA concerned shall be limited to identification of mixed use streets, and not for grant of permission in individual cases. However, RWAs shall have a right to be heard in cases of complains of public nuisance and non-permissible uses.

15.11 CONDITIONS FOR DENIAL / WITHDRAWAL / RESTRICTIONS OF MIXED USE

15.11.1. Permission or registration for mixed use can be cancelled or suspended by the concerned local body in case of violation of any of the conditions under which such mixed use is permissible/ permitted.

15.11.2. The following non-residential activities, not covered under the mixed use policy, shall be permissible in residential areas under the following conditions:

i. All such non-conforming schools operating on private lands and existing on or before 01.07.06 shall be required to conform to the prevailing norms within three years. Such schools shall apply to the concerned local body to consider for regularisation by modification in the layout plan, failing which these shall be closed down / shift to conforming premises.

ii. In addition, coaching centers and tuition centers referred to in para 15.7.1, running in residential premises, shall be allowed to continue till the end of May 2008.

15.12 COMMERCIAL STREETS AND AREAS

15.12.1. The following streets / stretches of streets or areas may be notified as commercial streets or commercial areas by the local authority*:

(a) Where more than 70% of the plots abutting roads of ROW of 24m or more, in a stretch of at least 300m, in regular plotted development are under commercial use, provided that no street in colonies in A and B categories shall be notified as commercial street.

(b) Where more than 70% of the properties abutting roads of less width than 24m ROW, in a stretch of at least 100m, in rehabilitation colonies, regularized-unauthorized colonies, resettlement colonies, Walled City, Special Area and urban villages and local commercial streets /areas declared under MPD-1962 as per para 15.3.1; and

(c) In E, F and G category colonies, where, 80% of residential plots are under mixed use, or if there are 300 shops, within a contiguous area of 1 hectare.

(d) Any street less than 6m ROW if declared as commercial streets shall be a pedestrian shopping street and not open to motorized transport.

*Provided that consistency shall be maintained by the local body in determining the ROW whether the street is bordered by service road, green verge, park or not.

15.12.2. For the notification of commercial streets/areas, in areas that have not been surveyed or have been surveyed but streets have not been notified pursuant to notification dated 7.9.2006, local bodies shall be required to carry out within a reasonable time of the notification coming into force, and with due expedition, and not later than 90 days, a survey of all streets of the above-mentioned width/ areas, if not already done, with a view to identifying stretches of such streets/areas as commercial streets/areas.

15.12.3 After identification is done, notification of commercial stretches / streets by the Urban Development Department, GNCTD would necessitate compliance to the following terms and conditions:

i. Preparation of revised layout plan / Scheme for such areas / streets with the approval of the local body/ Authority;

ii. The lay-out plan / Scheme for such areas / streets should indicate adequate provision for circulation, parking, open spaces and other planning norms;

iii. Common parking areas would be earmarked taking into account the additional load on traffic and parking consequent upon notification of the street as commercial area / street. If no parking space is available, land / plot on the said street / area may be made available by traders association, wherever possible, or acquired for construction of parking facilities, preferably, multi level parking. Development of such parking facilities may be done by either the traders association or by local bodies and may include public-private partnership as a model for implementation.

iv. On notification of a commercial street / area under this clause, such streets / areas shall be considered as local shopping centres as mentioned in Chapter 5.0 of this Plan. The plot owners / allottees on these commercial streets / areas shall have to pay special converse-on charges at rates approved by the Central Government, in respect of the built up area used for commercial purpose, provided that such built up area shall not exceed the residential development control norms applicable to the plot. This is a one-time facility for plot allottees/ owners in such commercial areas/ streets and shall not be construed as relaxation of the development control norms in future.

v. Any other condition that may be prescribed by Government from time to time.

vi. One time facility for all activities permitted in Local Shopping Centres shall be permissible in commercial streets and areas including multi-level parking. In addition, banquet halls shall also be permissible for which regulations may be prepared.

vii. Shops operating from basement on such streets may continue, subject to relevant provisions of building bye laws, structural safety and fire safety clearance. However if such use of basement leads to exceeding the permissible FAR on the plot, such FAR in excess shall be used subject to payment of appropriate charges prescribed with the approval of Government.

ANNEXURE I

LIST OF PRE-1962 BUILT UP RESIDENTIAL AND REHABILITATION COLONIES

1. Aliganj
2. Andha Mughal
3. Balbir Nagar
4. Bharat Nagar
5. B. K. Dutt Colony
6. Dishad Garden
7. Gandhi Nagar
8. Geeta Colony
9. Gulabi Bagh
10. Inderpuri
11. Jangpura - A
12. Jangpura - B
13. Jangpura Extn.
14. Jawahar Nagar
15. Kalkaji
16. Kamla Nagar
17. Karol Bagh
18. Kingsway Camp
19. Kirti Nagar
20. Kishan Ganj
21. Kishan Nagar
22. Lajpat Nagar - I to IV
23. Malka Ganj
24. Malviya Nagar
25. Mansarovar Garden
26. Model Basti
27. Model Town
28. Moti Nagar
29. Multan Nagar
30. Nanakpura
31. Nicholson Marg
32. New Rajinder Nagar
33. Old Rajinder Nagar
34. Outram Lines
35. Patel Nagar (E)
36. Patel Nagar (W)
37. Patel Nagar (S)
38. Pratap Nagar
39. Prem Nagar
40. Punjabi Bagh
41. Rajouri Garden
42. Rana Pratap Bagh
43. Ramesh Nagar
44. Ram Nagar
45. Rohtas nagar
46. Roop Nagar
47. Sarai Rohilla
48. Shahdara
49. Shakti Nagar
50. Sheikh Sarai
51. Shivaji Park
52. Subhash Nagar
53. Tilak Nagar
54. Timar Pur
55. Tihar - I & II
56. Vinoba Puri
57. Vijay Nagar

16. LANDUSE PLAN

16.0 LAND USE PLAN-2021

The Land Use Plan-2021 has been prepared based on

(i) The policies enunciated for different urban activities,

(ii) Requirement of additional social and physical infrastructure,

(iii) Transportation and work centres,

(iv) Already approved Zonal Development Plans and land use modifications.

In order to control the development, the areas have been designated as one of the 27 use zones identified in the Development Code. These use zones have been classified broadly in nine categories of land uses namely Residential, Commercial, Industrial, Recreational, Transportation, Utility, Government, Public & Semi - Public Facilities and Agriculture & Water Body. The development in these use zones would be carried out in accordance with the regulations as laid down in the Development Code and respective chapters.

16.1 ZONAL DEVELOPMENT PLANS

The NCTD has been divided in 15 Zones (Divisions) designated 'A' to 'P' (except Zone 'I') in the Master Plan 2021. The Zonal Plans of eleven zones for the perspective year 2001 have been approved and notified whereas the Zonal Plans for the zones 'N (North West Delhi-III)', 'K' (part) between Dwarka & Rohini, 'J' (South Delhi- II), L (West Delhi -III), O (River Yamuna), P- II (North Delhi) are at various stages of preparation and process. The boundaries of the zones 'O', 'P' and 'N' as given in the MPD-2001 have been modified and accordingly the areas have been computed approximately as given in the Table 16.1

Table 16.1: Zone wise Area

Zone	Name of Zone	Area (Ha.)
A	Old City	1159
B	City Extn. (Karol Bagh)	2304
C	Civil Line	3959
D	New Delhi	6855
E	Trans Yamuna	8797
F	South Delhi-I	11958
G	West Delhi-I	11865
H	North West Delhi-I	5677
J	South Delhi-II	15178
K	K-I West Delhi-II	5782
	K-II Dwarka	6408
L	West Delhi-III	22840
M	North West Delhi-II	5073
N	North West Delhi-III	13975
*O	River Yamuna / River Front	8070
P	P-I Narela	9866
	P-II North Delhi	8534

* The above areas are approximate and the re-delineation and rezoning of the zones can be done with the approval of the Authority.

Mapping of the NCT of Delhi would be done using remote sensing and GIS tools and will also be updated from time to time to have valuable data as regards ground situation and also to have inputs to detect and prevent unauthorised development and encroachment on public land and to facilitate the protection of greens. The Zonal plans shall detail out the policies of the Master Plan 2021and act as link between the Layout Plan and Master Plan. The development schemes and layout plans indicating various use premises shall conform to the Master Plan / Zonal Plans. The Zonal Plans of the areas shall be prepared under Section 8 and processed under Section 10 and simultaneously the modifications of land uses shall be processed under Section 11(A) of the Delhi Development Act 1957. Already approved Sub Zonal (earlier Zonal)

Plans in conformity with the Master Plan shall continue for the areas where the Zonal Plans have not been approved. The Zonal Plans in the form of structure plans shall be prepared within 12 months of the approval of the MPD-2021.

In absence of Zonal Plan of any area, the development shall be in accordance with the provisions of the Master Plan. No urban activity shall be permitted in the proposed Urban Extension without change of land use/ modification to the Master Plan as per the Delhi Development Act, 1957.

16.2 SPECIAL AREA REGULATIONS

The Walled City and its Extensions, Karol Bagh and the contiguous area in between has been designated as Special Area for the purpose of development since this area cannot be developed on the basis of normal regulations given in the development code. The Redevelopment Scheme for this Special Area should be prepared and notified by the MCD within three years. Special Area Building regulations shall be prepared by the Authority in consultation with the local body within a period of three years and notified with the approval of the Central Government.

The Authority may declare other historical / pre-1962 developed areas as Special Area.

The development within these areas shall be governed as per the following norms and regulations (also refer 3.3.2. 'Guidelines for Redevelopment Schemes' and 4.2.2. 'Restructuring and Upgradation of the existing areas).

Permission of use / use activities in use premises :

1. The noxious industries and hazardous trades shall be shifted from the Special Area within a maximum period of five years, and shall be replaced by other compatible uses.

2. The Public and Semi-public uses and services like Hospitals, Dispensaries, Colleges, Schools, Police Stations, Fire Stations, Post Offices, Local Government Offices, Parking etc. shall be retained in their present locations and additional sites could be indicated in the Redevelopment Schemes / Zonal Plans. Any change or additions thereof shall be in accordance with the overall policy frame prescribed in the plan.

3. Special Area building Regulations shall be framed for special area, unauthorised regularised colonies and village abadis. Owners in special area, unauthorised regularised colonies and village abadi shall register themselves with the local body within a period of four months indicating the existing extent of construction. Thereafter a certificate of structural safety by qualified engineers shall be submitted within the next 6 months. Subject to height restriction of 15 meters, all buildings covered by such registration shall be exempted from punitive action till Special Area Building Regulations for these areas are notified or maximum three years, whichever is earlier.

4. Regulations for special specific areas shall be as under:

(i) Lajpat Rai Market: The single storeyed market on either side of Chandni Chowk shall be retained.

(ii) The isolated use premises like School adjoining Jama Masjid, Presentation Convent School and the Church at Kashmere Gate, Municipal Offices at Old Hindu College Building Complex shall be retained with existing building volume. Any additions or alterations shall be within the overall policy frame of conservation.

(iii) Karol Bagh: Landuse and Development Code as per approved Zonal Development Plan and Local Area Plans.

(iv) The redevelopment schemes for different use zones generally shall adopt regulations prescribed in the Development Code. However, the Authority may adopt suitable regulations in case where either it is not feasible or not advisable to adopt the general regulations prescribed.

5. Re-development Plan and Schemes for the Special Area should be prepared by the local body within three years of approval of the MPD 2021. In this Plan, the Metropolitan City Centres as referred in 5.3, Chapter 5.0 Trade and Commerce, shall be delineated based on survey. Till such time, status quo shall be maintained.

17. DEVELOPMENT CODE

INTRODUCTION

The purpose of the code is to promote quality of built environment by organising the most appropriate development of land in accordance with the development policies and land use proposals contained in the Plan.

It is a systematic code to ascertain the use activity (use) at two levels:

(i) Conversion of Use Zone into Use Premises (layout); and

(ii) Permission of Use Activities on Use Premises. The code differentiates between the Use Zone and Use Premises.

ENFORCEMENT OF THE CODE

To regulate development in the National Capital Territory of Delhi within the framework of the land use plan, the following shall be observed :

CLAUSE 1.0 TITLES AND EXTENT

1(1) This code may be called the Development Code.

1(2) It covers the National Capital Territory of Delhi.

CLAUSE 2.0 DEFINITIONS

In this code unless the context otherwise require:

2(1) Land use Plan means the plan indicating Use Zones as defined in Clause 4.0.

2(2) Zonal Development Plan means a plan for one of the zones (divisions) of the National Capital Territory of Delhi containing detailed information regarding provision of social infrastructure, parks and open spaces, circulation system, etc.

2(3) Local Area Plan means the plan of a Ward / Sub Zone to be prepared and approved by the concerned local body.

2(4) Layout Plan means a Plan indicating configuration and sizes of all Use Premises. Each Use Zone may have one or more than one Layout Plan depending upon the extensiveness of the area under the specific Use Zones and vice-versa. A layout plan shall have at least two use premises (apart from Recreational, utilities and transportation) and a minimum area of 1 Ha. below which it shall be termed as site plan or sub division plan.

Layout Plan will indicate the location of all proposed and existing roads with their widths, dimensions of plots along with building lines and setbacks, location of drains, public facilities and services and electric lines etc, statement indicating the total area of the site, area under roads, open spaces for parks, playground, recreational spaces and other public places, as required by specific sections of the development code.

2(5) Site Plan: A Detailed Plan showing the proposed placement of structures, parking areas, open space, landscaping, and other development features, on a parcel of land, as required by specific sections of the development code.

2(6) Use Zone means an area for any one of the Specified Use Category of the urban functions as provided for in Clause 4.0.

2(7) Use Premises means one of the many sub divisions of a Use Zone, designated in an approved layout plan, for a specific Use. Land use of a premise has to be determined on the basis of an approved layout plan.

2(8) Special Area means an area with special characteristics designated as such in the Plan for development / redevelopment.

2(9) Commercial Centres include a Metropolitan City Centre, District Centre, Community Centre, Local Shopping Centre, Convenience Shopping Centre and Non-Hierarchical Commercial Centres wholesale and warehousing.

2(10) Conversion charges / other levies shall be payable wherever landuse conversion is enabled at premise level by the Master Plan / Zonal Plan, Mixed Use Regulations and other Regulations.

CLAUSE 3.0 ESTABLISHMENT OF USE ZONES AND USE PREMISES

3(1) The National Capital Territory of Delhi is divided into 9 land use categories as mentioned in clause 4.0

3(2) Each land Use category is assigned number of use zones, which shall be further subdivided into required number of Use Premises with or without conditions in Layout Plans.

3(3) Each use premises shall be permitted to have specific uses/ use activities out of the prescribed uses/ use activities with or without conditions.

3(4) The Layout Plans already approved by the Authority or any other local authority concerned in accordance with law shall be deemed to have been approved under this code.

3(5) An area in respect of which there is no approved Layout Plan shall be governed by the provisions of the Master Plan/Zonal Development Plan.

3(6) In case of Urban Design schemes, Redevelopment along MRTS Corridor, Urban Renewal schemes etc. on comprehensive basis the minimum area prescribed for planning and approval:

(a) Scheme area for redevelopment - 4 Ha.

(b) Plot area for redevelopment - 3000 sqm.

3(7) Accommodation Reservation (AR) and Transfer of Development Control Rights (TDR) are used as development control tools for implementing plans for redevelopment schemes in urban areas.

3(8) A landscape plan shall be prepared in case of the premises of size 3000 sqm. and above.

3(9) The natural drainage pattern shall not be disturbed.

3(10) Rainwater harvesting shall form an integral part of the storm water drainage plan, at the time of sanction of any layout plan.

SANCTION OF PLANS

3(11) Layout Plans / Site Plans and Building plans shall be approved by the Local Bodies and Authority in their areas of jurisdiction.

3(12) Authority/Local Body(s) shall be empowered after levying penalty to compound deviations from limits of coverage/ FAR to the extent of 5% of the permissible coverage and FAR, subject to maximum of 13.5 sqm. in building(s) / premises at the time of considering the completion / occupancy certificate. In Group Housing schemes and Public & semi-public facilities, 5% FAR beyond permissible FAR can be compounded by the authority/Local Body at the time of considering the completion/occupancy certificate.

3(13) Wherever required, the Technical Committee of the DDA shall formulate policy guidelines for the sanctioning of local area plans, layout plans, comprehensive schemes, re-development schemes, urban renewal schemes and multi-storeyed buildings in all land use categories. The Technical Committee shall be empowered to call for the plans from the development organisations / Local Bodies and would give directions / recommendations wherever necessary.

CLAUSE 4.0 USE ZONES DESIGNATED

There shall be 9 Land Use categories subdivided into use Zones as given below:

- RESIDENTIAL

RD Residential area

RF Foreign Mission

- COMMERCIAL

C1 Retail Shopping, General Business and Commerce, District Centre, Community Centre, Non Hierarchical Commercial Centre.

C2 Wholesale, Warehousing, Cold Storage and Oil Depot

C3 Hotels

- INDUSTRIAL

M1 Manufacturing, Service and Repair Industry.

- RECREATIONAL

P1 Regional Park

P2 City Park, District Park, Community Park.

P3 Historical Monuments

- TRANSPORTATION

T1 Airport

T2 Terminal / Depot - Rail / MRTS / Bus/ Truck

T3 Circulation - Rail / MRTS / Road

- UTILITY

U1 Water (Treatment Plant etc.),

U2 Sewerage (Treatment Plant etc.),

U3 Electricity (Power House, Sub-Station etc.)

U4 Solid Waste (Sanitary landfill etc.)

U5 Drain

- GOVERNMENT

G1 President Estate and Parliament House

G2 Government Office / Courts

G3 Government Land (use undetermined)

- PUBLIC AND SEMI PUBLIC FACILITES

PS1 Hospital, Education and Research University / University centre, College, Social - Cultural, Socio Cultural Complex/ Centre, Police/ Police Headquarter/ Police Lines, Fire Stations / Disaster Management Centres, Religious, Burial Ground / Cremation.

PS2 Transmission Site/ Centre

PS3 Sports Facilities/ Complex / Stadium/ Sports Centre.

- GREEN BELT / AND WATER BODY

A1 Plant Nursery

A2 Green Belt / Agricultural Green

A3 River and Water body

Mixed Use Zone

A use zone in the Land Use Plan could be indicated as consisting of more than one use zones.

CLAUSE 5.0 USE PREMISES DESIGNATED

The use premises and Uses/Use Activities with similar nomenclature are given with the controls of specific premises in the respective chapters.

CLAUSE 6.0 LOCATION AND BOUNDARIES FOR USE ZONES

6(1) Any one of the use zones may be located at one or more than one places as shown in the Land Use Plan.

6(2) The boundaries of various pockets of use zones are defined in land Use Plan by features like roads, railway tracks, drains etc.

CLAUSE 7.0 LOCATION AND BOUNDARIES OF USE PREMISES

7(1) The location and boundaries of each use premises shall conform to as specified in the layout plan with reference to important bench mark like road, drain or other physical features.

7(2) Any change in the location, boundaries and predominant use of use premises due to any reason whatsoever and duly approved shall be incorporated in layout plan.

CLAUSE 8.0 SUB DIVISION OF USE ZONES, PERMISSION OF USE PREMISES IN USE ZONES AND CONTROL OF BUILDINGS

8(1) SUB-DIVISON OF USE ZONES INTO USE PREMISES

The objective of these regulations is to guide the preparation of layout plants for residential and industrial use zones. These regulations include norms for provision of facilities and circulation system. The service plans corresponding to these layout plans for provision of physical infrastructure like water supply, sewerage drainage, etc., shall conform to municipal byelaws.

The use zone other than residential and industrial shall have integrated plans governed by respective building control regulations.

Integrated plan differs from customary layout plan as in the former the regulations are for the total plot and sub-divisions are done for the development purpose. The norms for sub-division of residential and manufacturing use zone into use premises are given in respective chapters.

SUB/CLAUSE 8 (2) PERMISSION OF USE PREMISES IN USE ZONES

(As part of approval of layout plan or as a case of special permission from the Authority)

Permission of selected Use Premises in Use Zones RD, C_1, C_2, M, PS

S.No.	Use Premises	Use Zones				
		RD	C1	C2	M	PS
RD	RESIDENTIAL					
(i)	Residential plot - Plotted Housing	P	P**	NP	NP	NP
(ii)	Residential plot - Group Housing	P	P	NP	NP	P
(iii)	Residence - cum - Work Plot	P	P	NP	NP	NP
(iv)	Foreign mission	P	P	NP	NP	NP
(v)	Hostel / Old age home	P	P	NP	P	P

(vi)	Guest House, Boarding and Lodging House	P	P	P	NP	P
(vii)	Dharamshala and its equivalent	P	P	NP	NP	P
(viii)	Community Hall / Barat Ghar	P	P	NP	NP	P
(ix)	Night Shelter	P	P	P	P	P
(x)	Community / Recreational Hall, Library, Reading Room, Society Office, Crèche and Day Care Centre.	P	P	P	P	P
C	COMMERCIAL					
(i)	Local Level (Convenience / Local shopping centre)	P	P	P	P	P
(ii)	Cinema / Multiplexes	NP	P	P	P*	NP
(iii)	Service markets / Informal Bazaars	P	P	P	P	NP
(iv)	Wholesale Trade	NP	P	P	NP	NP
(v)	Storage, godown and warehousing, cold storage & Ice factory, gas godown.	NP	NP	P	P	NP
R	RECREATIONAL					
	Recreational (Park, Play grounds, Swimming Pool)/ Sports Complex/ Stadium/Amusement parks/ Recreational Clubs etc.	P	P	P	P	P
M	INDUSTRY					
(i)	Industrial plot, flatted group industry	NP	NP	NP	P	NP
(ii)	Service centre & Service industry	NP	P	P	P	NP
T	TRANSPORTATION					
	Circulation (Road network with street furniture, Bus terminal, MRTS stations, Parking etc.	P	P	P	P	P
	Bus depot & Workshop	NP	NP	NP	P	NP
G	GOVERNMENT					
(i)	Local / Government maintenance Offices	P	P	P	P	P
(ii)	Offices of utility services providing agencies	P	P	P	P	P
PS	PUBLIC AND SEMI PUBLIC FACILITIES					
(i)	Hospital (upto 100 beds)	P	P	NP	NP	P
(ii)	Primary Health Centre/Family Welfare Centre/ Maternity Home/dispensary etc.	P	P	NP	P	P
(iii)	Nursing Home/poly clinic/clinic/clinical laboratory etc.	P	P	NP	P*	P
(iv)	Dispensary for pet and animals	P	P	P	P	P
(v)	Primary school / Middle school	P	NP	NP	NP	P
(vi)	School for Mentally / Physically Challenged	P	NP	NP	NP	P
(viii)	Technical Training centre (ITI / Polytechnic/Vocational/ Training Institute/ Management institute/Teacher Training Institute, etc.)	P	P	NP	NP	P
(ix)	Facilities - Bus terminal, taxi stand, milk / vegetable booths, religious premises, vending booth, petrol / CNG filling pump, recreational club, police post, police station, fire station, post office, & telegraph office and telephone exchange.	P	P	P	P	P

P : Permitted P*: Permitted only in Commercial Centres

NP: Not Permitted P**: Special permission as per Mixed use / Special Area Regulations

Notes :

(i) Park, Open Parking, Circulation and Public Utilities are permitted in all use zones

(ii) Limited remunerative uses may be permitted for making environmental upgradation of social upliftment projects such as covering of drains, in-situ rehabilitation schemes etc. financially viable. The activities and extent of the use permitted to be decided by DDA.

(iii) Property development in area aound Metro Stations (composite) upto a maximum area of 3.0 Ha., shall be permitted in all use zones, except Recreational and Ridge/ regional park use zone subject to approval of the Technical Committee of DDA.

(iv) The permission of use premise in the following use zones shall be governed by the specific function of the use zone.

C3- Hotel, P3- Historical Monuments, T1- Airport, T2- Terminal / Depot - Rail / MRTS / Bus/ Truck, T3- Circulation - Rail / MRTS / Road, U1-Water, U2-Sewerage, U3-Electricity, U4-Solid Waste, U5-Drain, G1-president Estate & Parliament House, G3-Government Land (Use Undetermined), PS1 -Cremation and Burial Ground, Religious, A2-Green Belt and A3-River & Water Body.

(vi) Land use of Village Abadi (Lal Dora) located in any use zone is residential.

8 (3) REGULATIONS FOR BUILDING CONTROLS WITHIN USE PREMISES

The objective of these regulations is to provide controls for building(s) within use premises excluding the internal arrangement, which are covered in Building Bye-laws.

General Notes

1. Where development controls are not stipulated for any use premise, the same can be formulated by the Authority.
2. The mezzanine floor and service floor wherever provided shall be considered as a part of the total FAR.
3. If the building is constructed with stilt area of non-habitable height (2.4 mts) and is proposed to be used for parking, landscaping, etc. the stilt floor need not be included in FAR.
4. Wherever the building regulations are given for different categories of plots, the area covered and the floor area shall in no case be less than the permissible covered area and floor area respectively for the largest size of plot in the lower category.

Table 17.1: Minimum Setbacks (Other than Residential Plotted Development)

S.No.	Plot size (in sq.m)	Minimum Setbacks			
		Front (m)	Rear (m)	Side (m) (1)	Side (m) (2)
1.	Upto 60	0	0	0	0
2.	Above 60 & upto 150	3	1.5 (avg.)	-	-
3.	Above150 & upto 300	4	2 (avg.)	-	-
4.	Above 300 upto 500	4	3	3	-
5.	Above 500 upto 2,000	6	3	3	3
6.	Above 2,000 upto 10,000	9	6	6	6
7.	Above 10,000	15	12	12	12

Note:

(i) In case the permissible coverage is not achieved with the above given setbacks, the setbacks of the preceding category may be followed.

(ii) The setbacks are subject to requirements of height and ventilation as per building byelaws.

(iii) In case a layout is sanctioned with more than the minimum prescribed setbacks, the same shall be followed in the sanction of the building plans.

(iv) The Technical Committee of DDA may relax setbacks, ground coverage and height in special circumstances.

(v) ESS wherever required to be provided within the plot, is allowed by shifting of side / rear setbacks.

8 (4) PARKING STANDARDS

Parking Standards have been prescribed in each use premises however, where it is not prescribed, it will be followed as given in the Table 17.2.

Table 17.2: Parking Standards

S.No	Use Premises	Permissible Equivalent Car Spaces (ECS) per 100 sqm. of floor area
1.	Residential	2.0
2.	Commercial	3.0
3.	Manufacturing	2.0
4.	Government	1.8
5.	Public and Semi Public-Facilities	2.0

(i) In existing buildings having plot area of more than 2000 sqm., an extra ground coverage of 5% shall be permissible for construction of automated multi-level parking to provide dedicated parking structures for additional needs.

(ii) For the provision of car parking spaces, the space standards shall be as given in Table 17.3.

Table 17.3: Space Standards for Car Parking

S.No	Type of Parking	Area in sqm. per ECS
1.	Open	23
2.	Ground floor covered	28
3.	Basement	32
4.	Multi level with ramps	30
5.	Automated multilevel with lifts	16

(iii) In the use premises, parking on the above standards shall be provided within the plot.

8 (5) BASEMENTS

(a) Basement(s) upto the setback line maximum equivalent to parking and services requirement, such as Air Conditioning Plant and equipment, water storage, Boiler, Electric Sub-Station HT and LT Panel rooms, Transformer Compartment, Control Room, Pump House, Generator Room and other mechanical services and installation of electrical and fire fighting equipments, and other services required for the maintenance of the building with prior approval of the concerned agencies, could be permitted and not to be counted in FAR. However, the area provided for services should not exceed 30 % of the basement area.

(b) The basement(s) above the plot level shall be kept flushed with the ground and shall be ventilated with mechanical means of ventilation; and

(c) Basement(s) shall be designed to take full load of the fire tender, wherever required and subject to adequate safety measures.

(d) In case the basement is used for activity in conformity with the use premises; wherever permitted, the same shall be counted in FAR subject to clearance from the Fire Authorities and other statutory bodies.

(e) Parking area, if misused, is liable to be municipalized / taken over by the Local Body / Authority.

(f) The ESS, fire fighting installations and underground water tank shall neither be counted in ground coverage nor in FAR.

18. PLAN REVIEW AND MONITORING

Plan Monitoring is essential to evaluate the changes required to improve the quality of life in the city. Properly phased monitoring makes the plan responsive to the emerging socio-economic forces. Implementation of the plan can be effective only when monitored and reviewed at appropriate periods.

No long-range plan can be implemented as it is. The process of implementation has to be divided into various time frames depending on the projects & schemes. To study the effect of implementation of these projects, monitoring is required from time to time for each of the various aspects of the master plan. A scientific monitoring framework is essential for:

(1) Effective implementation of plan within the plan period, thereby achieving the intended targets.

(2) Respond to the changing socio-economic needs of the people of the city.

(3) To check unintended growth within the city.

(4) Time lags between various implementation schemes and emerging needs of the people.

(5) Review the appropriateness of the plan policies.

Monitoring framework for targets of the master plan helps in judging the performance of various sectors, which need priority. Critical aspects and their targets need shorter monitoring period so that they can be constantly reviewed from time to time.

The Plan period is proposed to be divided in three phases taking 2006 as the base year. However, the targets, which are not achieved within the defined period, shall be carried forward in the next phase.

The following table lists the different sectors, their targets to be achieved and the period of monitoring. This table is however, not a programme of development but it provides a scale to assess the achievements in different sectors for the city development.

However, infrastructure facilities at neighbourhood level should be monitored in consonance with neighbourhood development / redevelopment scheme.

Table 18.1 Monitoring Framework for Development

Components	Unit	Period of Monitoring	Phase I Upto 2011		Phase II 2011-2016		Phase III 2016-2021		Target Upto 2021	
I. POPULATION	Lakhs		138-182		182-199		199-230		230	
(For Infrastructure Provision)										
II. NEW HOUSING	No. in lakhs DUs		7		9.0		8.0		24lakhs DUs	
			R*	N*	R	N	R	N	R	N
			3.5	3.5	3.5	5.5	3.0	5.0	10	14
a. Housing for Urban poor through Slum & JJ approaches	No. in lakhs	2 years	0.7	1.0	0.7	1.6	0.6	1.4	2.0	4.0
b. Houses as Independent Plots and Redevelopment	No. in lakhs	2 years	0.35	0.2	0.35	0.3	0.3	0.3	1.0	0.8
c. Group Housing (35% of total DU's mandatory not to exceed 2 room or less)	No. in lakhs	2 years	0.84	1.9	0.84	3.0	0.72	2.7	2.4	7.6
d. Employer Housing	No. in lakhs	1 year	0.14	0.15	0.14	0.25	0.12	0.2	0.4	0.6
e. Unauthorized Regularised colonies**	No. in lakhs	1 year	1.05	0.15	1.05	0.25	0.9	0.2	3.0	0.6
f. Other Housing areas Upgradation of Old areas Traditional/Villages**	No. in lakhs	4 years	0.42	0.1	0.42	0.16	0.36	0.14	1.2	0.4
* Includes backlog housing stock & replacement										
III. PHYSICAL INFRASTRUCTURE										
a. Augmentation of water distribution	Mgd	5 years	351		139		240		730	
b. Construction of new treatment plants	Mgd	5 years	129		51		89		269	
c. Augmentation of sewerage T Plants.	Mgd	15 years	282		112		194		588	
d. Construction of new sewerage treatment plants	Mgd	5 years	140		56		97		293	
e. Augmentation of power distribution system	MW	2 years	3744		1447		2639		7830	
f Development of sanitary landfill sites	Ha	5 years	98		39		68		205	
g. Construction/ development of compost/ incineration plants	Ha	5 years	15		6		11		32.0	
h. Municipal Solid Waste	Tons	1 Year	4900		1939		3368		10207	
IV. SOCIAL INFRASTRUCTURE										
a. Health										
(i) Hospital A (501 beds & above)	No.	2 years	9		3		6		18	
(ii) Hospital B (201 beds to 500 beds)	No.	1 year	18		6		12		36	
(iii) Hospital C (101 beds to 200 beds)	No.	1 year	43		17		30		90	
(iv) Hospital D (Upto 100 beds)	No.	1 year	43		17		30		90	
(v) Veterinary hospitals	No.	1 year	6		6		6		18	

(vi) Dispensary for pet animals	No.	1 year	43	17	30	90
b. Education						
(i) School for physically handicapped	No.	2 year	4	2	3	9
(ii) School for mentally handicapped	No.	2 year	4	2	3	9
(iii) Vocational Training Centre	No.	1 year	9	3	6	18
(iv) General college	No.	5 year	9	3	6	18
(v) Professional College	No.	10 years	9	3	6	18
(vi) Medical college	No.	10 year	4	2	3	9
(vii) Nursing and Paramedic Institute	No.	5 year	4	2	3	9
(viii) Training -Cum-Research Institute in Veterinary Sciences				As per requirement		
(ix) University Campus Including International Education Centre (IEC)	No.	10 years		4 sites in Urban Extension		
c. Communication						
(i) Head post office-administrative office	No.	5 year	4	2	3	9
(ii) Telephone Exchange	No.	5 year	4	2	3	9
d. Security- Police						
(i) Police Station	No.	1 year	17	7	12	36
(ii) Police line	No.	1 year		1 for each administrative zone		
(iii) District jail	No.	5 years	1	1	1	4
(iv) District office and battalion	No.	1 year		I for each administrative Zone		
(v) Police training institute/ college	City level	5 years		As per demand		
(vi) Police firing range	City level	5 years		As per demand		
(vii) Traffic and police control room	City level	5 years		As per demand		
e. Safety- Fire						
(i) Fire station	No.	1 year		As per demand		
(ii) Disaster Management Centre	No.	1 year	1 in each administrative Zone			
(iii) Fire Training Institute	No.	1 year	City level (One site in Urban Extension)			
f. Socio-cultural facilities						
(i) Multipurpose community hall	No.	5 years	As per residential development phase			
(ii) Community Recreational Club	No.	5 years				
(iii) Recreational Club	No.	5 years	9	3	6	18
(iv) Socio Cultural Activities Centre	No.	5 years	43	17	30	90
(v) Exhibition sites	No.	5 years	2 sites in Urban Extension			
g. Other community facilities						
(i) Old Age Home	No.	5 years	9	3	6	18
(ii) Working women hostels	No.	5 years	9	3	6	18
(iii) Night Shelters	No.	5 years	9	3	6	18
(iv) Care centre for mentally and physically challenged	No.	5 years	9	3	6	18
(v) Adult Educational centres	No.	5 years	9	3	6	18
(vi) Orphanage	No.	5 years	9	3	6	18
(vii) Science Centre	No		4	2	3	9
(viii) Religious Premises						
At sub city level in urban extension	No	10 years	5	2	2	9
i. Cremation grounds	No.	10 years	9	3	6	18
• Cemetery / burial grounds	No.	10 years	4	2	3	9
V. TRADE AND COMMERCE						
a. Metropolitan City Centre						
(i) Preparation of integrated schemes & specific projects	No.	5 years	1	-	1	2

b. District Centre/ Sub CBD						
(i) Upgradation of existing areas	No.	5 Years	6	2	2	10
(ii) Under implementation	No.	5 Years	9	2	2	13
(iii) New locations in urban extension		To be located along major arterial road as per norms.				
c. Community Centre						
(i) Upgradation of existing areas	No.	5 Years	20	10	10	40
(ii) Under implementation in DUA-81	No.	5 Years	22	10	10	42
(iii) New locations in urban extension/ Projects	To be located along major arterial road as per norms					
VI. TRANSPORT						
a. Fully/Partially segregated cycle tracks.	No.	1year		As per requirements		
b. MRTS	Length in K.m.	5 years	120	47.5	82.5	250
c. Construction of grade separators	No.	2 years	Should coincide with 5 year plan and monitored on regular basis.			
d. Development of urban relief roads	No.	2 Years				
e. Construction of interstate bus terminals	No.	1 Year				
f. Construction of Metropolitan Passenger Terminals	No.	5 Years				5
g. Integrated Freight Complexes	No.	1 Year				5
h. Petrol pumps & CNG stations	No.	1 Year	As per norms			
VII. RESTRUCTURING ALONG MRTS NETWORK						
(i) Upgradation of existing areas	No.	2 years	As per phasing of MRTS Network			
(ii) New locations in urban extension	No.	2 years				
VIII. INDUSTRIES						
(i) Redeveloped / Upgradation	No.	3 years	To be Redeveloped / Upgraded as per norms			
(ii) New locations in urban extension	No.	3 years	To be located as per norms			
IX. GOVERNMENT OFFICES/DISTRICT COURT						
(i) Redeveloped / Upgradation	No.	3 years	Area located in MRTS influence zone			
(ii) New locations in urban extension	No.	3 years				
X. ENVIRONMENT						
New landscape/Recreational area.						
(i) City park	No.	10 years	4	2	3	9
(ii) District Park	No.	5 years	9	3	6	18
(iii) Community Park	No.	1 year	43	17	30	90
(iv) City Multipurpose ground	No.	10 years	4	2	3	9
(v) District Multipurpose ground	No.	5 years	9	3	6	18
(vi) Community Multipurpose ground	No.	1 year	43	17	30	90
(vii) Divisional Sports Centres	No.	5 years	4	2	3	9
(viii) District Sports Centres	No.	1 year	9	3	6	18
(ix) Community Sports Centres	No.	5 years	43	17	30	90

*R- Redevelopment

N- New Housing

**No additional land required

18.2 MAJOR ISSUES

1. The Planning process needs reforms and capacity building to meet projected targets adequately, such as preparation of Sub-Regional Plan, Zonal Plans etc.

2. Local level participation in the planning process, its coordination, planning and building approvals, slum rehabilitation, social housing and legal reforms also requires attention for implementation of provisions of the Master Plans.

3. Monitoring & Review of Master Plan should be done through indicators of physical and socio-economic changes.

Taking into account the above, it is proposed to formulate a separate Monitoring Unit and a team of action groups which will function within the specified prescribed norms and social indicators within the over all framework of the Master Plan.

18.3 MONITORING UNIT

A dedicated Monitoring Unit with modern data processing facilities should be set up which would be responsible for collection and analysis of primary and secondary data and bringing the important changes to the notice of the authority comprehensively. This unit should also be in-charge of overall monitoring of implementation of the approved development plans and layout plans.

A suitable mechanism by way of high-level committee under Lt. Governor, Delhi is also proposed to be set up for periodic review and monitoring of the plan. To enable this, apart from targets arising from various infrastructure plans etc., other action points emerging from the proposals made in the plan for various sectors would also be listed out, to enable monitoring of timely implementation / identifying the need for any changes/ corrections.

18.4 MANAGEMENT ACTION GROUPS

It is proposed that for participatory planning, the following management action groups and initiatives are taken for addressing the major issues. These groups would work on following Planning indicators.

18.4.1 PLANNING INDICATORS

The following would be the indicators of physical and socio-economic changes to be monitored periodically :

(1) **Demographic:** Population size, Population distribution in relation to holding capacity, Age sex structure, Household size, Rate of migration, Causes of migration etc.

(2) **Landuse:** Landuse pattern, Development / Layout plans etc.

(3) **Housing:** Slum and squatter settlements, Household with essential services

(4) **Social Infrastructure:** Mortality Rate and Infant Mortality Rate, access of population to safe drinking water, access to low cost sanitation, removal of solid waste per capita, distribution of police and fire services, requirement of old age homes, working women's hostels, adult education centres etc.

(5) **Transport:** Percentage trips by public transport (modal split), cost of using and operating different modes, passenger capacity and distance traveled by public transport per year in relation to population, facilities provided on railways / metro stations / I.S.B.T, Requirement of petrol pumps & CNG stations.

(6) **Economic Aspects:** Distribution of households by income, consumption expenditure, employment, participation rate, employment in different sectors, shifting/ relocation of industries, growth of informal sector, shifting of government offices etc.

(7) **Environment:** Air pollution, Water pollution, Noise, Quality of water of River Yamuna, Ridge area conservation etc

(8) **Natural Disasters:** Floods intensity areas & effected population, any other natural disasters etc.

It is proposed to organize the following groups for follow up planning and integrated implementation of the Plan:

18.4.2 HIGH LEVEL GROUP FOR SUB-REGIONAL PLAN FOR DELHI

As a follow up of the Regional Plan-2021 and in consonance with Section 17 of the NCRPB Act, 1985, a Sub-Regional Plan for Delhi is to be prepared by GNCT-Delhi.

18.4.3 ENVIRONMENT PLANNING AND COORDINATION GROUP

The Group will evolve strategies for sustainable development, with major issues as conservation of Yamuna River bed and flood plain (including defining the same), Ridge etc. It will evolve a mechanism to coordinate the interventions of the several organizations involved in this cross-cutting task.

18.4.4 DELHI UNIFIED METROPOLITAN TRANSPORT GROUP

This group shall be responsible to prepare an action programme to coordinate a sustainable and balanced public transport system and will prepare traffic management strategic action plans with emphasis on movement of people and goods. The group will also evolve a parking policy and identify a Parking Authority for Delhi.

18.4.5 INFRASTRUCTURE DEVELOPMENT GROUP

The Infrastructure Development Group (IDG) will comprise of experts and agencies namely the PWD, MCD, NDMC, NHAI, DMRC, I&F Deptt, DJB, Power Companies, DDA, etc. This group will streamline infrastructure planning strategies and practices and formulate projects with latest technological and management interventions.

18.4.6 ENFORCEMENT AND PLAN MONITORING GROUP

The Enforcement and Plan Monitoring Group (EG) may comprise of the professionals, concerned local bodies and residents and evolve strategic action plans to ensure enforcement of the Plan. It will work out the implementation strategy and Monitoring System to review the progress periodically.

18.4.7 SPATIAL DATA INFRASTRUCTURE (SDI) GROUP

The SDI Group will ensure that the documentation, information with respect to settlements, colonies, villages, buildings, utilities, transport network, land use etc. incorporating upto date Geographical Information System, land/ground surveys, layout plans and land use plans are systematically organized and disseminated. This will develop a common database and provide a platform for documentation, planning and timely implementation of the Plan.

18.4.8 LOCAL LEVEL PARTICIPATORY PLANNING GROUP

The Group will define local areas and work out systems and procedures so that the local governments could take up the preparation of local level plans by participatory process. The institutional capacity building for this purpose should be taken up as a priority.

18.4.9 COMMON PLATFORM FOR BUILDING APPROVALS

To streamline the process of building approvals and to bring together many agencies involved in planning permissions and approvals, the Group shall work out the establishment of a common platform. The aim will be to devolve the process of building approvals and to deregulate, wherever necessary, and to review the Building Bye-laws and procedures.

18.4.10 SLUM REHABILITATION AND SOCIAL HOUSING GROUP

The Group will work out policies, physical and financial strategies and organizational structure for slum & JJ rehabilitation with the objective to make Delhi Slum free within a time frame.

18.4.11 LEGAL FRAMEWORK REVIEW GROUP

It is time that the present legal framework is reviewed and the framing of the following Regulations are taken up:

(a) Land Assembly and Private Sector Participation in Housing and Land Development.

(b) Regularisation & Up-gradation of Unauthorised Colonies and areas of mixed use.

(c) Local level Planning Regulations.

18.5 REVIEW

Timely review of the plan with the help of above groups and monitoring unit shall ensure mid-term correction and modifications if needed in the Plan Policies as well as the implementation procedures, which will help to re-adjust the events in the plan that could not be foreseen or anticipated during the Plan Formulation. If the plan is timely monitored and appropriately reviewed, the policies can be moulded in the right direction according to the present needs of the people of the city.

18.6 PROGRAMME OF ACTION

Chapter No.	Title	Programme of Action	Instrument/ Agency
2.0	Population & Employment	The projected population for NCT Delhi will BE reviewed after Census figures of 201 are published.	DDA and concerned agencies
3.0	Population Holding Capacity of Delhi	Redevelopment areas should be identified and Special Redevelopment Schemes should be prepared for implementation within a stipulated time framework.	DDA, MCD, NDMC & Cantonment Board
4.1	Housing Need	In order to ensure that housing need is accommodated in the Urban Extension, the Zonal Plans for 2021 should be prepared within 12 months.	DDA

4.2	Housing Strategy		
4.2.1	New Housing Areas	A suitable policy and guidelines involving Public Private Sectors is to be framed. The policy should ensure that a min. provision of 55% percent of the housing is for EWS & LIG.	DDA in collaboration with the Government of NCT of Delhi and the Ministry of Urban Development
4.2.2.2 A.	Restructuring and Upgradation of the Existing Areas • Traditional Inner City and Unplanned Areas • Special Area and Villages • Heritage Conservation Zone	Special Area Redevelopment Schemes must be prepared for traditional areas, giving the development control parameters for the heritage areas keeping in view archeological norms / architectural character and general parameters for the non-heritage segment of the traditional area. Each Special Area Redevelopment Scheme for a traditional area should entail an enumeration of the monuments and old buildings within the heritage areas which must be conserved.	MCD, DDA & ASI
4.2.2.2 b.	Unauthorized / Regularised Colonies	In all unauthorised colonies, whether on private or public land, regularization should be done as per the government orders issued from time to time. It must be ensured that for improvement of physical and social infrastructure, the minimum necessary / feasible level of services and community facilities are provided.	DDA, MCD & GNCTD
4.2.3.4	Housing for the Urban Poor Guidelines for Collective Community Rehabilitation/ Relocation-In-situ Upgradation/ Rehabilitation of Slum & JJ Clusters & Resettlement Colonies	The concerned implementing agency/ corporate body should work out schemes for collective communit rehabilitation/ relocation and explore the possibility of involving private sector/slum cooperatives. In existing resettlement colonies, redevelopment, regular servicing and maintenance, are to be based on the guidelines and incentives as applicable for the Squatter Rehabilitation Scheme.	DDA, MCD, GNCTD
4.3	Night Shelters	On the basis of 2001 Census of Houseless population at least 25 sites should earmarked in Delhi for Night Shelters.	DDA, MCD, NDMC & GNCTD.
14.0	Physical Infrastructure	Provision of physical infrastructure like power, water, sewerage and solid waste disposal to be ensured for the projected population.	DJB, Delhi Transco Ltd., MCD, GNCTD and other concerned agencies.
16.0	Landuse	Zonal Development Plans of MPD-2021 should be prepared and notified within 1 year of approval of the MPD-2021.	DDA

Note:

Detailed Action Plans shall be prepared by the concerned departments/organizations/local bodies specifying time lines.

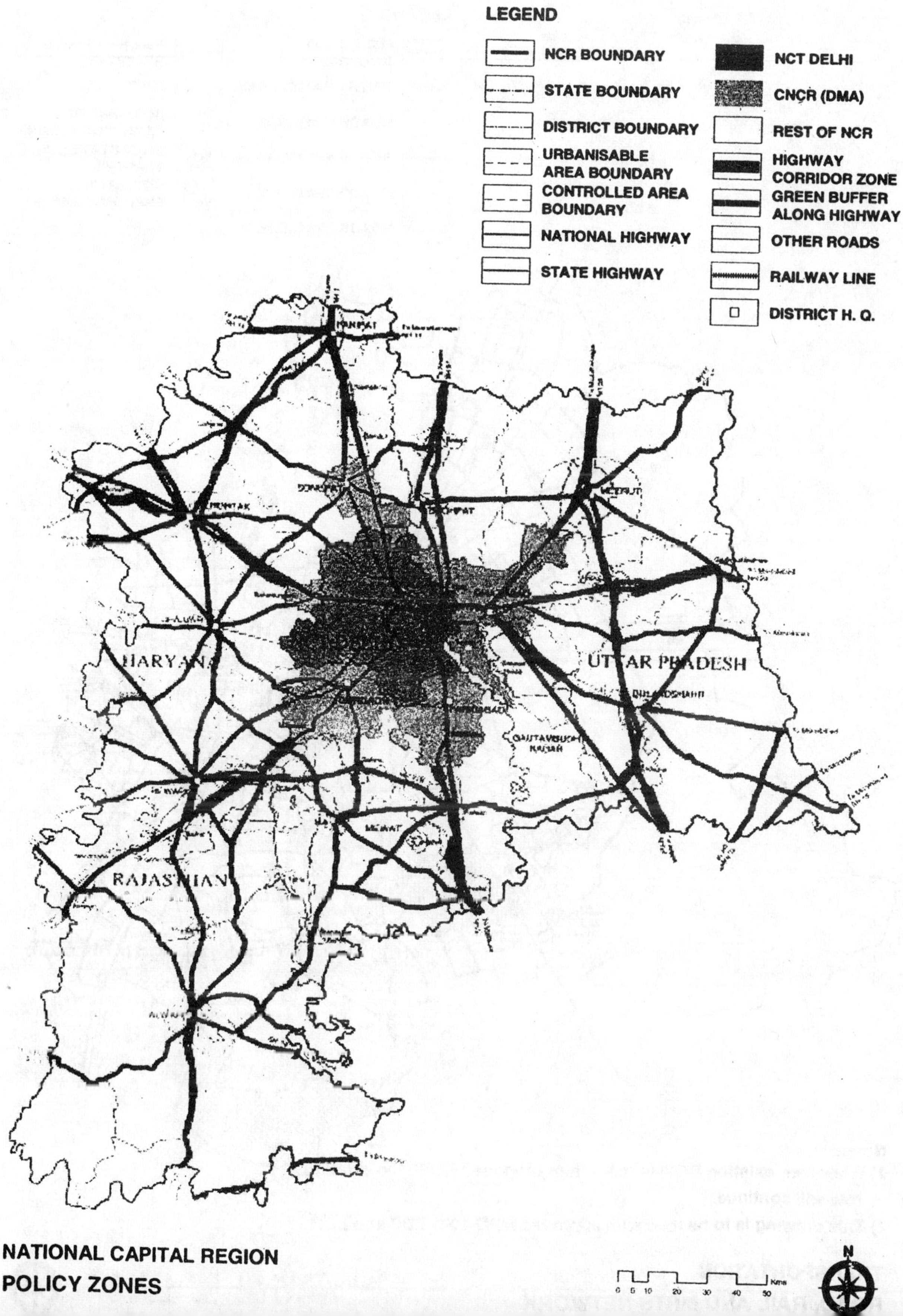

NATIONAL CAPITAL REGION
POLICY ZONES

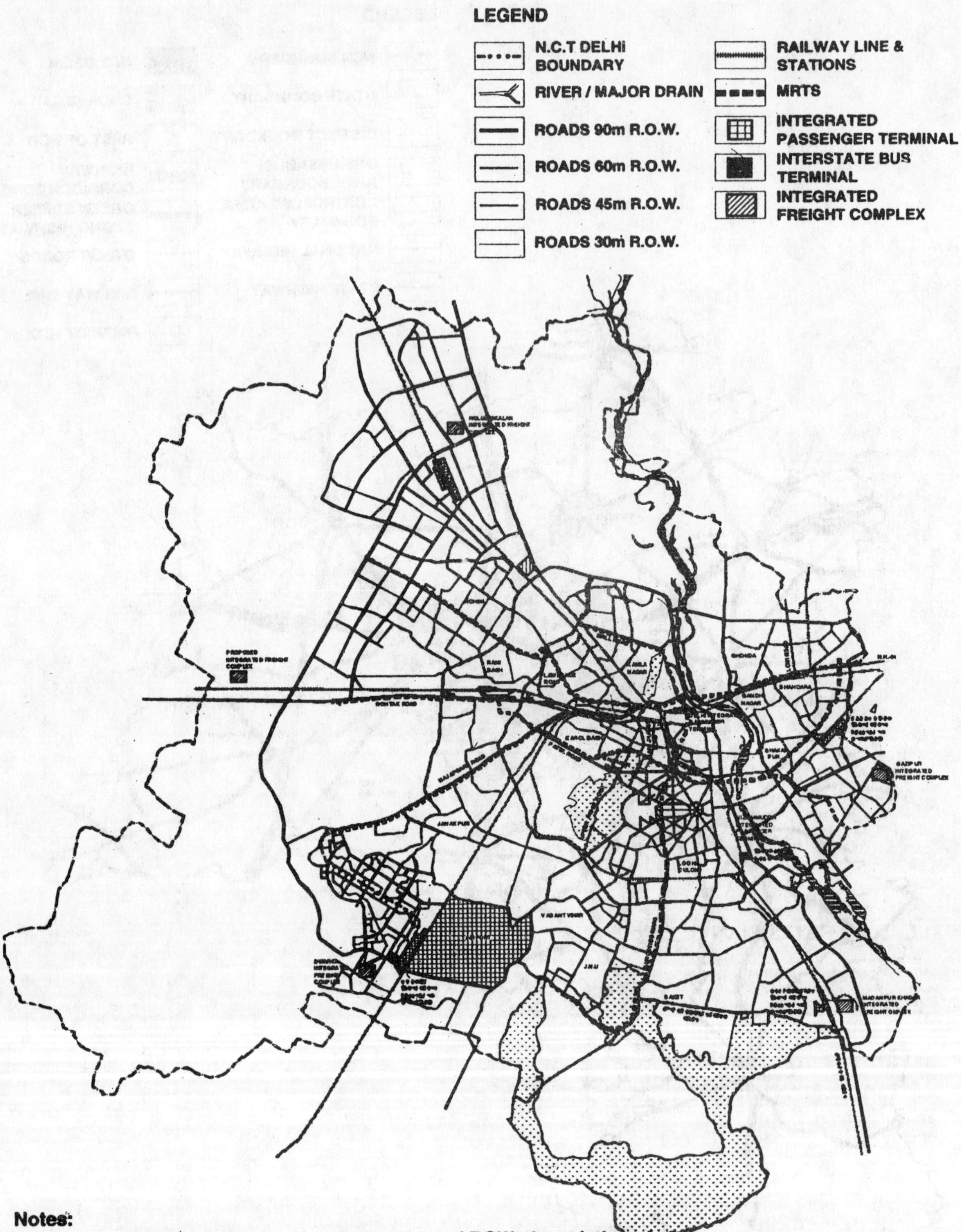

Notes:

1) Wherever, existing ROW is more than proposed ROW, the existing row will continue.

2) This drawing is to be read with approved MPD-2001 ZDP and LOP.

TRANSPORTATION

ROAD, RAIL AND MRTS NETWORK

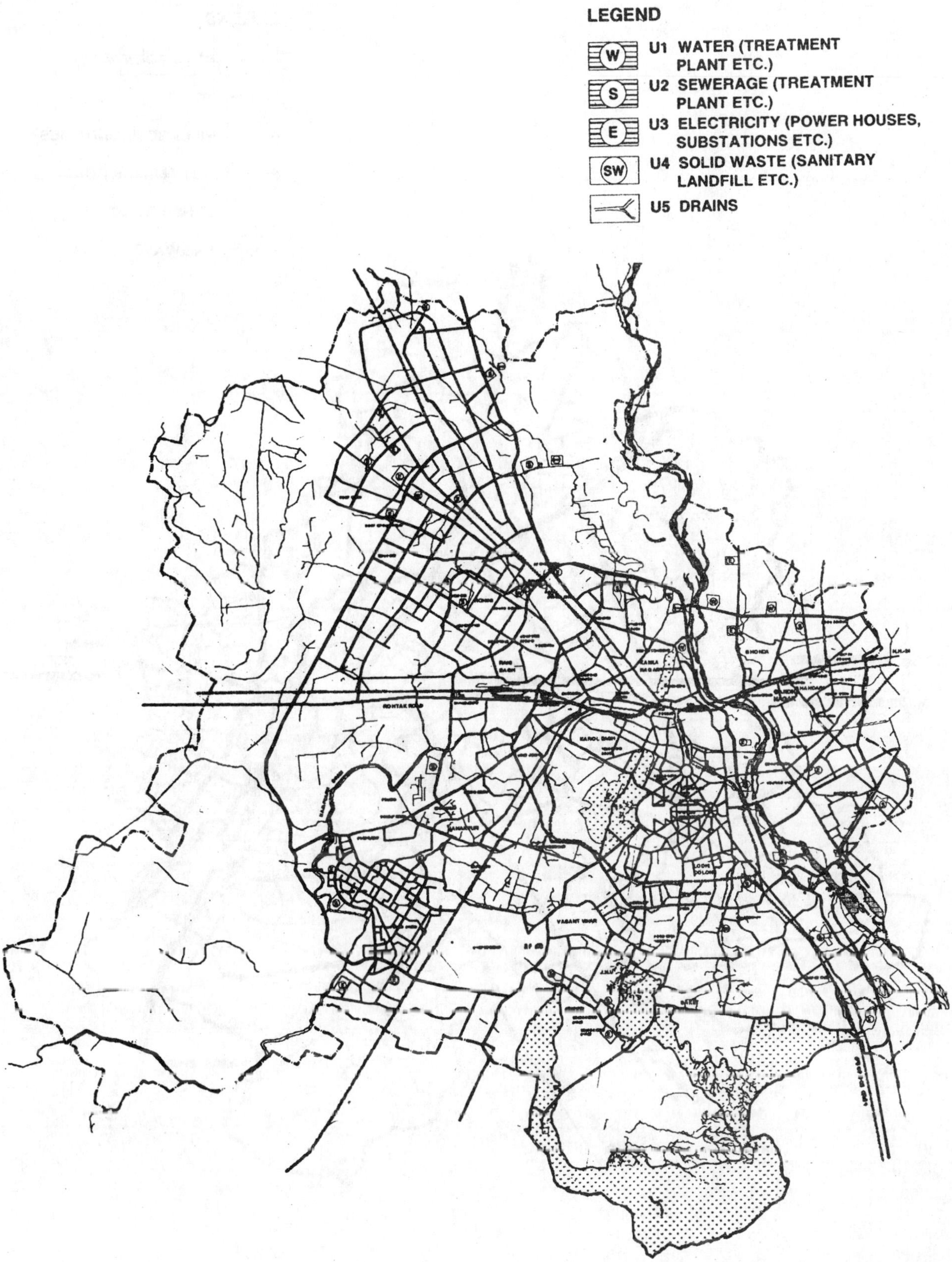

PHYSICAL INFRASTRUCTURE UTILITIES

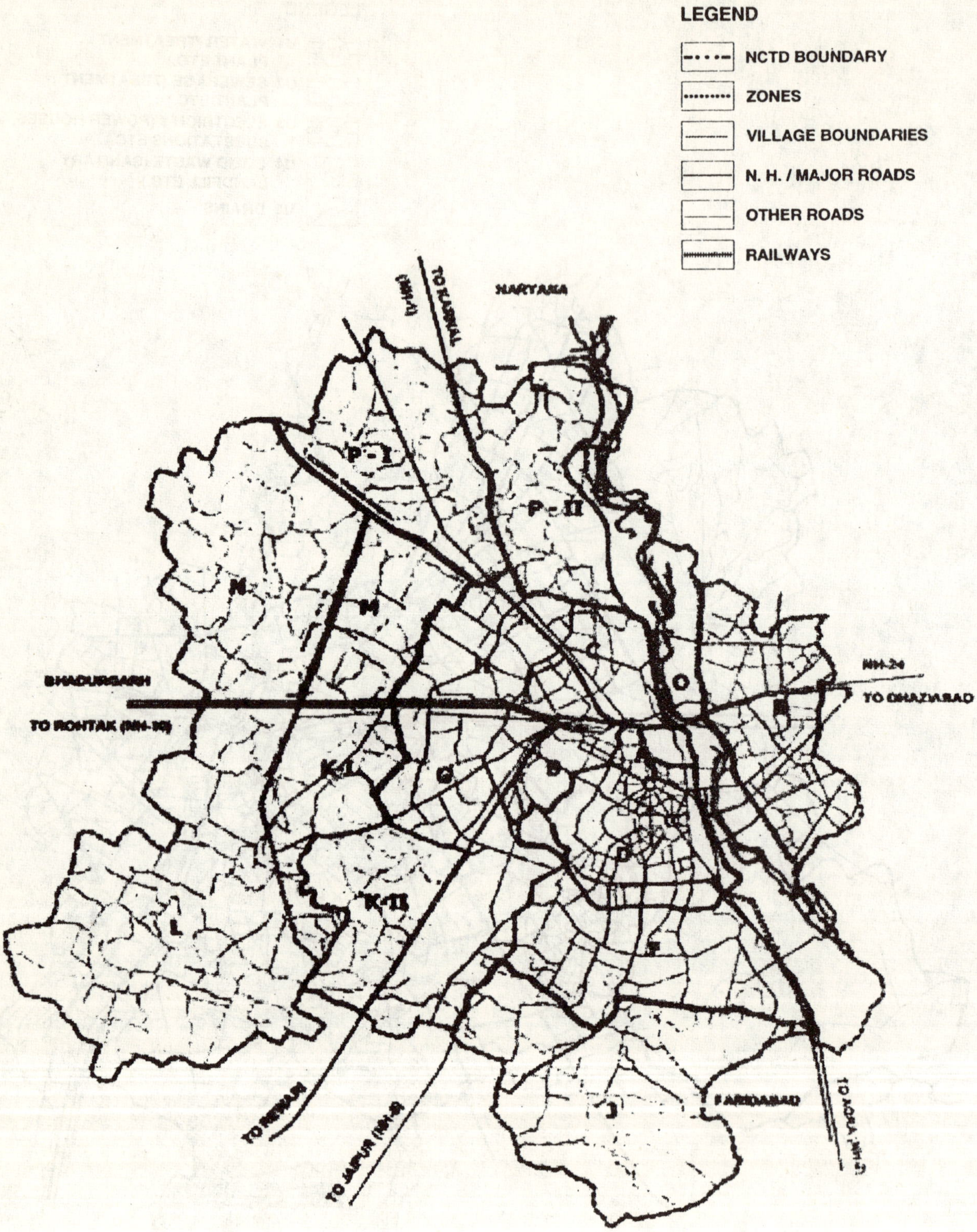

NATIONAL CAPITAL TERRITORY OF DELHI
ZONES (DIVISIONS)

SUB DIVISIONS FOR ZONES (DIVISIONS) A TO H

DRAWING NOT TO SCALE

N

ANNEXURE-I

DELHI JAL BOARD, GOVT. OF NCT OF DELHI

OFFICE OF THE SUPERINTENDING ENGINEER (P) WATER

VARUNALAYA BUILDING, KAROL BAGH, NEW DELHI.

No: DJB/SE (P) W/06/2402 Dated: 29-12-06

To

The Commissioner (Planning)

Vikas Sadan, INA,

New Delhi.

Sub:-MPD 2021 - Perspective Plan for Infrastructural Services - Water Supply.

Sir,

DDA is in the process of preparing the Master Plan 2021 for Delhi. A meeting had been held in a few days back with the representative of DDA to discuss connected issues. Accordingly, enclosed please find herewith our comments and perspective Plan for Infrastructural Services for Delhi - 2021 - water supply.

Thanking you,

Yours faithfully,

(G.R.K. Bansal)

S.E. (P) Water

Copy to :-

1. Member (WS) for information please.
2. C.E. (Project) Water for information please.
3. E.E. (P) Water-III

S.E. (P) Water

Perspective Plan For Infrastructural Services For Delhi -2021

Water Supply

The total area of the National Capital Territory of Delhi (N.C.T.D) is 1,48,639 Ha. As per 2001 census, the population of Delhi is 137.8 lacs. Taking into account, the past trends, the population of Delhi is estimated to be around 190 lacs by 2011 & 230 lacs by 2021.

PRESENT WATER AVAILABILITY

The Delhi Jal Board has an installed capacity of 805 MGD against which on an average 800 to 820 MGD potable water is expected to be produced by optimization of Water Treatment Plants.

PRESENT WATER DEMAND

The present water demand for potable water in Delhi has been assessed as 990 MGD @ 60 gpcd for all uses. No allowance is made for use of potable water for parks & lawns/horticulture/agriculture purposes due to water shortage.

PROJECTED WATER DEMAND 2011

The Delhi Jal Board anticipates that by the year 2011 about 1140 MGD potable water @ 60 gpcd for a population of 190 lacs shall be required. However, the DDA has projected the 2011 water demand as 1520 MGD @ 80 gpcd.

PROJECTED WATER DEMAND IN 2021

The Delhi Jal Board anticipates that by the year 2021 about 1380 MGD potable water @ 60 gpcd for a population of 230 lacs shall be required. However, the DDA has projected the 2021 water demand as 1840 MGD @ 80 gpcd.

BASIS FOR ADOPTING PER CAPITA WATER REQUIREMENT

a) Delhi Jal Board

The Delhi Jal Board is adopting the domestic consumption as per C.P.H.E.E.O Manual 1999 on water supply which provides for domestic consumption in Metropolitan & mega cities as 150 LPCD plus 15% losses. As per the Manual, the water requirement for other uses is to be assessed separately. To assess the water demand for other uses, the Delhi Jal Board has followed the Master Plan Document - 2001. Consequently, the per capita water requirement works out as follows:

I.	Domestic (150 + 22)	172 LPCD
II.	Industrial, commercial and community requirement at 45,000 lts. Per Ha. Per day	47 LPCD.
III.	Special uses, embassies, floating population, hotels, airports and railway stations etc.	52 LPCD.
IV.	Fire protection @ 1% of total demand	3 LPCD
		Total - 274 LPCD

(Say 60 gallons per capita per day (GPCD).

(b) Delhi Development Authority

The total city requirement is considered as 80 gpcd out of which 50 gpcd is for domestic requirement and 30 gpcd for non-domestic purposes. The domestic water requirement of 50 gpcd comprises of 30 gpcd for potable needs and 20 gpcd for non-potable water. The requirement of potable water out of total requirement of 80 gpcd has been assessed as 35 gpcd (30 gpcd for domestic and 5 gpcd for non-domestic demand) while the demand for non-potable water has been assessed as 45 gpcd i.e 20 gpcd for domestic and 25 gpcd for non-domestic purposes.

However, the stand of DJB is that it is more realistic to calculate demand projection @ 60 gpcd., as 80 gpcd is unrealistic to achieve.

PRESENT SOURCES OF RAW WATER

The present sources of raw water available to Delhi are as under:-

Yamuna Water	-	750 cusec (Includes 130 cusec transit losses from Tajewala to Haiderpur)
Ganga water	-	470 cusec at Bhagirathi and Sonia Vihar Water Works.
BBMB Water	-	225 cusec (Ex. Nangal 371 cusec)
BBMB Water	-	40 cusec (Ex. Nanagla 60 cusec)
Ground Water	-	185 cusec.

Based on the availability of above raw water, following water treatment plants are functioning:—

Sl. No.	Source of Raw Water	Name of the Plant	Installed Capacity
1.	River Yamuna	Chandrawal I & II	90 MGD
2.	River Yamuna	Wazirabad I, II & III	120 MGD
3.	Bhakra Storage	Haiderpur I	100 MGD
4.	Yamuna	Haidepur II	100 MGD
5.	Bhakra Storage	Nangloi	40 MGD
6.	Upper Ganga Canal	Bhagirathi	100 MGD
7.	Upper Ganga Canal	Sonia Vihar	140 MGD
8.	Sub-Surface Water	Ranney Wells/Tube wells	115 MGD
		Total	805 MGD

Although, installed capacity of Nangloi Water Treatment Plant is 40 MGD, but presently it is treating only 20 MGD, due to raw water constraints. Balance 20 MGD water is likely to be available for this plant after the commissioning of Parallel lined channel by Haryana Government.

SHARE IN YAMUNA WATER

A MoU for sharing of Yamuna water between five riparian states, Haryana, U.P., Himachal Pradesh, Rajasthan & N.C.T. of Delhi has been signed on 12.05.1994 and Delhi share in Yamuna water has been fixed as 0.724 BCM (consumptive). The above allocation is subject to construction of Renuka Dam, Kishau Dam, Lakhwar Vyasi Project. Pending construction of these dams, following seasonal allocations have been made: —

S. No.	States	July to Oct.	Nov. to Feb.	Mar. to June	Total
1.	Haryana	4.107	0.686	0.937	5.730
2.	Uttar Pradesh	3.216	0.343	0.473	4.032
3.	Rajashthan	0.963	0.070	0.086	1.119
4.	Himachal	0.190	0.108	0.080	0.378
5.	Delhi	0.580	0.068	0.076	0.724
		(1926 cusec)	(231 cusec)	(255 cusec)	(808 cusec)

Presently, Delhi is getting about 750 cusecs of raw water during the lean season against a consumptive allocation of 255 cusecs. After fulfilling the consumptive need, 495 cusecs flows back in the river as return flow.

With the construction of the dams in the upper reaches of river Yamuna, Delhi's consumptive allocation will be 808 cusecs and total allocation will be 2400 cusecs.

POLICY DECISIONS NEED TO BE TAKEN IMMEDIATELY FOR EFFICIENT WATER MANAGEMENT

Requirement of potable water for significant years are discussed later in this plan. However, seeing to the gap in the present demand and supply and for the overall efficient management of water resources, the following policy decisions needs to be taken/implemented on priority:-

i) Regulation and control of under ground water:-

Presently, there is no control over the extraction of underground water except banning of new bore wells in selected pockets by C.G.W.A. This has led to depletion of water table at an accelerating pace and in future large area well be affected. Depletion of water table would lead to enhancement of demand from the D.J.B.

The continued abstraction of groundwater in urban areas has led to severe depletion of groundwater levels. Unrestricted and unregulated abstraction of groundwater has serious long term environmental implications. Over extraction of ground water can result in drying up of resources and may also affect water quality. The National Water Policy 2002, issued by the Ministry of Water Resources, GOI emphasizes that 'Exploitation of groundwater should be so regulated as not to exceed recharging possibilities, as also to ensure social equity. The detrimental environmental consequences of overexploitation of groundwater need to be effectively prevented by the Central and state governments. The Central government has set up a Central Ground Water Authority, under the MOWR under the Environment (Protection) Act 1986. Its powers, among other things include the power to regulate and control management and development of ground water in the country and to issue necessary regulatory directions for the purpose. CGWA had in the year 2000 notified the South and South West districts of Delhi as critical areas where regulation had become necessary due to over exploitation of groundwater. Subsequently, through a notification in March 2006, it has notified East district, New Delhi district, North East district, North West District and West district as over exploited areas needing regulation. Now 7 out of 9 districts have been deemed to be overexploited zones in the state of Delhi. This makes the need for regulation of exploitation of ground water critically imperative.

The MOWR, GOI had prepared a model groundwater bill way back in 1996 and circulated it for enactment to various state governments. So far the states of Andhra Pradesh, Goa, Tamil Nadu, Kerala and Union territories of Lakshadweep and Pondicherry have enacted and implemented ground water legislation. Subsequently, keeping in view of the provisions of National Water Policy, 2002, MOWR, GOI circulated revised Model Bill 2005 to regulate and control the development and management of Ground Water in February, 2005. Delhi Jal Board has also formulated a draft bill namely the Delhi Water

Board Act (Amendment) Bill-2006 to régulate and control the development and management of ground water in NCT, Delhi. A preamble of the amendment bill is annexed as Annexure - A to the plan.

(ii) Cost of enhancement:—

Marginal cost of further enhancements of water is going to be substantial, as it will involve construction of huge reservoirs in the form of dams, construction of conveyance system, construction of transmission, peripheral and distribution main and underground reservoirs in the city. At present, infrastructure development fund is being charged from the Developing Agencies for developed areas @ Rs. 15/- per litre of average daily demand, but the same is not enough to finance the cost of the huge reservoirs and dams. So, it is necessary to enhance the same to finance the construction of dams and transmission of bulk/raw water. The quantum of levy and detail modalities can be worked out subsequently.

(iii) Prevention of wastage and theft of water:—

Wastage and theft of water will have to be curbed mercilessly. Suitable amendments are necessary in Delhi Water Board Act to provide for stringent measures for enforcing curbs on theft/wastage of water. Simultaneously, it would be necessary to evolve more intelligent system of leak detection and control which would require investments for metering at all levels, segregation of district metering areas, setting of up of pressure gauges etc.

WATER SUPPLY SCENARIO IN 2011

Sl. No.	Source of Raw Water	Name of the Plant	Installed Capacity in 2011
1.	River Yamuna	Chandrawal I & II	90 MGD
2.	River Yamuna	Wazirabad I, II, & III	120 MGD
3.	Bhakra Storage	Haiderpur I	100 MGD
4.	Yamuna	Haidepur II	100 MGD
5.	Bhakra Storage	Nangloi	40 MGD
6.	Upper Ganga Canal	Bhagirathi	100 MGD
7.	Sub-Surface Water	Ranney Wells/Tubewells	125 MGD
8.	Upper Ganga Canal	Sonia Vihar	140 MGD
9.	Saving from seepage losses with the construction of new parallel lined channel	Dwarka	40 MGD
10.	-do-	Bawana	20 MGD
11.	-do-	Okhla	20 MGD
12.	---	Recycling of wastewater at water treatment plants	45 MGD
			Total:— 940 MGD

PROPOSED STEPS TO BE TAKEN TO MEET THE SHORTFALL UPTO 2011

As seen from the above table, Delhi Jal Board will be able to increase its treatment capacity of 805 MGD at the end of 2006 to 940 MGD by the year 2011 against the projected demand of 1140 MGD by taking following steps:—

(i) Water Treatment Plant at Dwarka, Bawana & Okhla

The existing parallel lined channel from Munak to Haiderpur water treatment plant is having seepage losses to the tune of 30%. It is proposed to construct a parallel lined channel from Munak to Haiderpur water treatment plant. With the construction of this channel, there will be saving of about 160 cusecs of raw water and Delhi Jal Board has proposed construction of water treatment plants of 40 MGD at Dwarka, 20 MGD at Bawana and 20 MGD at Okhla.

Even after the commissioning of above Projects, there is shortfall of about 200 MGD. To meet this shortfall, the following steps are proposed to be taken up:-

(a) Govt. of NCT of Delhi may approach Ministry of Water Resources for increase in raw water allocation of Yamuna water by 370 cusecs during the lean period to meet the drinking water requirement of Delhi during the above period.

(b) Govt. of NCT of Delhi has made a request to Ministry of Water Resources for additional allocation for surplus Ravi-Vyas Water.

(c) Govt. of NCT of Delhi has initiated rain water harvesting in Delhi which will help in sustaining the present availability of ground water. These efforts shall be continued thereafter also.

(d) In addition to sustaining sub-surface water availability of 115 MGD at the end of 2006 by rain water harvesting, the D.J.B. can extract additional 10 MGD as suggested by C.G.W.B. from the following locations:—

(ii) 5 MGD can be extracted from flood plains of river Yamuna in NCT of Delhi along Okhla barrage-Kalindi Kunj reach through a battery of about 25 tubewells.

(iii) 5 MGD can be extracted from flood plains of river Yamuna in NCT of Delhi along Akshar Dham Mandir-Nizamuddin bridge reach through a battery of about 25 tubewells.

Common Wealth Village is likely to come up near Aksha Dhakm Mandir for the proposed Common Wealth Games to be held in 2010. The entire village can be fed though a battery of 25 tubewells and a small treatment plant of 5 MGD. The D.D.A. will have to reserve about 7.5 acres of land for the treatment plant in the vicinity of the area.

(iv) It is recommended that D.D.A. may explore possibility of dual pipe system in limited way for flushing purpose only, in all group housing societies and new colonies. The idea is to collect the waste water from bathrooms in a storage tank and pump it to separate overhead storage tank for this purpose at roof-top and then connect the same with cisterns in the toilets for flushing purpose only.

The present population of Delhi is 165 lacs and it is projected to be 190 lacs by 2011 which means the population will increase by 25 lacs. Now, assuming that 60% of this population will come up in new planned colonies the population works out to be about 15 lacs. As per D.D.A., the domestic non-potable consumption is 20 gpcd. Out of this 20 gpcd it can be safely assumed that 10 gpcd will be for washing/cleaning purposes and 10 gpcd for toilet and flushing purposes. This means that saving on water by application of partial dual piping system will be 15 MGD.

(v) Although, there is no further scope of augmenting the present sub-surface water in NCT of Delhi, due to lack of both quantity and quality, the N.C.R. region in the neighboring states have promising prospects. The entire projected shortfall of 200 MGD by 2011 can be met by developing a system of tubewells in following regions in the NCR:-

(a) **Yamuna Flood Plains of NCR** - This area falls in Panipat & Sonepat districts of Haryan and Baghpat district of Uttar Pradesh. The area extends from Karaina in the North to Palla in the South.

(b) **The Area along Upper Ganga Canal in NCR** - This area extends from Jani (located on Baghpat-Meerut road) in the North and Muradnagar in the South. The demarcated area is in a length & width of about 20 Kms. and 50 Kms. respectively on either side of Upper Ganga canal.

(c) **The Ganga Flood Plains in NCR** - The C.G.W.B. has earmarked the area along the Ganga River as one of the most potential for development of ground water to be supplied to NCT of Delhi. The khaddar zone on the Western side of Ganga River extend up to 15 Kms. from Parichatgarh in the North to Syana in the South and falls in Parichat Development Block of Ghaziabad district of Uttar Pradesh. The area is bounded by Madhya Ganga Canal in the West and Ganga River in the East.

(vi) **Water Reclamation**

The D.J.B. shall also explore the possibility of reclamation of sewage water on the lines of NE Water of Singapore using ultra-filtration, reverse osmosis and UV treatment processes by going through a pilot project of 6 MGD at Okhla S.T.P. If, it is found techno-economically feasible, then large scale reclamation of sewage water at Treatment Plants can be taken up in phases. The first plant for such large scale tertiary treatment of water will be at Rithala sewage treatment plant, which can add upto 40 MGD of treated water. This can be further taken to Hyderpur WTP for distribution.

In view of above, it is obvious that the shortfall of 200 MGD by 2011 can only be met either by increased allocation of Delhi during lean period or by developing a system of tube wells in the NCR or by combination of two as an interim measure till the dams in Upper Reaches in Yamuna are completed. The intervention of Ministry of Water Resources is needed for both cases. The existing corridor for raw water transportation after the lining of Western Yamuna Canal and completion of parallel lined channel will be more or less sufficient to carry the additional requirement of 2011. The D.D.A. will have to allocate the land measuring about 300 acres @ 1.5 acres/mgd (That is 1.5 Acres for every additional population of 15000 persons) also the equal amount of land may also be kept reserved for construction of UGR's and Pumping station at strategic locations for the construction of additional 200 mgd treatment plants and its allied works. While allocating the land for additional treatment capacity, location of new developing colonies and sources of raw water shall have to be kept in view.

WATER SUPPLY SCENARIO IN 2021

Sl. No.	Source of Raw Water	Name of the Plant	Installed Capacdity in 2021
1.	River Yamuna	Chandrawal I & II	90 MGD
2.	River Yamuna	Wazirabad I, II, & III	120 MGD
3.	Bhakra Storage	Haiderpur I	100 MGD
4.	Yamuna	Haidepur II	100 MGD
5.	Bhakra Storage	NanglOi	40 MGD
6.	Upper Ganga Canal	Bhagirathi	100 MGD
7.	Sub-Surface Water	Ranney Wells/Tubewells	125 MGD
8.	Upper Ganga Canal	Sonia Vihar	140 MGD
9.	Saving from seepage losses with the construction of new parallel lined channel	Dwarka	40 MGD
10.	-do-	Bawana	20 MGD
11.	-do-	Okhla	20 MGD
12.	-	Recycling of wastewater at water treatment plants	45 MGD
		Total	940 MGD

PROPOSED STEPS TO BE TAKEN TO MEET THE SHORTFALL UPTO 2021

As seen from the above table, Delhi Jal Board will not be in a position to increase its treatment capacity of 941 MGD by the year 2011 from the existing resources and raw water sources. The projected demand in 2021 will be of 1380 MGD @ 60 gpcd for 230 lacs population, thus, there will be a shortfall of about 440 MGD. To meet this shortfall, the work on following dams has to be expedited. There seems to be no other alternative.

On completion of above projects, Delhi will receive its full share of 0.724 BCM(808 Cusecs Consumptive). The total allocation works out to 2400 cusecs that means an additional 1600 cusecs (865 MGD) will be available to Delhi which is more than enough to meet the projected shortfall of 440 MGD by 2021.

(A) Renuka Dam

Renuka is contemplated as a 148 meter high rock fill dam on River Giri, a tributary of Yamuna, in Sirmour district of Himanchal Pradesh, mainly to augment water supply to Delhi, estimated cost is Rs 1225 crores at May 1997 price level. The project has been cleared by CEC and approval of MoE&F is likely to be obtained shortly.

(B) Kishau Dam

This dam is to be constructed on the River Tons in Uttranchal. Kishau Dam project has been examined in C.W.C. for broad technical and economic aspects and was found technically and economically feasible. It was recommended for consideration by the Advisory Committee at an estimated cost of Rs. 35,662 million (December 1998 price level). The Kishau Dam project was taken up in the 72nd meeting of the advisory Committee on Irrigation, Flood Control and Multipurpose Projects, on 18 January 2000. After discussion, it was decided that consideration of the project be deferred until a further elaboration of the economic viability has been prepared, including apportioning project costs among the irrigation, power and water supply components. As per latest information from Utranchal govt. it has been informed that a MOU has been signed with the Tehri Hydro Development Corporation (THDC) for construction of the dam.

(C) Lakhwar Vyasi Dam

This project envisages construction of 204 m high concrete dam on river Yamuna near Lakhwar Village in Dehradoon district of Uttranchal, and another dam down stream at Vyasi, for providing drinking water, irrigation and power generation. This Project was approved by the planning commission way back in 1976. However, the State Government submitted revised estimate in 1979, 1994 and 1998. Uttrânchal Government has entrusted the construction of the project and preparation of its revised DPR to NHPC.

The preparation of DPR is in advanced stage by NHPC, but the sharing of cost for project for Irrigation and Drinking water is yet to be agreed by the beneficiary states. Thereafter, NHPC has to sign MOU with other basin states on cost sharing of Irrigation and Drinking water components.

The D.D.A. may reserve the land measuring 600 acres by 2011 and additional 1320 acres by 2021 to construct the additional water treatment plants and its allied works. While allocating the land for additional treatment capacity, location of new developing colonies and sources of raw water shall have to be kept in view.

ANNEXURE- 'A'

Proposed Draft Delhi Water Board (Amendment) Bill, 2006

BACKGROUND

The continued abstraction of groundwater in urban areas has led to severe depletion of groundwater levels. Unrestricted and unregulated abstraction of groundwater has serious long term environmental implications. Over extraction of ground water can result in drying up of resources and may also affect water quality. The National Water Policy 2002, issued by the Ministry of Water Resources, GOI emphasizes that 'Exploitation of groundwater should be so regulated as not to exceed recharging possibilities, as also to ensure social equity. The detrimental environmental consequences of overexploitation of groundwater need to be effectively prevented by the Central and State Governments. The Central Government has set up a Central Ground Water Authority, under the MOWR under the Environment (Protection) Act 1986. Its powers, among other things include the power to regulate and control management and development of ground water in the country and to issue necessary regulatory directions for the purpose. CGWA had in the year 2000 notified the South and South West Districts of Delhi as critical areas where regulation had become necessary due to over exploitation of groundwater. Subsequently, through a notification in March 2006, it has notified East district, New Delhi district, North East district, North West district and West District as over exploited areas needing regulation. Now 7 out of 9 districts have been deemed to be overexploited zones in the state of Delhi. This makes the need for regulation of exploitation of ground water critically imperative.

LEGISLATIVE ARRANGEMENTS

The MOWR, GOI had prepared a model groundwater bill way back in 1996 and circulated it for enactment to various State Governments. We have been receiving continuous references in this regard ever since. So far, the states of Andhra Pradesh, Goa, Tamil Nadu, Kerala and Union Territories of Lakshadweep and Pondicherry have enacted and implemented ground water legislation.

Presently, section 9(1) of the Delhi Water Board act 1998 defines as one of the functions of the Board to 'Plan for, regulate and manage the exploitation of groundwater in Delhi, in consultation with the Central Ground Water Authority and also to give advice in this regard to the New Delhi Municipal Council, the Delhi Cantonment Board or any other local authority:

Provided that the Board shall not license or levy user charge for exploitation of groundwater in any area for the time being falling in the jurisdiction of the New Delhi Municipal Council, the Delhi Cantonment Board, or any other local authority, expect with the prior approval of Central Government.' Based on the principles enunciated in the model bill circulated by Central government, Delhi Jal Board vide its resolution number 204, dated 8th May 2002 approved the Delhi Water Board (Amendment) Bill 2002. The draft Bill was given an in principle approval by the Delhi Council of Ministers vide decision number 861 in 2004. While discussing the Bill, the Council of Ministers had suggested that the need for rainwater harvesting as a mandatory provision prior to grant of permission for new wells or registration of existing ones should be given primacy. The revised Bill was resubmitted and approved by the Council of Ministers meeting on 13th June 2005, with certain proposed amendments. Finally, the Delhi Water Board (Amendment) Bill 2005 was introduced in the Assembly on 22nd September 2005. Several legislators had suggested amendments to the Bill and had raised objections to certain provisions.

The objections were raised by Mr. Mukesh Sharma, MLA and Mr. Vijay Jolly, MLA. Principally the objections raised by the two members pertained to the following:

Mr. Mukesh Sharma:

- The definition of user of groundwater should exclude domestic and agricultural users
- For publication of notice, it was suggested that is should be published in 2 regional language papers and two English language dailies instead of one each.
- The extent of penalties was proposed to be reduced
- The section dealing with the powers of the Board to enter the premises and search and seize equipment should be deleted

Mr. Vijay Jolly:

- The entry inside a premises for search and seizure should be with the prior permission of the property owner
- Power to break open premises for seizing illegal equipment may be dispensed with.

These objections were examined by a committee of DJB headed by Member (W) and the committee felt that the basic intention of the proposed amendment would be affected by accepting the suggestions made by legislators.

Thereafter, the Bill was referred to a Select committee of the Assembly, which in its meeting in 2nd February 2006 decided that the Bill in its present shape was not accepted and should be withdrawn.

However, the need and urgency if ground water regulation is clearly the need of the hour for a sustainable water resource management in Delhi. With fresh raw water resources becoming available in the near future being a remote possibility, the need for an integrated water resource management is essential. The Commissioning of Sonia Vihar treatment plant had increased the availability of filtered water supply to the extent of 30% in hitherto water deficit areas of Delhi. Therefore, now the timing is right to introduce an institutional arrangement of effectively regulating groundwater abstraction.

Meanwhile, a letter was received in February 2005 from Secretary, Ministry of Water Resources, GOI, addressed to the Chief Secretary of Delhi, wherein it was indicated that the Model Bill of 1996 had been revised in light of the NWP 2002 shifting the focus of the Bill from mere regulation to regulation, development and augmentation of groundwater resources. Letters have also been written by the Honorable Prime Minister of India and the Union Minister of Water Resources to the Chief Minister of Delhi, highlighting the urgency of introducing legislation for regulation of groundwater usage.

It is felt that perhaps it would be prudent to re introduce the amendment of the Delhi Water Board Act, incorporating the salient features of the Model Bill circulated by GOI. This would avoid the need to set up a separate Groundwater Regulation Authority because in a small state like Delhi there is perhaps no need to have a separate authority for this purpose. Given below are the key variants in this Bill from the Previous Delhi Water Board (Amendment) Bill 2005.

- Some definitions like 'groundwater', 'sink', 'user of groundwater' have been slightly modified keeping in line with the way it is defined in the Model Bill
- A new section 35 D has been added, in line with the Model Bill, which mandates that even users of new wells in non notified areas would have to get themselves registered with the DJB. This does not mean that they would have to seek permission in non notified areas, but would have to register themselves. This would help the DJB to track the extent of exploitation of groundwater even in non notified areas in the future, so that if even some non notified areas to be regulated in future, sufficient data should be available for the same. It would also help in integrated water resource management to enable a correct mix of filtered water supplies and groundwater supplies.
- A new section 35 E has been added, as per the Model Bill 2005, mandating that all drilling agencies would have to get themselves registered with the Board. This would enable a parallel check on the extent of underground drilling being undertaken through these rig owners.
- Section 35 H defines the powers of the Board. This section actually merges the provision of the previous section 35 F and section 35 H (power to levy user charges) in a common heading. However, this section authorizes the Board to enter premises, for investigation and measurement between 9 am and 5 pm, in presence of the occupier or a duly authorized person, after giving a due notice. Further, it authorizes the Board from time to time prescribe the basis of collection of user charges, the categories of customers to be charged, areas where such charges shall be levied. In due course, it may evolve a sound basis of regulating multiple usages of groundwater through a mix of policy and pricing mechanisms.
- Section 35 J has been added as a new section to specifically deal with rainwater harvesting. This has been done in line with the provisions of the Model Bill 2005. The introduction of a specific legislative sanction for rainwater harvesting will be a major step in promoting rainwater harvesting. The GNCT of Delhi has so far been promoting rainwater harvesting through executive orders and budgetary layouts. But this section would give a legislative backing to scale up the rainwater harvesting efforts.
- Penalties defined in the Schedules have been enhanced keeping in view the fact that they should serve as a sufficient deterrent.

ANNEXURE 'B'

Water Management By Use Of Recycled Waste Water

Concept of water management includes water conservation, water harvesting and water recycling for sustainable water management. In India traditional water conservation and water harvesting have been in practice and many cities have modified their byelaws to encourage water harvesting in residential buildings of new development. But little have been done in water reuse and recycling within the building as a strategy to reduce the water demand.

Delhi, the capital of India, is experiencing a rapid population increase from 0.4 million in 1911 to 13.8 million in 2001. The Delhi Development Authority is projecting a population of 23 million in 2021 and water requirement of 1150 million gallon per day (MGD). On the other hand Delhi Jal Board's (DJB) capacity augmentation plan 2021 says the capacity can be increased to a maximum of 919MGD by all possible sources (Table 1) Inadequate and intermittent supply of piped water has led unchecked exploitation of ground water resources in different parts of the city.

Table 1: Water Augmentation Plan of Delhi Jal Board

S.No.	Water treatment Plants	Capacity 2001 in MGD	Capacity *2021 in mgd
1.	Chandrawal I & II	90	100
2.	Wazirabad	120	130
3.	Haiderpur I & II	200	216
4.	Bhagirathi	100	110
5.	Dwarka	-	40
6.	Sonia Vihar	-	140
7.	Nangloi	40	40
8.	Bawana	-	20
9.	Okhla	-	20
10.	Ranney wells at Okhla	100	12
11.	Palla and other ground water sources		91
	Total	650	919

*Capacity proposed by DJB in case non construction of Dams by 2021

About 40 percent of the treated water supplied by the DJB daily is never used for drinking. Instead it is used for domestic chores, including flushing of toilets. The avoidable wastage has continued for years even as the city's demand for drinking water is rising by 20MGD per year. From the breakup of use of water required for different activity in our day-to-day like-viz for drinking and cooking, for washing, for toilet flushing, for industries, for recreation, for maintaining garden and urban green, it can be seen that 90 lpcd is absolutely waste is about 40% of the total demand.

Table 2 : Breakup of water usage for 50 gpcd is as under:

`Purpose		Potable @ 30 gpcd (135 lpcd)	Non-potable @ gpcd (90 lpcd)
1.	Drinking	05	
2.	Cooking	10	
3.	Washing clothes	30	
4.	Washing utensil	20	
5.	Washing hand and faces	10	
6.	Bathing	60	
7.	Floor washing		30
8.	Flushing of toilets		60
	Total @ 225 lpcd	135 lpcd	90 lpcd

As per the new building byelaws in Delhi, all the buildings having a minimum discharge of 10,000 or above liters per day shall incorporate wastewater recycling system. The recycled water would be used for horticulture purpose (GOI notification, 28th July 2001). Although the agencies are taking care while sanctioning the plans but enforcement of the provisions are to be strengthened at ground. The figure of 10,000 liter discharge generated from a plot would mean it should have at least 32 dwelling units with a total population of 144 persons. The group housing societies, shopping malls, institutions, hotels etc are suitable to implement the provisions.

Group Housing Societies and other institutions mentioned above have bore wells of their own, which rather made their supply 24 hours in spite of the intermittent supply by Delhi Jal Board. In these societies / institutions the Jal Board water is collected in the under ground reservoir (Wherever possible) from where the water is pumped to the overhead tanks from where connection to the residents are provided. These overhead tanks are also filled with ground water whenever required and hence water is made available 24 hours. Due to the absence of adequate water supply there is over exploitation of ground water. The level of groundwater is decreasing at a rate of 0.5 m per annum. Therefore immediate measure should be taken to discourage the resident to extract ground water for residential use. Thus there is a need for alternative methods to reduce the residential water demand in such institutions viz-a-viz abstraction of ground water.

WATER MANAGEMENT IN INSTITUTION & GROUP HOUSING SOCIETIES

It is found from a primary survey conducted (in 2005) by a group of planning students from School of Planning and Architecture, New Delhi (sample from group housing apartments) that most of these group-societies are spending on an average Rs.20,000/- per month to collect water (an average of @ Rs.600/- per dwelling unit per month) from the sources other than the supply from Delhi Jal Board. The 27 percent reduction in domestic demand will lead to a saving of Rs.5400/- per month and Rs.64,800/- per year. Factor 27% has been assumed on the basis that 80% of 90 lpcd shall be converted into sewage and out of remaining another 5% has been discounted for other losses.

Requirement of Space

The major component of such recycle system is Septic tank, disinfections chamber, simple sand filters (at least two, one for sand by) and pump sets and pipe systems. The septic tank should be able to retain 11,450 liters for two days. The capacity required for the same should be around 24 k-liters and size=3x4.5x2 m3 will be sufficient. The total area required for all other components can be located within the plot.

The recycled water can be pumped to the tank over the apartment blocks and connected to the toilet/flush with totally separate plumbing system.

Economics of the System

The construction of the underground septic tank of capacity of 27k-liters (@2/ per liter)	=Rs. 54,000/-
Construction of Sand filter two in number	=Rs. 40,000/-
Cost of pump + additional plumbing etc.	= Rs. 26,000/-
The total capital cost of the system	=Rs. 1,20,000/-

After discounting a saving of Rs. 64,800/- per year from the procurement of additional water, the total capital cost will be recovered within two year.

ANNEXURE-II

DELHI JAL BOARD

OFFICE OF THE MEMBER (Dr)

VARUNALAYA PHASE-II : KAROL BAGH : NEW DELHI

No: DJB/Mem(Dr)/2004/ Dated: 18.06.04

Kindly refer to your letter no. Dir/MPD-2021/DDA/F-298/607EP dated 11.06.2004 addressed to Chief Secretary with a copy to CEO regarding Perspective Plan for Infrastructure Services for Delhi-2021 pertaining to Sewerage Sector from DJB side. This is in continuation to our letter no. DJB/CE(C) III/F 46/2003/2150-53 dated 21.07.2003 on the same subject with further details.

Sd/-

(RAKESH SETH)

MEMBER (D.R.)

Encl: As above.

Sh. Madhukar Gupta, Vice Chairman,

Vikas Sadan, INA, New Delhi-110023.

Perspective Plan for Infrastructure Services for Delhi-2021-Sewerage

The total area of the National Capital Territory of Delhi (NCTD) is 148639 Hac. As per 2001 Census the population of Delhi is 137.8 Lacs. Taking into account, the past trends, the population of Delhi is estimated to be around 190 Lacs by 2011 & 230 Lacs by 2021.

PRESENT WATER AVAILABILITY:

The Delhi Jal Board having an installed capacity of 650 MGD against which on an average 670 MGD potable water is being produced by optimization of Water Treatment Plants.

PRESENT WATER DEMAND:

The present water demand for potable water in Delhi has been assessed as 828 MGD @ 60 gpcd for all uses. No allowance is made for use of potable water for parks and lawns/horticulture/agriculture purposed due to water shortage.

PROJECTED WATER DEMAND IN 2006:

The Delhi Jal Board anticipates that by the year 2006 about 990 MGD potable water @ 60 gpcd for a population of 165 Lacs shall be required. However, the DDA has projected the 2006 water demand as 1320 MGD @ 80 gpcd.

PROJECTED WATER DEMAND IN 2011:

The Delhi Jal Board anticipates that buy the year 2011 about 1140 MGD potable water @ 60 gpcd for a population of 230 Lacs shall be required. However, the DDA has projected the 2021 water demand as 1840 MGD @ 80 gpcd.

BASIS FOR ADOPTING PER CAPITA WATER REQUIREMENT:

The Delhi Jal Board is adopting domestic consumption as per CPHEEO Manual-1999 on water supply which provides for domestic consumption in Metropolitan and Mega Cities as 150 LPCD plus 15% losses. As per the Manual, the water requirement for other uses is to be assessed separately. To assess the water demand for other uses, the Delhi Jal Board has followed the Master Plan Document-2001. Consequently, the per capita water requirement works out as follows:

(i)	Domestic (150+22)	172 LPCD
(ii)	Industrial, Commercial & community requirement at 45,000 ltrs. per Ha. Per day	47 LPCD
(iii)	Special uses, embassies floating population, hotels, Airports and Railway Stations etc.	52 LPCD
(iv)	Fire protection @ 1% of total demand	3 LPCD
	Total	274 LPCD

(Say 60 gallons per capita per day (GPCD)

Delhi Jal Board have entrusted in December-2001.

PRESENT SOURCES OF RAW WATER:

The present sources of raw water available to Delhi are as under:

Yamuna Water	- 750 cusec (includes 130 cusec transit losses from Tajewala to Haiderpur)
Ganga Water	- 200 cusec at Bhagirathi Water Works.
BBMB Water	- 225 cusecs (Ex. Nangal 371 cusec).
Ground Water	- 185 cusec.

Based on the availability of above raw water, following Water Treatment Plants are functioning:

S.No.	Source of Raw Water	Name of the Plant	Installed Capacity
1.	River Yamuna	Chandrawal-I & II	90 MGD
2.	River Yamuna	Wazirabad-I, II & III	120 MGD
3.	Bhakhra Storage	Haider Pur-I	100 MGD
4.	Yamuna	Haider Pur-II	100 MGD
5.	Bhakhra Storage	Nangloi	40 MGD
6.	Upper Ganga Canal	Bhagirathi	100 MGD
7.	Sub-Surface Water	Ranney Wells/Tubewells	100 MGD
	Total		650 MGD

1. INFRASTRUCTURE: PHYSICAL

1.1 Physical infrastructure 2021 projections:

It has been projected by DDA that for 2021 projected population of the city will be 230 Lacs and requirement of potable water is 805 MGD and non-potable water is 1035 MGD. Total sewage generated has been worked out to 1012 MGD by DDA which seems to be on the lower side keeping in view of the requirement of water worked out by DDA to the tune of (805 MGD + 1035 MGD) 1840 MGD whether it is potable or non-potable because both the water will generate the waste water.

1.2 Resources requirement for year - 2021 :

SEWERAGE:

Sewage quantum is worked out @ 80% of domestic water requirement per capita (50 gpcd) catering to 40 gpcd (180 lpcd) excluding handling of animal, commercial and industrial waste water.

PRESENT STATUS:

The present water supply in Delhi is 640 MGD. At present, the details of sewage generation are as under:

(i)	Water supplied by DJB = 640 x 0.8	= 512.4 MGD
(ii)	Estimated sewage generated From extraction of water from Private bore holes / tube wells:	=100.0 MGD
(iii)	Industrial waste water	= 40.0 MGD
		652.4 MGD

To cater to the growing population, the water supply will be augmented to 919 MGD in 2011/2021.

The wastewater that will be generated will be of the order of 806 MGD for the year 2011 for total water supply of 919 MGD by DJB. As additional sources of water have not been identified for supply of water to DJB upto 2021, it can be seen that population growth results in reduced per capita water supply and corresponding reduction in per capita waste water generation. The total quantum of wastewater however is not expected to change.

The details regarding sewage treatment capacities are as under:

SEWAGE TREATMENT PLANTS (CAPACITY IN MGD)

S.NO.	NAME OF STP	EXISTING CAPACITY	ADDITIONAL CAPACITY PROPOSED UPTO YEAR 2011
1.	Rithala	80	30
2.	Rohini	15	40
3.	Yamuna Vihar	20	25
4.	Kondli	45	45
5.	Narela	10	40
6.	Pappan Kalan (Dwarka)	20	20
7.	Najafgarh	5	-
8.	Vasant Kunj	5	-
9.	Mehrauli	5	-
10	Ghitorni	5	-
11.	Keshopur	12	-
12.	Nilothi	40	30
13.	Cantonment	-	8
14.	Okhla	140	30
15.	Delhi Gate	2.2	15
16.	Sen Nursing Home	2.2	-
17.	Coronation Pillar	40	10
18.	Timar Pur	6	-
	TOTAL :	512.4	293

Total proposed capacity in year 2011 : 512.4 MGD

293.0 MGD

805.4 MGD

The DSIDC is constructing 14 CETPs for Industrial Waste Water for a total capacity of 40 MGD.

PROPOSED STRATEGIES FOR DIFFERENT ASPECTS:

(i) Drawing up a detailed blue print for augmenting sewerage system of Delhi, which may include following key proposals.

(ii) Phasing of new work for total coverage of city with interim arrangements.

(iii) In the old city and other areas identified in some places, new sewerage lines can not be laid and the existing sewer lines have to be de-silted and rehabilitated.

(iv) Technological changes :

The Delhi Jal Board has switched over to the DBO Contracts for setting up the STPs. In these cases, availability of land with the DJB is mentioned and the contractor has the option for offering the suitable technology, which can fulfill other specified parameters.

Sewerage system in the whole Delhi, except NDMC and Cantt. areas is being laid and maintained by Delhi Jal Board where surface drains are being constructed and maintained by General Wing, MCD, CSE (MCD), DDA, PWD, Irrigation and Flood Department, Govt. of NCT of Delhi etc.

Decentralised STPs with capacity of 3-5 MLD at the sub-city level, (10-15 Lacs population) and at community level if environmentally sustainable (mandatory for new developments). Decentralised STPs for smaller capacities can be set up keeping in view the techno economically feasibility and viability and availability of land by the DDA.

INSTITUTIONAL IMPROVEMENT:

The DJB has already set up 21 divisions by restructuring for the maintenance of water distribution system and sewage network. Suggestion for implementation of principle of "polluter pays" is very good and can be examined by Delhi Jal Board. As far as to create one single agency for the management of surface drainage and sewerage is a cumbersome subject because lot of agencies are involved in the management of surface drainage whereas sewerage system is managed by DJB except in NDMC and Cantt areas.

ENCOURAGING PUBLIC PRIVATE PARTNERSHIPS:

Public Private Partnership for the collection of sewerage, its treatment and disposal of treated effluents can be adopted in phases. DJB has already adopted the public private partnership for the maintenance of Sonia Vihar Water Treatment Plant (under construction) and at some places, newly constructed Sewage Treatment Plants are being operated and maintained by some private agencies at present.

PRESENT STATUS OF SEWERAGE SYSTEM:

Sewage treatment plant & ancillary works:

Out of 17 STPs under construction all the 17 STPs have been completed. In east Delhi, Delhi Jal Board has planned to augment the capacity of Sewage Treatment Plant by 45 MGD at Kondli and 25 MGD at Yamuna Vihar. The tenders of Kondli Plant are before the Evaluation Committee. An effluent Pumping Station at Yamuna Vihar is proposed for which short listing of firms had been done and offers are being invited.

The existing Sewerage Conveyance System is a large network of branch peripheral and Trunk Sewers. There are 28 main Trunk Sewers with sizes ranging from 700mm dia. to 2400 mm dia. with a total length of about 130 kms. The balance length of sewage conveyance system comprises of peripheral sewers and internal sewers of small sizes and a total length of approximate 6000 kms. The Trunk Sewers have been laid over the years at different stages. Some of these are as old as 40-60 years old. The condition of Trunk Sewers specially the older one has deteriorated as a result of silting and settlements.

Trunk sewers:

It is estimated that about 91 kms. of Trunk Sewers need desilting and rehabilitation including repair of settlement. Work for desilting/rehabilitation in 22 kms. length has already been completed.

The following major works of rehabilitation of Trunk Sewers is in progress:

(i) Desilting of Trunk Sewer No. 4 from Gurudwara Rashid Market to Preet Vihar SPS Shahdara.

(ii) Desilting of Trunk Sewer No. 5 Shahdara.

(iii) Rehabilitation through Trenchless technology of 600 mms dia. sewer from Gautam Nagar culvert to Ch. Dilip

Singh Marg crossing along Aurobindo Marg.

(iv) Rehabilitation through Trenchless technology of 900 mm dia. Sewer Line from T-junction Shekh Sarai to Madangir along Road no. 13.

(v) Rehabilitation of 1600mm dia. Trunk Sewer from Harsh Vihar to Haider Puri SPS.

(vi) Rehabilitation/renovation of 1600-1900 mm dia brick barrel Trunk Sewer from Delhi Gate to College lane and egg shape Sita Ram brick sewer from Turkman Gate to Ajmeri Gate.

(vii) Rehabilitation of 1650 mm dia. old brick barrel from Q-point to SPS Kilokari and 1200 mm dia cross connection no. 4 from 66" dia. brick barrel to Railway Bridge Nizamuddin.

While the following works of rehabilitation of Trunk Sewer will be carried out after approval of Delhi Jal Board :-

(i) Desilting of Trunk Sewer (1600-2100 mm dia) from Jhilmil Colony to Jagriti SPS Shahdara.

(ii) Desilting and sealing of joints of Punjabi Bagh and Jail Road Trunk Sewer in West Zone.

(iii) Improvement of peripheral sewer of 600-800-1000 mm dia. from T-point Red Light at Laxmi Nagar to Madhuban Chowk and 450-700-800 mm dia from Ramesh Park to Kanishka Emporium, Laxmi Nagar, AC-40 Shahdara.

(iv) Desilting, CCTV survey and sealing of joints of 1200 mm dia. UTS line from manhole no. 64 to 72 near DRDO Complex.

Laying of sewer lines:

There are 567 unauthorised / regularized colonies in Delhi. The status of sewerage system in Unauthorised / Regularised Colonies, Resettlement Colonies and Urban Villages are as under :-

S. No.	Status	Total Nos.	Sewer lines laid
1.	Unauthorised/Regularised Colonies	567	482
2.	Resettlement Colonies	44	44
3.	Urban Villages	135	98

Replacement of sewer lines:

Old/damaged sewer lines are being replaced in a phased manner. It is targeted to replace 585 kms. of existing sewer lines. Replacement of old/damaged sewer line is 116.15 kms.

Non-conventional source of energy:

Vaish Committee has recommended for utilization of Bio-Gas at various sewage Treatment Plants for generation of electricity which can be utilized for operating the STPs. 1440 Lac cft of Bio-Gas generated from Okhla Sewage Treatment Plant was supplied to residents having sewage gas connection in adjacent Colonies and revenue of Rs. 32 Lacs was collected. Bio-Gas Engines at new Plants of Rithala were commissioned in September-2002 to generate the electricity. Which in turn is utilized for operating the plants itself, there saving of Rs. 35 Lacs P.M. in electricity bill was possible.

PROPOSED STEPS TO BE TAKEN, HEAD WISE TO MEET THE REQUIREMENTS FOR 2021:

1. TRUNK SEWERS:

There are 28 main Trunk Sewers with sizes ranging from 700 mm dia. to 2400 mm dia. with a total length of 130 kms. The condition of these Trunk Sewers has deteriorated considerably and also silted up to large extent, so DJB has been rehabilitating these sewers in a phased manner. All Trunk Sewers will be desilted in a phased manner.

2. LAYING OF SEWER LINE IN UNAUTHORISED / REGULARIZED COLONIES:

At present there are 567 unauthorised/regularized colonies. Sewage facilities will be provided in all the colonies subject to technical feasibility.

3. LAYING OF SEWER LINE IN URBAN VILLAGES :

At present there are 135 Urban Villages. Efforts will be made to provide sewage facilities in all the villages, subject to technical feasibility.

4. LAYING OF SEWER LINES IN RESETTLEMENT COLONIES :

Sewage facilities have been provided in all the Resettlement Colonies.

5. PERIPHERAL AND BRANCH SEWERS :

Old Sewer Lines are either inadequate or silted. This results in less discharge to SPS / STPs. It is proposed to replace old 4" dia. and 6" dia. sewer lines.

6. NON CONVENTIONAL SOURCE OF ENERGY :

It is proposed that all major STPs will be provided with Gas Engines so that they are self sufficient with the power supply.

7. SEWAGE TREATMENT - AUGMENTATION WORKS :

M/s.TCE was given study for various augmentation works. Draft Final Report has been submitted by M/s. TCE. The augmentation work will be completed in a time bound manner.

8. SEWAGE FACILITIES IN RURAL VILLAGES :

At present DJB is not laying sewerage system in Rural Villages. Matter will be taken up with Govt. of NCT of Delhi to provide sufficient funds for laying of sewers and treatment of generated sewage on the basis of schemes under-Grant-in-Aid.

9. SEWAGE FACILITIES IN UNAUTHORISED COLONIES :

At present as per the instructions of Hon'ble High Court, Sewer facilities cannot be provided in these colonies. These Colonies are Regularised by Delhi Govt. from time to time. Sewerage system will be laid in these colonies on there being regularized or if Govt. approves laying of sewer in these colonies. Sewerage system will be provided wherever schemes are technically feasible.

In addition, following are the new initiatives taken by Delhi Jal Board.

- It is proposed to construct 6 STPs on the mouth of following drains:

  1. For the drains out falling into river Yamuna:

     (a) Civil Mill Drain

     (b) Additional STP on Delhi Gate Drain

     (c) Barapulla Nallah

  2. For the drains out falling into Najafgarh Drain:

     (a) Palam Drain

     (b) Ring Road Drain

     (c) Daryai Nallah

- We are setting up a Pilot Project in collaboration with CSIR to treat sewage flowing into the drains by using microbes wherever land is not available for constructing STPs.

- We have also used of enzymes in Balbir Nagar Drain to treat sewage. The results are encouraging. It is proposed to use enzymes at Kondli STP on regular basis. Its use will decrease consumption of air and consequently drastic saving in power consumption.

- On all water Treatment Plants wastewater is produced from backwashing of filters and desludging of clarifiers. These effluents carry various chemicals and at present are discharged into various drains, which ultimately pollutes river Yamuna.

  It is proposed to set up waste recovery/recycling plants on all the water Treatment Plants by the end of 2011 so that effluent is stopped from reaching drains/Yamuna and recovery of potable water is benefited.

- It is proposed to set up power plants based on sludge gas being produced at Okhla sewage disposal works, so that sufficient power is produced at the plant itself. This plant will be constructed on BOOT basis. This will be source of power generation based on non-conventional source of energy.

  The list of major works to be completed by 2021 is given at Annexure - A.

FOR SHAHDARA ZONE :

Proposed Pumping Stations :

- Yamuna Vihar 60 MGD (peak)
- New Preet Vihar 48 MGD (peak)

Proposed Treatment Plants :

- Yamuna Vihar 26 MGD (av.)
- Kondli 45 MGD (av.)

FOR RITHALA ROHINI ZONE:

Proposed Pumping Stations :

- Kishan Ganj 36 MGD (peak)
- Anand Vihar 18 MGD (peak)
- Shalimar Bagh 6 MGD (peak)
- New Rithala 22 MGD (peak)
- Nangloi Extn. 22 MGD (peak)

Proposed Treatment Plants :

- Rithala 30 MGD (av.)

FOR OKHLA ZONE:

Proposed Pumping Stations :

- Pahari Dhiraj 21 MGD (peak)
- Police Colony, 36 MGD (peak)
- Seva Nagar 31 MGD (peak)
- Barapulla Nalla, 43 MGD (peak)

Proposed Treatment Plants :

- Okhla 30 MGD (av.)
- Barapulla Nallah 20 MGD (av.)

FOR KESHOPUR ZONE:

Proposed Pumping Stations:

- Raja Garden 48 MGD (peak)
- Poshangipur 11 MGD (peak)
- Punjabi Bagh 7 MGD (peak)
- Delhi Cantonment 17 MGD (peak)

Proposed Treatment Plant:

- Delhi Cantonment 8 MGD (av.)

FOR CORONATION PILLAR ZONE:

Proposed Pumping Stations:

- Roshan Pura 7 MGD (peak)
- New University 7 MGD (peak)
- SGT Nagar Extn. 9 MGD (peak)
- Dhir Pur 6 MGD (peak)
- Rana Pratab Bagh 2.5 MGD (peak)

Proposed Treatment Plant

- Coronation Pillar 10 MGD (av.)

FOR OUTER DELHI ZONE:

Proposed Treatment Plants:

- Pappan Kalan (Dwarka) 18 MGD (av.)
- Nilothi 24 MGD (av.)
- Rohini Ph-IV & V 40 MGD (av.)
- Narela Subcity-I 26 MGD (av.)
- Narela Subcity-II 15 MGD (av.)
- **Decentralised system for group of villages in Outer Delhi (capacity range between 0.5 MGD to 2.5 MGD).**

ANNEXURE-III

DELHI TRANSCO LIMITED

OFFICE OF GENERAL MANAGER (PLANNING)

Shakti Deep Building, Jhandewalan Extension, New Delhi-110055

Phone 23536469, 23552070 Fax 23622707

Email Address- gm.plg.@delhitransco.com

No. F.DTL/202/Oprs. (Plg.)/2006/F-28/216 Dated 28/29/Nov.,2006

Director (Plg.),

Delhi Development Authority,

Master Plan for Delhi-2021

D-6, Vasant Kunj, Near Flyover,

New Delhi-110070.

Sub: **Draft MPD-2021.**

Sir,

Kindly refer to the meeting convened by Hon'ble CMD, DTL on 15th November 2006 with the officers of DDA and DTL on the subject. The Revised Write-up on 'Power' under chapter 14.5 has been updated and the same is enclosed herewith for inclusion in the MPD-2021.

Sd/- 28/11/06

(Raj Bhartiya)

General Manager (Plg.)

Encls. As above

POWER:

Central Electricity Authority has estimated Power requirement of 10,708 MW in the 17th Draft Annual Survey for the year 2021. However, the actual demand may be higher in view of the realistic growth related to Commonwealth Games 2010, Asian Games 2014 which Delhi is competing to host. To meet this demand; there is a need to augment the Power Generation, Transmission, Sub-Transmission & Distribution Capacity within the State.

As per Govt. of India Policy 60-70% of the load demand is required to be met through core generation within the State. However, local generation is limited to only about 17% of the requirement. Since Coal based generation in Delhi is not permitted due to environmental and ash disposal constraints only Gas based Power Plants are envisaged to be installed in Delhi. Recently 10 mcmd of Gas has been allotted for Delhi, which will facilitate to establish the Power Plants of about 2000 MW capacity.

Table be low indicates the existing and the proposed Power Plants/ Generation Capacity within Delhi:

Existing Power Stations

S. No.	Name of the Station	Installed Capacity (MW)
1.	I.P. Station	147.5
2.	RPH	135.0
3.	GT	182.0
4.	Pragati-I	330.0
5.	BTPS	720.0
	Total	1514.5

Proposed Power Stations

S. No.	Name of the Station	Installed Capacity (MW)
1.	Pragati-II	330.0
2.	Pragati-III	1000.0
3.	I.P.	700.0
	Total	2030
	Grand Total	3545

Since the projected load demand is expected to reach 11,000 MW by 2021, the existing generation capacity in Delhi including the proposed additional 2000 MW capacity at Pragati Ph.II, Pragati Ph. III and Replacement units at I.P. will not be sufficient and the gap between the core generation and the load demand will further increase. To reduce this gap, at least 3 Nos. generating stations each of 1000 MW capacity shall be required. About 40 hectares of land would be required for each of such facilities. This could be compacted by going for higher generation for each of such facilities. This could be compacted by going for higher generation in one place provided gas is available as required. Balance generation could be brought from outside Delhi for which following arrangements have been made: —

Location	Generation	For Delhi	Year of Commissioning
Jhajjar (Haryana)	1500 MW	750 MW	2010
DVC (West Bengal)	2600 MW	2600 MW	2007-11
THDC (Uttranchal)	1000MW	600 MW	2010
TOTAL		3950 MW	2011

TRANSMISSION NETWORK:

Though 400KV D/C Transmission Ring around Delhi has been established to draw Power from the Northern Grid but this Transmission Network is inadequate to draw required Power from Northern Grid to meet the load of about 11,000 MW keeping in view the N -1 Criteria at outage of one largest Transformer in each Sub-Stn. and other redundancies as per CEA's planning norms.

Existing number of Grid Stations of 400/220KV, 220/66-33KV are as follows:

(a) 400KV Sub-Stns. - 2 Nos.

400/220KV Sub-Stn. at Bamnauli (4x315 MVA)

400/220KV Sub-Stn. at Bawana (4x315 MVA)

(b) 220 KV Sub-Stns. - 20 Nos. (6300 MVA)

Two more Grid Stations one at Maharani Bagh and other at Mundka are under execution. 400/220KV Grid Sub-Stn. at Maharani Bagh is under construction while work at 400/220KV Grid Sub-Stn. at Mundka is expected to start in 2007-08.

Thus in order to draw Power from the Northern Grid to meet the expected Load requirement and to keep contingencies and margins, 4 No. new 400KV Grid Stations would require to be established. The locations of two Grid Stations have already been identified in East Delhi and in South East Delhi. Location of other two Stations would be identified based upon the load development plans as per the proposed Master Plan.

In addition, in feeds from 765 KV proposed ring in NCR Region would also be required to be established. On an average 400/220KV out door Grid would be established in 60 acres.

Further, keeping in view the long-term requirements of Power in Delhi provision of at least 2 no. 765/800 KV Grid Stations would also required to be kept. The land requirement would be 100 acres/40 Ha. for each of the station.

Correspondingly, 220 KV Grid Stations and down stream 66KV 1KV Grid Station would also require to be established to meet the load requirement of newly developed areas and increasing demand in the existing developed areas. About 40 no. 220/66KV and 220/33KV Grid Station would be required while at present only 22 Stations are existing. As such land requirement for at least 20 more 220KV Grid Stations would be required.

Further, in the developed areas where the load growth is taking place, indoor 220KV Grid Stations would be established while in the out skirts and the newly developed areas proposed in the Master Plan of 220 KV outdoor Grid Stations are proposed.

CEA has prepared the norms for the land requirement of the various sub-stations. As per details below:

- 220 KV Sub-Stn. - 180 X 165 Sq. mtrs. (2.96 hectares)
- 66 KV Sub-Stn. - 90 X 95 Sq. mtrs. (0.86 hectares)
- 33KV Sub-Stn. - 60 X 45 Sq.mtrs. (0.3 hectares)
- 11 KV Sub-Stn. - 10 X 8 Sq. mtrs.

66/ 11KV, 33/11 KV and 11/11.4 KV Grid Stations would require to be established at the load centers and adequate provisions for the land would be kept in the Master Plan.

DEMAND SIDE MANAGEMENT AND ENERGY CONSERVATION MEASURES:

In order to arrest the run away load demand, Demand Side Management is also considered very necessary which could result from adopting the following:

➲ **Green Building Bylaws to reduce the Energy requirement of the new Buildings:**

Energy efficient building Bylaws/ Building Code has been drafted by Bureau of Energy Efficiency, which may be considered mandatory in the Master Plan.

➲ **Use of Energy Efficient Devices:**

Use of CFLs, Electronic Chokes and Solar Water Heaters have been made mandatory by Notification of GNCTD for all Govt. Buildings. These measures could be considered for adoption for all new buildings including Institutional, Commercial and Private.

ANNEXURE-IV (i)

MUNICIPAL CORPORATION OF DELHI

OFFICE OF THE DIRECTOR-IN-CHIEF (CSE)

TOWN HALL: DELHI

No. F-406/DNC/2003/44 Dated: 28/04/2004

To,

The Member Secretary,
N.C.R. Planning Board,
India Habitat Centre,
New Delhi.

Sub:—**Strategies / Master Plan-2021 for Solid Waste for Delhi City.**

Sir,

A telephonic message has been received from N.C.R. Planning Board that they are preparing the Master Plan-2021 for NCR Region pertaining to Solid Waste for Delhi City. The Municipal Corporation of Delhi has already forwarded the same to the Delhi Development Authority for incorporating the same in Master Plan-2021. A copy of the same is attached herewith, for ready reference.

Encl: As above. Sd/-

Director-in-Chief
(CSE)

Copy to:—

(i) P.S. (U.D.) for f/o information.
(ii) Commissioner, MCD
(iii) Addl. Commer. (CSE)

Director-in-Chief
(CSE)

MUNICIPAL CORPORATION OF DELHI

CONSERVANCY & SANITATION ENGINEERING DEPARTMENT

The CSE Department of Municipal Corporation of Delhi is one of the important departments and responsible for management and handling of solid waste as well as disposal of storm water drainage form its jurisdiction which is about 94% of the total area of Delhi. This department is carrying out sweeping from the streets, lanes & roads and collecting garbage received from the residents in its Dhalaos, besides storage, transportation and disposal of waste at Sanitary Land Fill sites. Considering the present population of 14 millions and 500 grams of domestic waste per capita (NEERI study), the garbage generated is 6000 to 7000 M.T. per day. With the present pace of growth of population, the population by 2021 shall be around 22 million and garbage generation shall be around 20,000 M.T. per day with an increase @ 5% approximately (NEERI study).

STRATEGIES FOR MPD-2021 FOR SOLID WASTE

Collection / Storage:

(a) Community Bins / Receptacles:

Presently, the MCD have provided Dhalaos and receptacles/community bins at different locations in the colonies/areas for collection and storage of municipal waste. It is generally found that the DDA does not adequately provide such kind of spaces in the existing as well as in new colonies. It is proposed that a space measuring 100 sq.mt. may be provided on every 8 to 10 thousand population in the colonies /areas to cater to the needs of storage of garbage. In addition to this, spaces measuring around 200 sq.mt. are to be provided for segregation of different kind of non-biodegradable waste.

(b) Attendance Office:

The collection of solid waste is one of the crucial components of the solid waste management. To have effective control in the field as well as on the work, the office of Assistant Sanitary Inspector, a small office, consisting of 100 sq. meter is to be provided in each colony to have effective attendance system and interface with the Residents Welfare Associations. This projection is based on the recommendations of DUEIIP.

(c) Facilities for Kabariwalas:

It has been observed that the recyclable waste is being sold to Kabariwalas, whichis subsequently recycled depending upon its uses. It would be necessary to have at least two markets in each zone for all 12 zones of MCD, i.e. recycling centers/kabari markets are to be developed by the DDA or MCD to reduce and re-use the recyclable part of the municipal garbage. For developing this kind of facility close to business district centers or near markets, a space of about 1000 sq.mt. shall be required.

(d) Space for Storage:

The Municipal Corporation of Delhi has recently handed over the land for development of Millennium Park on Ring Road to the DDA under the orders of the Hon'ble L.G. Delhi, measuring 4 Acres. In lieu of this land, it was promised by the Engineer Member, DDA that land measuring 2 Acres will be provided to MCD by the DDA, but, unfortunately, this could not be materialized. Space measuring around 2 Acres is to be provided in central location for storage of tools and equipments of the CSE Department, in lieu of the land already handed over to DDA for Millennium Park.

Transportation:

(a) Workshop & Parking facilities:

A space for providing adequate shelter for repair and maintenance of vehicles and other heavy equipments is required to have effective transportation system. Presently, the CSE Department is having about 700 refuse removal trucks and 100 Front-end-Loaders for transportation of waste being generated by the city, which is likely to increase further based on the quantum of garbage generation by 2021. To rationalize the pace of garbage generation, it is required to have 2200 vehicles (NEERI report), for which parking and workshop facility in the existing as well as new colonies likely to come up by 2021 is required to be provided. On an average, a space of area measuring 3000 sq.mt. for at least 5 of the existing areas of different zones, namely Shahdara (South) Zone, Narela Zone, Najafgarh Zone, South Zone and S.P. Zone, is required. For further development of colonies, additional space @ 3000 sq.mt. is required to be given for developing parking and workshop facilities for transportation of garbage.

(b) Transfer Stations:

To have effective and economical transportation system, intermediate transfer stations are required to be made. It is proposed that at least land for six transfer stations measuring 5000 Sq. Mtr. each may be provided in each of the 12 zones spreading in north, south, east and west directions of the city.

Disposal:

(a) **Landfill Sites:**

Presently, the solid waste is being dumped at three SLF sites, namely Bhalswa, Ghazipur and Okhla. These landfill sites have saturated and outlived their normal life. As per Solid Waste (Management & Handling) Rules, 2000 notified by the Ministry of Environment and Forest, Govt. of India, the Engineered Sanitary Land Fill sites are required to be developed in each direction of the city to have economical and effective solid waste management. Recently, the Hon'ble Supreme Court of India in its order has pointed out that at least 10 garbage processing facilities are to be provided. The requirement of land for development of engineered S.L.F. site should preferably be in low lying areas and the agency / MCD would be developing it with proper liner for gases and leaches management as per guidelines issued by the Ministry of Environment & Forest, Govt. of India. The approximate area of each landfill site should at least take care of next 20-25 years and garbage intake capacity of 2000 M.T. daily and the area of proposed land for SLF should preferably be around 1500 acres in totality.

(b) Processing facilities:

For developing processing facilities for different kind of waste and specialized waste, like Slaughter House Waste and Cow dung, Composting/Pellets etc. by opting various technologies, space measuring about 10 acres for each facility is required. These processing facilities should be closed to the waste generating centers namely Dairy colonies or near Slaughter House. Thus, making the total requirement of land as 100 acres for 10 Processing Units. All these processing facilities are likely to come up on public private partnership basis, as they are highly capital-intensive units.

Disposal of Storm Water Drainage:

The disposal of storm water is one of the crucial components for the urban structure services. In most part of the city wherever low lying colonies have been developed by the Agencies, the responsibility of disposal of storm water lies on the shoulders of the Municipal Corporation of Delhi, for which pumping facilities within the Complex are required. In some colonies, on account of non-availability of space, the problem of water stagnation persists and the residents have to suffer a lot. Considering human factors, it is proposed that wherever low habitation exists in the approved area, the space of 1000 sq.mt. should be provided to MCD for setting up pumping facilities for proposal disposal of storm water.

ANNEXURE-IV(ii)

RAKESH MEHTA, IAS
COMMISSIONER

MUNICIPAL CORPORATION OF DELHI
Town Hall, Chandni Chowk,
Delhi-110006

Dear,

You had made observations that you would like to have Master Plan for Treatment and Disposal 2005-2024, which has been prepared by COWI Consultants, so that the same can be incorporated in the Master Plan 2021. As per the Master Plan 2005-2024, a number of activities have been listed in various sites and a number of new technologies have been suggested by the COWI, which includes the following:-

(i) Setting up Construction and Demolition Waste Treatment Facility
(ii) Methanisation Plants
(iii) Compost Plants
(iv) Bio-Cell Technology
(v) Refuse Derived Fuels
(vi) Home Composting

I am enclosing herewith the relevant copies of the Master Plan, which can be included in the Master Plan, 2021. Action Plan for proposed facilities for Waste Treatment and Disposal during the Master Plan Period 2005-2024 is attached at Annexure - 'I'. The details of time frame required for implementing various waste treatment project is attached at Annexure - 'II'. The requirement of land area for various waste treatment facilities for Municipal Solid Waste Management may be seen at Annexure - 'III'.

The total area of land requirement as per the Master Plan is 65.6 hectares, whereas the total area currently available is 41.2 hectares. In the Annexure - III, it has been estimated that the total investment for the above facilities upto 2024 would be Rs.3719.88 crores. The revenue scheme on account of these facilities as has been listed in the Master Plan would amount to Rs.2855.70 crores.

With regards,

Yours sincerely,

Sd/

(RAKESH MEHTA)

Shri A. K. Jain,
Commissioner (Planning),
Delhi Development Authority,
Vikas Minar, I.P. Estate, New Delhi - 110002.

ACTION PLAN

NEED FOR THE ACTION PLAN:

A Plan of Action has been developed to provide a time schedule and overall breakdown of the main activities for implementation of the Master Plan. The format of the Plan of Action is in such a way that provides an overview of the implementation rather than engages in too many details and inter-linkages between tasks. The aim is to develop a format that can be taken over by MCD, revised and used for monitoring purposes.

The purpose of Action Plan is to evaluate in detail the actions required to convert strategy into practice. The Action plan sets out in detail the steps taken in implementing each component of the overall strategy over a period of time.

Structure of the Action Plan:

The Action Plan provides a list of activities for management of municipal solid waste in Delhi and assigns a time frame for implementation of the specified activity. The Action Plan is divided into three time segments:

- The short-term period 2005-2009 (5 years);
- The medium-term period 2010-2014 (5 years);
- The long-term period 2015-2024 (10 years).

The Action Plan is more detailed in its provisions for the short term i.e. for a period of five years. The medium and long-term provisions are less detailed and focus on the major objectives and targets as the detail of the plan will have to take into account the success of the implementation of the objectives for the short term as well as the actual developments.

Development of the Action Plan:

Action Plan is a result of continuous interaction with the consultants and the MCD officials. The listed out activities and their time frame of implementation was discussed with MCD officials to arrive at realistic targets. The Action Plan has been developed by the consultants on the basis of "Financial Model", the details of which are provided in Volume 7, Master Plan Appendices. The Financial model provides forecast for municipal solid waste quantities, waste flow and land requirements for treatment facilities. It also provides forecast for revenue and the overall costing and financial analysis.

Features of the Action Plan:

The key components of the Action Plan are summarised below:

- Institutional Developments of the Conservancy and Sanitation Engineering (CSE) department (e.g. new management principles and new units).
- Development of new sanitary landfills with adequate capacities to cater for municipal solid waste arising in the study area over five year planning period.
- Closure and restoration of existing landfills to minimise the potential for further pollution from these sites.
- New composting schemes/facilities to minimise the demand for sanitary landfill facilities.
- New treatment options of Refuse Derived Fuel (RDF) and Methanisation to minimise the demand for sanitary landfill facilities.
- Public-Private-Partnership for waste treatment projects.

Action Plan 2005 - 2009

The major projects listed out in the Action Plan 2005-2009 are as follows:

- New organisational structure and capacity building in CSE.
- Commissioning of first two pilot facilities based on Methanisation and RDF with daily capacities of 50 and 100 tonnes respectively through a renewed call for proposals from the private sector and rigorous scrutiny in MCD.
- Commissioning of two facilities for processing of Construction and Demolition (C & D) waste.
- Revamping and operation of MCD composting plant at Okhla at a capacity of 200 tonnes per day (tpd).
- Planning of new composting plant with a capacity of approx. 600 tpd.
- Operation of Bhalswa Compost plant (privately operated) at full capacity (500 tpd).
- Operation of NDMC compost plan at full capacity (200 tpd) after discussions between MCD and NDMC.
- Financial and technical support by MCD for two local composting projects implemented by Resident Welfare Association (s) (RWA) and NON Government Organisations (NGOs) at neighbourhood level.
- Commissioning of new sanitary landfills at Jaitpur, Narela Bawana Road and Bhatti Mines of Design, Build and Operate basis.
- Closure of existing three landfills and development of restoration projects.
- Changes to the street sweeping procedures in order to keep this waste separate from other waste streams throughout the storage and transportation process.

Action Plan 2010 - 2014

The major projects listed out in the Action Plan 2010-2014 are as follows:

- Commissioning of the composting plant planned in the first phase 2005 - 2009.
- Planning of an additional 600 tpd composting plant.
- Commissioning of extension of the planned methanisation plant at Narela Bawana Road to an operating capacity of 250 tpd from 2011.
- Commissioning o additional methanisation plant of 250 tpd capacity, thereby bringing the total capacity for methanisation to a total of 500 tpd.
- Development of a third methanisation facility (also 250 tpd) to be commissioned in 2015.
- Commissioning of extension of the planned RDF facility to an operating capacity of 500 tpd from 2011.
- Designing of a new RDF plant to be tendered for Commissioning in 2015.
- Commissioning of an additional treatment facility in the Bhatti Mines areas for processing approx. 1000 tpd of C & D waste.
- Closure of sanitary landfill at Jaitpur.
- Continuous scheduled extensions of Narela Bawana Road and Bhatti Mines landfills including use of bio-cell technology.
- Finalisation of new landfill site to take over from Jaitpur with all permits obtained.
- Mining of Okhla landfill by a private developer identified through a competitive bidding procedure and the site cleared and used for development of offices and institutions.
- Sites at Gazipur and Bhalswa transformed into recreational areas with landfill gas being utilised at Gazipur.
- Supporting of several local composting projects implemented by RWAs and NGOs through an incentive scheme that provides financial and technical support from MCD.

Action Plan 2015 - 2024

The major projects listed out in the Action Plan 2015 - 2024 are as follows:

- Operation of a total of five composting plants (2100 tpd), three C&D waste processing plants (2000 - 2500 tpd), four methanisation plants (1000 tpd), and three RDF plants (1500 tpd) with a total daily capacity of more than 6600 tonnes.
- Closure and restoration of sanitary landfill at Narela Bawana Road.
- Continuous scheduled extensions of Bhatti Mines and the new landfill with the use of bio-cell technology.
- Finalisation of third new landfill site to take over from Narela Bawana landfill with all permits obtained.
- Supporting of local composting projects implemented by RWAs and NGOs through an incentive scheme that provides financial and technical support from MCD.

  The following table provides details of different projects required to be planned, executed and operated with overall supervision of the MCD during the entire Master Plan period (2005 - 2024).

Proposed Facilities for Waste Treatment and Disposal during the Master Plan Period (2005-2024)

Sr. No.	Facility	Proposed Location	Waste Treatment Capacity (tpd)	Area Required (ha)	Area Available (ha)	Start Year of Operation	Project cost (INR)	Remarks
1.	Landfill	Jaitpur	-	10	10	2005	24,00,00,000	Project underway, to be speeded up
2.	Compost (Upgrade)	Okhla, MCD,	200	3.2	3.2	2006	14,02,50,000	Work to start next year
3.	Compost (Upgrade)	Okhla, NDMC,	200	3.4	3.4	2006	14,02,50,000	Discussion required with NDMC
4.	Landfill	Narela Bawana Road	-	112	62	2007	168,00,00,000	Work to be speeded up urgently, addl land requirement to be addressed.
5.	C & D	Burari, Jahangirpuri	500	3.92	20.98	2007	15,00,00,000	Project to commence next year
6.	C & D	Bakarwala	500	3.92	2.1	2007	15,00,00,000	Project to commence next year
7.	Methanisation (Pilot)	Narela Bawana Road	50	2.5	2	2007	16,00,00,000	Project to commence next year
8.	RDF (Pilot)	Burari, Jahangirpuri	100	5.	5	2007	15,00,00,000	Project to commence next year
9.	Landfill	Bhatti Mines	-	73	0	2008	224,00,00,000	Work to be speeded up, land acquisition is a priority.
10.	Compost	To be identified	600	12		2010	30,60,00,000	Land identification to begin in 2004.
11.	Methanisation (upgrade)	Narela Bawana Road	250	-	-	2011	72,00,00,000	Project to commence in 2009.
12.	Methanisation	To be identified	250	2.5		2011	72,00,00,000	Land identification to begin in 2004.
13.	RDF (upgrade)	Burari Jahangirpuri	500	-		2011	60,00,00,000	Project to commence in 2011.
14.	Compost	Bhalswa, private	500	4.9	4.9	2013	0	Assuming 25% investment by MCD.
15.	C & D	Bhatti Mines	1000	7.85	2.5	2014	15,00,00,000	Project to commence in 2013.
16.	Compost	To be identified	600	12		2015	30,60,00,000	Land identification by 2010, Project to commence in 2013.
17.	Methanisation	To be identified	250	2.5		2015	80,00,00,000	Land identification by 2010, Project to commence in 2013.
18.	RDF	To be identified	500	5		2015	75,00,00,000	Land identification by 2010, Project to commence in 2013.
19.	Methanisation	To be identified	250	2.5		2020	80,00,00,000	Land identification by 2010, Project to commence in 2018.
20.	RDF	To be identified	500	5.		2020	75,00,00,000	Land identification by 2010, Project to commence in 2018.
	Total		**6750**	**271.19**	**116.08**		**1071,25,00,000**	

Proposed Projects and Facilities for Waste Treatment and Disposal as suggested by the Master Plan (2005-2024)

Facility/Project	Proposed Location	Start	Finish	Remarks
Capacity Building in CSE of MCD	-	Jun-04	May-05	
Waste management unit in CSE	-	Jun-04	May-05	
Upgrade of Existing and Establishment of new Compost Plants				
Okhla MCD Plant upgrade	Okhla	Jun-04	Dec-05	
Okhla, NDMC Plant upgrade	Okhla	Jan-06	Jan-06	Discussion with NDMC
Bhalswa Compost Plant upgrade	Bhalswa	Jan-06	Jan-06	Discussion with plant operator
New Plant I	To be identified	Jan-07	Dec-09	Land acquisition is a priority
New Plant II	To be identified	Jan-17	Dec-19	Land acquisition is a priority
Construction, Demolition Waste Processing (C&D) Plants				
Phase I (two facilities)	Burari, Bakarwala	Jan-05	Dec-06	
Phase II	To be identified	Jul-13	Dec-14	
Bio-methanisation Plants				
Pilot Plant	Narela Bawana Road	Dec-04	Dec-06	
Upgrade of Pilot Plant	Narela Bawana Road	May-09	Dec-10	
Plant II	To be identified	Nov-08	Dec-10	Land acquisition is a priority
Plant III	To be identified	Nov-12	Dec-14	Land acquisition is a priority
Plant IV	To be identified	Nov-17	Dec-19	Land acquisition is a priority
Refuse Derived Fuel (RDF) Plants				
Pilot Plant	Burari,	Nov-04	Dec-06	
Upgrade of Pilot Plant	Burari,	May-09	Dec-10	
Plant II	To be identified	Nov-12	Dec-14	Land acquisition is a priority
Plant III	To be identified	Nov-17	Dec-19	Land acquisition is a priority

Facility/Project	Proposed Location	Start	Finish	Remarks
Existing and New Sanitary Landfills				
New landfill at Narela Bawana Road	Narela Bawana Road	May-04	Jun-06	
Closure of Bhalswa Landfill	Bhalswa	Jul-05	Feb-08	
New landfill at Jaitpur	Jaitpur	Jul-04	Jul-05	
Closure of Okhla landfill	Okhla	Feb-06	Sep-08	
New landfill at Bhatti Mines	Bhatti Mines	Aug-06	Aug-08	Land acquisition is a priority
Closure of Gazipur landfill	Gazipur	Aug-08	Apr-11	
Street Sweeping				
Better procedures	Whole Delhi	May-05	Mar-07	
Neighborhood Composting				
Neighborhoods Projects	To be identified	Jan-06	Dec-06	
Public Information and Education				
Campaigns/source segregation	Whole Delhi	May-05	May-12	

Current Approval Procedure for Waste Facilities

An issue that is a serious hindrance for timely implementation of projects is the current approval procedure for waste management facilities (and others).

The procedures required in taking projects from concept to completion require several procedural issues to be completed, not only within MCD but also with other Authorities. Typical procedures followed in various projects along with timeframes required are stated in table. Time frames mentioned here are only an approximation on the basis of past experience, in the case of landfills and compost plants.

Table 3.2 : TIMEFRAME CURRENTLY REQUIRED BY CSE DEPARTMENT FOR IMPLEMENTING WASTE MANAGEMENT PROJECTS

Sr. No.	Activity	Time required in months
1.	Screening of suitable sites incorporating requirements of the MSW Rules, 2000 and preliminary feasibility assessment for acquisition of the land.	3
2.	Preparation of preliminary estimates, obtaining administrative and technical approval from within MCD.	2
3.	Preparation of detailed estimate, checking by the planning department and obtaining technical sanction.	2
4.	Notice inviting tender.	1
5.	Receipt and evaluation of tenders, checking by Planning Department.	2
6.	Approval by Finance Department.	1
7.	Preparation of preamble and approval by Standing Committee	2
8.	Carrying out rapid EIA of the selected site	6
9.	Survey of the selected site by the DPCC/CPCB and approval of the same by the DDA/DPCC/CPCB (possibly also by the central water commission – CWC)	3
10.	Confirmation of the land for the selected purpose by a echnical committee;	3
11.	Central ground water authority approval	3
12.	No objection certificate from Pollution Control Board	3
13.	Approval of the location by the DDA and its incorporation in the Master Plan	6
14.	The implementing agency will then approach the land owning agency for land allocation. These could be MCD / DDA / L& DO / Cantonment Board / DJB / private owners or others. (Land is to be given to the MCD for setting up treatment and disposal facilities on a priority basis under a recent ruling of the Hon'ble Supreme Court of India)	6
15.	Incorporation of the land in the MPD (DDA Master Plan)	6
16.	Planning, design and development of the area by the Conservancy and Sanitation Engineering (CSE) Department of the MCD considering the guidelines laid down by the MSW Rules, 2000.	6
17.	Construction and subsequent operation of the selected site with periodic inspection by the concerned agencies.	Variable
	Total	56

Under the current regime, it is thus likely that development of new treatment and disposal sites will take up to 56 months or almost 5 years from site identification to start of construction of the planned facility. However, this time may be reduced if some of the above activities are run in parallel, c.f. section 3.4.4.

TARGETS FOR WASTE TREATMENT (TPD)

	2005	2009	2014	2019	2024
Total daily waste quantity collected	5,711	7,086	9,000	11,345	14,302
Waste for treatment	850	1,882	3,350	4,797	5,839
Waste for landfill, direct supply	4,861	5,203	5,650	6,549	8,462
Waste for landfill including residues	4,949	5,431	6,246	7,483	9,613

The table provides an overview of the facilities for treatment and disposal proposed for the Master Plan Period.

PROPOSED FACILITIES FOR TREATMENT AND DISPOSAL

Facility	Location	Capacity tpd	Area Requirements (ha)	Total Area Available, ha	Start Year of Operation
Composting Plant	North Zone	500	4.9	4.9	2013
Composting Plant	Okhla, MCD (Upgrade)	200	3.2	3.2	2006
Composting Plant	Okhla, NDMC	200	3.4	3.4	2006
Composting Plant (s)	New site	600	12		2010
Composting Plant (s)	New site	600	12		2015
C & D Processing Plant	North Delhi	500	3.92	3.92	2007
C & D Processing Plant	West Zone	500	1.3	2.1	2007
C & D Processing Plant	South Zone	1000	2.5	2.5	2014
Methanisation Plant	North Zone	50	2.5	2	2007
Methanisation Plant	North Zone	250	-		2011
Methanisation Plant	New site	250	2.5		2011
Methanisation Plant	New site	250	2.5		2015
Methanisation Plant	New site	250	2.5		2020

Facility	Location	Capacity (tpd)	Area Requirements (ha)	Total Area Available, (ha)	Start Year of Operation
RDF Plant	North Zone	100	5	5	2007
RDF Plant	North Zone	500	-	-	2011
RDF Plant	New site	500	5		2015
RDF Plant	New site	500	5		2020
Total area requirement			65.6		
New Developments				41.2	

The table shows the accumulated landfill need for the Master Plan period as well as the corresponding area need assuming an average landfill height of 20 metres. The estimated landfill volumes at the three proposed sites at Jaitpur, Narela Bawana Road and Bhatti Mines are included as well.

LANDFILL VOLUME NEEDS IN THE MASTER PLAN PERIOD

The total landfill volume need in Master Plan Period 2005-2024	40,972,851 m^3
The total landfill area required in Master Plan Period 2005-2024	205 ha.
Estimated volume remaining at the three existing sites (from 2005);	~5,00,000 m^3
Estimated volume at the three proposed new sites;	
Jaitpur	25,00,000 m^3
Narela Bawana Road (assuming additional land near site is acquired)	150,00,000 m^3
Bhatti Mines (identified pits only)	200,00,000 m^3
Total volume identified for the Master Plan period	380,00,000 m^3
Landfill volume requirements for the Master Plan Period	445,16,237 m^3
Shortfall in volume after all identified volumes have been used	85.4%

COMMERCIAL ASPECTS OF THE RECOMMENDED MASTER PLAN FOR TREATMENT AND DISPOSAL

A number of assumptions were made to arrive at the capital costs for implementation of SWM master plan for Delhi. The total developmental costs, based on these assumptions, in the form of investments and annual operation and maintenance costs can be summarised.

ANNEXURE V

MEMBERS OF THE DELHI DEVELOPMENT AUTHORITY

1. Sh. B.L. Joshi

   Lt. Governor, Delhi

   Chairman, DDA
2. Sh. Dinesh Rai

   Vice-Chairman, DDA
3. Sh. A. K. Patnaik

   Finance Member, DDA
4. Sh. A.K. Sarin

   Engineer Member, DDA
5. Sh. Mahabal Mishra

   M.L.A
6. Sh. Jile Singh Chauhan

   M.L.A.
7. Sh. Mange Ram Garg

   M.L.A.
8. Ishwar Dass

   Councillor, MCD
9. Sh. Virender Kasana

   Councillor, MCD
10. Dr. M.M.Kutty

    Jt. Secretary (D&L), MOUD, GOI
11. Dr. H.S.Anand

    Member Secretary, NCRPB
12. Sh. A.K.Nigam

    Commissioner, MCD
13. Sh. J.B.Kshirsagar

    Chief Planner, T.C.P.O.
14. Sh. V.M. Bansal

    Pr. Commr. cum Secretary., DDA

MEMBERS OF BOARD OF ENQUIRY AND HEARING CONSTITUTED FOR DRAFT MPD-2021

Vice Chairman- Chairman

Members

1. Engineer Member, DDA
2. Commissioner, MCD
3. Chief Planner, TCPO
4. Sh. Virender Kasana, Councillor MCD & Authority Member

Co-Opted Member

1. Sh. R. K. Anand, M.P. & Member of the Advisory Council

Convener & Secretary

1. Commissioner (Planning), DDA

Special Invitees

1. Principal Secretary (UD)
2. Principal Secretary (Power)
3. Chief Executive Officer

MEMBERS OF ADVISORY COUNCIL

1. Sh. B.L. Joshi, President
2. Sh. Dinesh Rai

   Vice-Chairman, DDA
3. Sh. R.K. Anand

   M.P. (Rajya Sabha)
4. Sh. Kishan Singh Sangwan,

   M.P. (Lok Sabha)
5. Sh. Sajjan Kumar

   MP(Lok Sabha)
6. Sh. Hiren Tokas

   Councillor (MCD)
7. Sh. Sugreev Singh

   Councillor (MCD)
8. Sh. Rohit Manchanda

   Councillor (MCD)
9. Smt. Nirmala Vats

   Councillor (MCD)
10. Sh. J.P. Goel
11. Sh. Chattar Singh
12. Sh. Sunil Dev
13. Sh. Anshu Prakash

    Chairman cum Managing Director, DTC
14. Sh. H.L. Bajaj, Chairman, CEA
15. Mrs. Veena Maitra,

    D.G. (Defence Estate)

    Min. of Defence
16. Sh. N.K. Sinha,
17. D.G. (RD), Transport Bhawan, New Delhi
18. Sh J.B.Kshirsagar,

    Chief Planner, T.C.P.O.
19. Sh. R.P.S.Sinha,

    CMD, MTNL
20. Dr. N.K.Yadav,

    Municipal Health Officer, MCD

MPD-2021 SUB-GROUPS

Sub-group on Regional and Sub Regional Aspect

1. Prof. R.C. Gupta, Chairman
2. Sh. N.K. Aggarwal, former Addl. Commissioner (Plg.), DDA, Co-Chairman
3. Prof. J.H. Ansari, Director, S.P.A., Member
4. Dr. N.B. Johari, N.C.R. Planning Board, Member
5. Sh. Ved Mittal, former Chief Planner, G.D.A., Member
6. Dr. Amitabh Kundu, Member
7. Sh. Sabyasachi Das, Jt. Director (Plg.), DDA, Member
8. Smt. I.P. Parate, Jt. Director (Plg.), DDA, ; Member

Sub-Group on Demographic Profile and Population Projection

1. Dr. Ashish Bose, Chairman
2. Sh. Anil Barai, Director (Plg.), DDA, Co-Chairman
3. Dr. D. Roy Chaudhary, Member
4. Addl. Secretary (UD), Member
5. Sh. V.K. Thakore, Member
6. Dr. Aslam Mahmood, Member
7. Dr. K. Srinivasan, Member
8. Sh. P.N. Mari Bhat, Member
9. Dr. K.S. Natrajan, Expert Member
10. Dr. Arup Mitra, Expert Member
11. Sh. M.K. Premi, Expert Member
12. Sh. R.P. Tyagi, Editor Member
13. Smt. Meera Kanwaria, Councillor, MCD, Member
14. Dr. K. Srirangan, Asstt. Director (Plg.), DDA, Member

Sub-Group on Shelter

1. Sh. M.N. Joglekar, Advisor, HUDCO, Chairman
2. Sh. S.K. Agarwala, Sr. Architect, DDA, Co-Chairman
3. Sh. Kulwant Singh, Executive Director, HUDCO, Member
4. Shri V.K. Bugga, Chief Town Plannner, MCD, Member
5. Sh. Subir Saha, Head Housing Deptt., SPA, Member
6. Sh. V. K. Dhar, Associate Professor, NIUA, Member
7. Sh. S.K. Das, Member
8. Sh. K.P. Singh, Member
9. Sh. Mahinder Nagpal, Councillor, MCD, Member
10. Dr. H.S. Gill, Dy. Chief, HUDCO.
11. Sh. S.B. Khodankar, Jt. Director (Plg.), DDA, Member

Sub-Group on Trade and Commerce

1. Sh. D. S. Meshram, former Chief Town Planner, TCPO, Chairman
2. Sh. S.C. Karanwal, former Chief Architect, DDA Co-Chairman
3. Sh. Sunil Mehra, Addl. Town Planner, MCD, Member
4. Sh. M.M. Aggarwal, former President, New Delhi Traders Association, Member
5. Dr. Kiran Wadhwa, Chief Economist, HUDCO, Member
6. Sh. Sushil Nanda, Secretary, Delhi Chamber of Commerce, Member
7. Sh. Sita Ram Goyal, former President A.P.M.A, Member
8. Sh. Manoharlal Kumar, President Delhi Vyapar Mahasangh, Member
9. Sh. Vijender Kumar, Councillor (MCD), Dy. Chairman Standing Committee, Member.
10. Sh. Hitender K. Bharti, Asstt. Director (Plg.), DDA, Member

Sub-Group on Industrial Aspects

1. Sh. Dilip Biswas, Chairman, CPCB, Chairman.
2. Sh. D.K. Saluja, Director (Plg.), DDA, Co-Chairman
3. Sh. R.K. Gupta, CE, DSIDC, Member
4. Sh. H.L. Malik, JD (Indl.), GNCTD, Member
5. Sh. Anil Behl, Vice President (Technical), CII, Member
6. Sh. P.K. Rajgarhia, PHDCCI, Member
7. Sh. J.R. Jindal, President, Delhi Factory Owners Federation, Member
8. Sh. Ved Prakash Gupta, Former Dy. Chairman, MCD, Member
9. Sh. R. N. Jindal, Sr. Environmental Engineer, CPCB, Special Invitee
10. Sh. B. Kumar, Sr. Environmental Engineer, DPCC, Special Invitee
11. Sh. N. K. Garg, PHDCCI, Special Invitee.
12. Sh. H.S. Dhillon, Jt. Director (Plg.), DDA, Member

Sub-Group on Environment and Pollution

1. Ms. Sunita Narayan, Director, CSE, Chairman
2. Ms. Savita Bhandari, Director (Landscape), DDA, Co-Chairman
3. Member Secy. CPCB, Member
4. Member Secy., DPCC, Member
5. Sh. Mukesh Khare, Prof.IIT, Member

6. Prof. K.T. Ravindran, Head Urban Design, SPA, Member
7. Smt. Amarjeet Kaur, Advisor, School of Environment, Member
8. Smt. M.Z. Bawa, Jt. Director (Plg.), DDA Member
9. Sh. J.S. Sodhi, Jt. Director (Plg.), DDA Member

Sub-Group on Conservation and Urban Renewal

1. Prof. A.G.K. Menon, Director,TVB, Chairman
2. Sh. B.K. Jain, Director (DC&RYP), DDA, Co-Chairman
3. Dr. B.S.R. Babu, Archaeology Officer, Member
4. Superintending Archaeologist, Member
5. Prof. Nalini Thakur, Head Conservation Deptt, SPA, Member
6. Director, IHM, Member
7. Chairman, INTACH, Member
8. Sh. Raj Panjwani, Advocate, Member
9. Sh. V.D. Dewan, Chief Architect, DDA, Member
10. Sh. R.K. Jain, Director (Plg.), Member
11. Sh. P. S. Uttarwar, Jt. Director (Plg.), Member

Sub-Group on Traffic and Transportation

1. Dr. T.S. Reddy, Director, CRRI, Chairman
2. Sh. Prakash Narain, Addl. Commr. (Plg.), DDA Co-Chairman
3. DCP (Traffic), Delhi Police, Member
4. Sh. Piyush Kansal, AGM, RITES, Member
5. Prof. Dinesh Mohan, I.I.T., New Delhi, Member
6. Sh. S. Sanyal, Transportation Consultant, Member
7. Prof. A.K. Sharma, Head, Transport Planning, SPA, Member
8. Sh. B.I. Singhal, former CMD, RITES, Member
9. Sh. J.K. Mittu, Transport Consultant, Member
10. Sh. Tapan Mandal, Jt. Director (Plg.), DDA, Member

Sub-Group on Social Infrastructure

1. Prof. S.C. Gupta, former Addl. Commissioner (Plg.), DDA, Chairman
2. Sh. A.K. Jain, Commissioner (Plg.), DDA, Co-Chairman
3. Dr. S.K. Kulshrestha, former Director, CRDT, ITPI, Member
4. Sh. Anoop Kothari, Urban Designer, Member
5. Sh. Rajendra Kumar, Member
6. Dr. R.N. Baishya, Health Services, Member
7. Director (Social Welfare), GNCTD Member
8. General Secy. Indian Medical Association, Member
9. DCP (HQ), Member
10. Dr.K.Srirangan, Asstt. Director (Plg.), DDA, Member

Sub-Group on Physical Infrastructure

1. Sh. H.U. Bijlani, former CMD, HUDCO, Chairman
2. Dr. S.P. Bansal, Director (Plg.), DDA, Co-Chairman
3. Sh. Girish K. Mishra, Professor, IIPA, Member
4. Sh. Pradeep Singh, Chief Executive, IHC, Member
5. Sh. S. Prakash, former Engineer-in- Chief, MCD, Member
6. Sh. S.G. Deolalikar, Services Consultant, Member
7. Sh. Anil Bhargawa, Member
8. Sh. M.L. Kansal, Editor
9. Sh. Ram Kishan Singal, Councillor, MCD, Member
10. Mrs. M.Z. Bawa, Jt. Director (Plg.), DDA, Member

Sub-Group on Mixed Landuse

1. Sh. D.D. Mathur, Former Chief Town Planner, MCD, Chairman
2. Sh. Surender Srivastava, Director (Planning), D.D.A., Co-Chairman
3. Smt Asma Manzar, Commissioner (Lands), DDA, Member
4. Sh. Shamsher Singh, Add. Town Planner, M.C.D., Member.
5. Sh. Satish Chander Khandelwal, former M.L.A, Member
6. Prof. Veena Garella, SPA, Member
7. Sh. D. Banerjee, Vice-President, ORG, Member
8. Sh. S.C. Gupta, former Addl. Commissioner (Plg.), DDA, Expert Member
9. Dr. S.K. Kulshrestha, former Director, CRDT, ITPI, Expert Member
10. Sh. K.M. Saxena, Asstt. Director (Plg.), DDA, Member

Sub-Group on Development Control

1. Ar. Balbir Verma, President, AIIA, Chairman
2. Sh. Anil Barai, Director (Plg.), DDA, Co-Chairman
3. Ar. Anoop Kothari, Urban Designer, Member
4. Ar. Arun Rewal, Urban Designer, Member
5. Sh. R.K. Gupta, Ex. Engineer (MCD), Member
6. Sh. R.L. Aggarwal, Chief Architect, NDMC, Member
7. Sh. K.N. Saikia, Sr. Architect, CPWD, Ministry of UD, GOI, Member

8. Sh. Sanjib Sen Gupta, Sr. Architect, CPWD, Ministry of UD, GOI, Member
9. Sh. Rajesh Kaushal, Architect, CPWD, Member
10. Sh. Sanjay P. Pathak, Jt. Director (Plg.), DDA, Member

CONSULTANTS TO THE MPD-2021

1. Association of Municipalities and Development Authorities, New Delhi.
   — Prof. E.F.N.Ribeiro, Former Chief Planner, TCPO/ Director SPA
   — Prof. B. Misra, former Head Urban Planning, SPA
2. National Institute of Urban Affairs, New Delhi.
   — Dr. Vinod Tiwari, Ex. Director, NIUA
   — Prof. S. Shafi, former Chief Planner, TCPO
3. School of Planning & Architecture, New Delhi.
   — Prof A. K. Maitra, Ex. Director
   — Prof. A.K. Sharma, Head Transport Department
   — Prof. K.T. Ravindran, Head Urban Design Department

TEAM:

Vice-Chairman	**Dinesh Rai, IAS**
Commissioner (Planning)	**A. K. Jain**
Addl. Commissioner (Planning)	**Ashok Kumar**
Director (Planning)	**P. V. Mahashabdey**
Jt. Director (Planning)	**M. Z. Bawa** **Archana Mahapatra**
Dy. Director (Planning)	**Dr. K. Srirangan** **K. M. Saxena**
Asstt. Director (Planning)	**Anju Aggarwal** **S. P. Sharma**
Planning Assistant	**Sneh Lata** **Rinkoo Mahajan** **Kiran Jain**
Planning Draftsman	**Rajender Kumar** **S. P. Verma**
Surveyor / Field Investigators	**Jagdish Pr. Meena,** **Rajender Singh** **B. S. Negi** **Baleshwar Dayal**

P. V. Abraham
R. K. Sharma
Rajnesh Kr. Singh
Bindu Sharma
Abha Mathur
Hemant Rana

Planning Officers	**Uttam Gupta** **Rohini Belapurkar**

The following officers were also associated with the project at different times

Vice Chairman	**P. K. Ghosh, IAS** **P. K. Hota, IAS** **Subhash Sharma, IAS** **Anil Baijal, IAS** **Madhukar Gupta, IAS**
Commissioner (Planning)	**Vijay Lisbud**
Addl Commissioner (Planning)	**K.K. Bandhopadhyay** **Chandra Ballabh** **N. K. Agarwal**
Director (Planning)	**B.K. Jain, Kuldeep Raj, Anil Barai, J. S. Sodhi, Sanjay P. Pathak, P. S. Uttarwar**
Jt. Director (Planning)	**S. Khodankar**
Asstt. Director (Planning)	**H. Bedi, Hitender K. Bharti, Jyoti D. Iyer**
Planning Assistant	**Tulsi Mohan**
Field Investigators	**M. C. Sharma, R. P. Ram, Virender Panwar, Hans Raj, Vijay Shankar Sharma D.K. Jain, S. K. Gupta, B. B. Singh**

Planning Officers:- Sudeep Gupta, N.R. Aravind Rahul Jindal, Amit Arora, Jaspreet Bedi, Sheba Puji, Swati Gore, Chetan Sahastrabudhe, Arijita Bansal, Jayant Gahi, Sanika Jain, Guneet Kaur, A.L. Valliappan, Urmi Buragohain, Naveen Angurala, Himani Jain, Vikrant Kumar, Gagandeep Kaur, Damini Raina, Parvesh Siroha, Vibha Bagde, Mona Kalia, Ruchi Gupta, Monika Pahwa, Namita Kumar, Astha Balwani, Charu Dhawan, Sabiha Khan, Sakshi Walia, Ritu Srivastav, Sudhir Kain, Sudip K. Guin, Prerna Mehta, Shikha Gandhi, Shashank Patil, Priyanka Mishra, Viraj. L. Mishra.